TO FORGET IT ALL AND BEGIN ANEW

Reconciliation in Occupied Germany, 1944–1954

Germany's transition from Nazism to peaceful, if at times reluctant, integration into the Western and Soviet spheres during the decade immediately following the Second World War is one of the most remarkable events of the twentieth century. Shattered relations between Germans and their wartime enemies and victims had rendered prospects for peaceful relations between these groups unimaginable, or a dream belonging to the distant future. However, numerous grassroots initiatives found varying degrees of success in fostering reconciliation.

Drawing on underutilized archival materials, *To Forget It All and Begin Anew* reveals a nuanced mosaic of like-minded people – from Germany and other countries, and from a wide variety of backgrounds and motives – who worked against considerable odds to make right the wrongs of the Nazi era. While acknowledging the enormous obstacles and challenges to reconciliatory work in postwar Germany, Steven M. Schroeder highlights the tangible and lasting achievements of this work, which marked the first steps towards new modes of peaceful engagement and cooperation in Germany and Europe.

(German and European Studies)

STEVEN M. SCHROEDER is a faculty member in the History Department at the University of the Fraser Valley.

GERMAN AND EUROPEAN STUDIES

General Editor: Rebecca Whitmann

STEVEN M. SCHROEDER

To Forget It All and Begin Anew

Reconciliation in Occupied Germany, 1944–1954

UNIVERSITY OF TORONTO PRESS
Toronto Buffalo London

© University of Toronto Press 2013
Toronto Buffalo London
www.utppublishing.com

ISBN 978-1-4426-4575-2 (cloth)
ISBN 978-1-4426-1399-7 (paper)

German and European Studies

Library and Archives Canada Cataloguing in Publication

Schroeder, Steven M., 1969–
To forget it all and begin anew : reconciliation in Occupied
Germany, 1944–1954 / Steven M. Schroeder.

(German and European studies)
Includes bibliographical references and index.
ISBN 978-1-4426-4575-2 (bound)   ISBN 978-1-4426-1399-7 (pbk.)

1. Germany — History — 1945–1955. 2. Germany — Social conditions —
1945–1955. I. Title. II. Series: German and European studies

DD257.S37 2013   943.087'4   C2012-905644-8

University of Toronto Press acknowledges the financial assistance
to its publishing program of the Canada Council for the Arts
and the Ontario Arts Council.

 Canada Council   Conseil des Arts
for the Arts   du Canada

 ONTARIO ARTS COUNCIL
CONSEIL DES ARTS DE L'ONTARIO
50 YEARS OF ONTARIO GOVERNMENT SUPPORT OF THE ARTS
50 ANS DE SOUTIEN DU GOUVERNEMENT DE L'ONTARIO AUX ARTS

University of Toronto Press acknowledges the financial support of the
Government of Canada through the Canada Book Fund
for its publishing activities.

Contents

Preface vii

Abbreviations xiii

Introduction 3

1 The German People and Allied Demands: Pressures and Initiatives towards Reconciliation 13

2 German Church and Political Groups 41

3 Steps towards Christian-Jewish Reconciliation 69

4 Broadening International Contacts and Reconciliation Work 96

5 The Politics of Reconciliation in the Two Germanies, 1949–1954 127

Conclusion 161

Notes 165

References 217

Index 227

Preface

The research for this book was conducted throughout Germany during a ten-month period (September 2004 to July 2005) that coincided with the sixtieth anniversary of the end of the Second World War and its immediate aftermath. During that time, Germans revealed a preoccupation with their history, which was evident in the ubiquitous treatment of the Nazi era in media and popular culture, including articles in daily newspapers and periodicals, nightly television documentaries, popular music, and blockbuster movies such as Oliver Hirschbiegel's, *Der Untergang*. This period also witnessed increasing support for far-right groups and politicians throughout Germany. Apparently, the Nazi past continues to influence the German people in various ways, much as it did in the immediate aftermath of the war.

My own family history, trips to Germany over the years, and this research stay in particular have afforded me an appreciation for the difficulties Germans faced when confronting Nazism in 1945. These experiences have also underscored in my mind the truism that the contemporaneous handling of misdeeds affects directly the future lives of individuals, groups, and even entire nations.

Approaching the multifarious topic of how Germans and others attempted to address the evils of Nazism right after the war is a challenging endeavour. I chose the concept of reconciliation because it fit best as a central touchpoint for the diverse work highlighted in this book, even though these labours did not result in simple, happy endings, which the term 'reconciliation' often connotes.

Daniel Bishop's sketch, depicted in *Die Neue Zeitung* in the U.S. zone in October 1945 and on this book's cover, captures well the central components of this study.[1] Reconciliatory work engaged necessarily the complex issues that faced Germans and international military personnel and aid workers alike. Some of these challenges are evident in the image: the ruins of Nazi Germany remained in sight as an ever-present point of reference; Germans, and those assisting them, faced formidable challenges on the path to international acceptance; and the German people required assistance in leaving the past behind, and in the integration process. The thoughts, opinions, and motives of the Germans and their helpers are not apparent, nor is it clear who is helping the German people, and who is awaiting them under the banner of the 'United Nations' at the end of the struggle. The book that follows elucidates the work of a wide range of people who – with diverse views, motives, and approaches – succeeded in integrating peacefully the German people into the family of nations, and – more specifically – into the Western and Soviet blocs.

To address the central questions posed in this project, I realized the necessity of using a wide variety of sources. In examining the many dimensions of reconciliation, one must consider numerous standpoints, including those of Allied personnel, German and non-German relief workers and operatives from other non-government organizations (NGOs), German and international religious and political figures, and victims of Nazism, both within Germany and abroad. By looking at this wide array of individuals and groups, the combined sources can be used to test and confirm each other, and differences between them can be analysed.

The primary material that informs this book is found in numerous archives and private holdings in Germany, Switzerland, the United States, and Canada. The Bundesarchiv (German Federal Archives) in Koblenz was consulted for the records of the Allied Control Authority and for the files of the Western Allies. The Stiftung Archiv der Parteien und Massenorganisationen der DDR im Bundesarchiv (Archives of the Parties and Mass Organizations of the GDR) in Berlin provided the basis for my research on the Soviet zone and the German Democratic Republic. The research materials on German administrative bodies and government ministries were found at the same archives, respectively, with records from the Western zones and the Federal Republic of Germany in Koblenz, and Soviet zone records in Berlin. The combination of these sources provided the essential information for the bases of Allied-German relations.

The focus on NGOs in this book rendered vital research on many groups, whose records are scattered throughout Germany and Switzerland.

The records of the Church's Aid Society (Kirchliche Hilfsstelle) and the Societies for Christian-Jewish Cooperation (Gesellschaften für Christlich-Jüdische Zusammenarbeit) are located in the Federal Archives in Koblenz. The Pax Christi archives are located in Bad Vilbel, Germany, and the records of Moral Re-Armament are housed in the Cantonal Archive of Vaud in Lausanne, Switzerland. In Berlin, I consulted the Archiv des Diakonischen Werkes der EKD (Protestant Relief Work Archives, including records of Das Hilfswerk der Evangelischen Kirche in Deutschland), and the Evangelisches Zentralarchiv (Evangelical Central Archives), which holds the files of the International Fellowship of Reconciliation and Friedrich Siegmund-Schultze's personal papers, along with the records of the German Protestant Committee for Service towards Israel (Deutsche evangelische Ausschuss für Dienst an Israel). Together, these resources equipped me with the details regarding the personnel, vision, and practice of the NGOs that were most effective in reconciliatory work in occupied Western Germany. The records of the NGOs that were most active in numerous aspects of reconciliation in the Soviet zone – the Victims of Fascism (Opfer des Faschismus), the Association of Victims of Nazism (Vereinigung der Verfolgten Naziregimes, VVN), and the Society for German-Soviet Friendship (Gesellschaft für Deutsch-Sowjetische Freundschaft) – are all located in the Federal Archives in Berlin. These files revealed the control that both the Soviet Administration and the Eastern German government bodies had on NGOs, and correspondence between the groups exposes their respective priorities and objectives. Other useful resources that addressed important questions directly related to this project were found in the following locations: the Zentralarchiv zur Erforschung der Geschichte der Juden in Deutschland (Central Archives for Research on the History of Jews in Germany) in Heidelberg; the Centrum Judaicum Archiv (Jewish Center Archives) in Berlin, which holds the records of Jewish communities in Eastern Germany; the Archives of the University of Notre Dame in South Bend, Indiana (particularly the George Shuster Collection); and the Conway Collection in Vancouver, Canada, which holds a wide variety of primary documents on the German churches during the occupation era.

The support and assistance necessary to complete this book have come from numerous institutions and individuals to whom I would like to express my gratitude and appreciation. First, I am indebted beyond measure to Doris Bergen; her expertise in German history, the German churches, the Holocaust, and German reconstruction after the Second World War provided me with insights at crucial junctures during the writing process. I would like to express my deep gratitude to John Conway for reading chapter drafts and for taking the time to offer his insights and suggestions, which were invaluable, particularly regarding the role of religion and ecumenism in the reconstruction of Germany. Semion Lyandres helped me understand the multiple connections between Soviet and German history during the twentieth century, and Thomas Kselman's knowledge of European religion likewise proved critical to this study. Thanks to Wilson Miscamble, C.S.C., and Gary Hamburg for providing important perspectives on American and Soviet policies at the early stage of this project that checked my thoughts and assumptions regarding the activities of Allied powers.

Numerous institutions and individuals made possible the fieldwork for this project through grants and personal support. The Kellogg Institute for International Studies at the University of Notre Dame provided seed money for exploratory research, and participation in the German Historical Institute's Summer Seminar in Germany introduced me to archives, libraries, and important contacts in Germany. Generous funding from the German Academic Exchange Service (DAAD) made possible my ten-month research stay in Germany in 2004–2005, and Philipp Gassert offered personal assistance and a forum to present my work at the Heidelberg Center for American Studies at the University of Heidelberg, which was valuable during the research phase.

I thank Peter Franz at the Federal Archives in Koblenz for his numerous trips to the *Magazine* and ensuring that files and copies were delivered punctually, and thanks to Annegret Neupert for providing useful insights into the archival collections. Michael Häusler at the Archives of the Protestant Church's Diakonisches Werk, and Ruth Pabst at the Central Archives of the German Protestant Church in Berlin both did an excellent job in guiding me to important holdings in the respective archives. In researching Moral Re-Armament, thanks are due to Eliane and Andrew Stallybrass for providing the much-needed information regarding archival holdings and contacts. My interview of Pierre Spoerri resulted from that correspondence, and my gratitude is extended to him for taking the time to travel to Lausanne from Zurich to meet with me and to provide access to restricted documents in the Vaud Cantonal Archives. Thanks are due to Peter Hönigmann at the Central Jewish Archives in Heidelberg for his assistance and in providing information on the Societies for Christian-Jewish Cooperation. Finally, I would like to thank the staff at the Pax Christi archives in Bad

Vilbel, who provided me unlimited access to documents, including the personal papers of Manfred Hörhammer.

My deepest gratitude is reserved for my wife, Rebecca, whose unwavering love and support throughout all stages of this project made possible the completion of this book. I dedicate this book to her.

Abbreviations

CRALOG	Council of Relief Agencies Licensed for Operation in Germany
DM	German Mark (Deutschmark)
DP	Displaced Persons
EKD	German Protestant Church (Evangelische Kirche in Deutschland)
FRG	Federal Republic of Germany
GDR	German Democratic Republic
ICCJ	International Council of Christians and Jews
IFOR	International Fellowship of Reconciliation
MRA	Moral Re-Armament
NGO	non-government organization
OMGUS	Office of the Military Government, U.S.
POW	prisoner of war
SED	Socialist Unity Party of Germany (Sozialistische Einheitspartei Deutschlands)
SMAD	Soviet Military Administration in Germany
SPD	Social Democratic Party of Germany (Sozialdemokratische Partei Deutschlands)
UNRRA	United Nations Relief and Rehabilitation Administration
VVN	Association of Victims of Nazism (Vereinigung der Verfolgten Naziregimes)
WCC	World Council of Churches

TO FORGET IT ALL AND BEGIN ANEW

Reconciliation in Occupied Germany, 1944–1954

Introduction

> For what matters is not a man's motive but any practical result that may follow from his work.
>
> –Victor Gollancz, 1947[1]

When the Nazi leadership offered its unconditional surrender on 8 May 1945, Europe lay in ruins. Germans had succeeded in plunging Europe into total war, but had failed to reach their objectives of sustained continental domination. However, German-led commando units, the Wehrmacht, and the Schutzstaffel (SS) did realize some of their goals in their onslaught on civilians – mainly Jews and other 'undesirables' – resulting in millions dead. The survivors were living reminders of the communal and personal devastation left in the wake of German wartime aggression. The shattered relations between Germans and their wartime enemies and victims, compounded with a budding discourse of German victimhood, rendered prospects for peaceful relations between these groups impracticable, or as a dream belonging to the distant future.

The transformation that took place in Germany over the next decade, from Nazism to peaceful, if sometimes reluctant, integration into either the Western or the Soviet spheres, is one of the most remarkable events of the twentieth century. Today, Germany is a liberal democracy and a significant member of the European Union that labours, mostly with success, towards multiculturalism and tolerance. The Federal Republic of Germany (FRG) is also an exemplar to other nations in its long-standing, and ongoing, commitment to recognizing and compensating the victims of German aggression during the Second World War. This seismic shift towards reconciliation began during the first postwar decade and included a myriad of factors, among which German contrition ranked very low. Instead, it was foreign occupation, geopolitics, Cold War fault-lines, and grassroots initiatives stemming from many countries that factored significantly as Germans forged peaceful relations with their former enemies.

Although these transformative components are deeply enmeshed, the significance of grassroots initiatives has not been adequately reflected in postwar narratives. This book examines some of the grassroots initiatives that found varying degrees of success, despite their imperfections. Civilian work in relief organizations, non-government organizations (NGOs), churches, and Communist-directed front organizations began during the early weeks of the occupation, as the Allies wrestled with issues of responsibility and justice. The groups and individuals examined in this book do not comprise an exhaustive list. Rather, their initiatives form part of a mosaic that included, in most cases, like-minded people who worked on the margins in occupied Germany and had a common objective: to make right, in some way, the massive injustices and abuses of the Nazi era. With the assistance of the occupying powers, these initiatives found success, as long as they aligned with the Allies' policies in each respective zone. Whereas it did not overcome the Nazi past, or atone completely for the tremendous wrongdoing suffered by the victims of Nazism, this reconciliatory work – which began as marginal – initiated the interminable process of working through the widespread devastation of the Nazi era, and it had a profound impact on many people.

What Is Reconciliation?

The term 'reconciliation' has been applied commonly to a wide range of cases of human suffering throughout history, rendering the term ambiguous and, in some cases, trite. However, the term's ambiguity enables the inclusion of many different attempts to address positively past injustices; nevertheless, it needs to be defined clearly. In this book, *reconciliation* is defined as the establishment of peaceful – or at least non-hostile – relations between former enemies. Reconciliation in all of its facets is treated as a process rather than a one-time accomplishment, and it emerges from two different impulses: pragmatism and altruism. Achievements are measured in the development of peaceful relations between former enemies, with the assumption that maintenance of this success is an ongoing, long-term process. This book reveals that accomplishments in reconciliatory work stemmed from relationships that were aloof and official – resulting in pragmatic action – but also from deeply personal relationships, which engendered a genuine change of mind and action from both sides of the victim-perpetrator divide.

The most common approach to reconciliation in occupied Germany revolved around pragmatic concerns and was largely self-serving. For example, Germans in public administration, domestic NGOs, and churches engaged in this form of reconciliation when they acknowledged crimes of the Nazi era and victims of Nazism in order to win favour from their foreign occupiers and the international community who were demanding German accountability. Regardless of the motives behind them, these actions contributed to the discourse of reconciliation, because they acknowledged German responsibility for the crimes of the Nazi era. These coerced actions were mutually beneficial, because the Allies made strides towards German integration into their respective political spheres, and Germans gained favour with the Allies, which was a crucial step towards achieving control of their own domestic affairs.

The other side of reconciliation involved a more altruistic and idealistic approach, the proponents of which considered reconciliation to be an end in itself. Germans in this camp transcended pragmatic concerns to engage in more thoroughgoing reconciliatory encounters that created or re-established relationships of cooperation and trust with their former enemies. For example, Germans who were welcomed to participate in international NGO meetings were encouraged towards personal reflection and responsibility. Such encounters yielded significant results, seen in the Franco-German reconciliation brokered by Moral Re-Armament, and gentile-Jewish reconciliation evident in the work of the Societies for Christian-Jewish Cooperation. Although sincere motives were not a requirement for effective reconciliation work, efforts based on altruism and generosity did contribute to advancing processes of reconciliation and to sustaining them long term.

Taken together, these two approaches to reconciliation – and the contrast in practices between the three Western zones and the Soviet zone – give rise to the central questions addressed in this book: Did the Allies foster an environment conducive to reconciliation in occupied Germany? How did the Allied occupation impact Germans in their dealing with the Nazi past? What role did German and international grassroots initiatives play in postwar reconstruction in Germany and Europe? How successful were their initiatives? What were the long-term results of this activity, and what hindered it?

The book's title, 'To Forget It All and Begin Anew,' is an excerpt from a 1946 letter that German Protestant pastor Hans Asmussen wrote to the Allied Control Council. It captured how most Germans felt at the time: they wanted to get on with their lives, and they did not want to talk about their support for Nazism in any way. Together with the term 'reconciliation,' and Daniel Bishop's sketch that depicts the dire situation Germans faced in 1945, the book's cover reflects the multidimensional nature of occupied Germany. The argument of this book is that grassroots reconciliatory work between Germans and their former enemies yielded significant achievements during the troubled and turbulent decade following the end of the Second World War. To be sure, immense difficulties and obstacles – political, social, and ideological – were encountered during these decisive postwar years. These are fully described in the following chapters. But in the end, they were surmounted to a degree that allowed reconciliatory work to succeed, and to establish its varied modi operandi throughout the four zones.

All four Allied powers employed reconciliatory work striving towards German democratization, even though 'reconciliation' and 'democratization' were interpreted differently in the four zones. For the Soviets, democratization meant the establishment of a classless society, and a multi-party (though Communist-dominated) political system. Ironically, as Heinrich August Winkler has pointed out, it was the German Communist Party in the Soviet zone that espoused the foundation of 'a parliamentary-democratic republic with all the democratic rights and liberties for the people,' which did not include 'imposition of the Soviet system.'[2] This clash led to the Soviet takeover of German politics in the zone by early 1946. Thereafter, 'reconciliation' in the Soviet zone focused on justice for the political victims of Nazism – while ignoring other victims – and on building close ties with Soviet-friendly socialist states. For the Western Allies, democratization meant a thorough overhaul of all aspects of society, and reconciliation was much more thoroughgoing and involved. Germans were to create their own democratic, multi-party, parliamentary system, decartelize and privatize the economy, and recognize the suffering of a wide variety of victims through compensation.

This study illuminates the positive steps between Germans and the principal victims of Nazi persecution, including Jews, victims of racial 'purification' policies, political prisoners, and people who suffered under Nazi occupation. It also illuminates the limits of reconciliatory work at this time, as homosexuals, Gypsies, and a variety of other victims of Nazi racial policies were ignored in reparations discussions, and even persecuted in postwar Germany. The views of the few idealists who promoted reconciliation, on both the German and non-German sides, were often snubbed, but they eventually won out. By such means the evils of Nazism and the hatreds induced by its nefarious ideology were at first outlawed and later more or less eradicated. This was to be the most momentous step forward and the major achievement of right-thinking Germans in the second half of the twentieth century.

Essential to comprehending the paradox of the rapid, and peaceful, integration of Germany into the Eastern and Western blocs is an understanding of how the German people changed in their actions and, in many cases, in their thoughts and beliefs. Whereas diplomacy and issues of responsibility and justice are crucial to this book's chief queries, they only tell fragments of the story. Another fragment – reconciliatory work at the grassroots level – broadens the scope considerably. Indeed, reconciliation, whether sought overtly or found inadvertently, was complementary to the diplomatic and legal endeavours. Interactions between the Allies and Germans, who all held a wide variety of motives, encouraged reconciliation from the outset of the occupation of Germany. In many cases, it was grassroots initiatives that were able to foster reconciliation in ways that governments and military personnel did not. This work progressed from distanced, official contacts to deeper relationships of trust throughout the occupation era. By the summer of 1945, grassroots initiatives had led some Germans in all four zones of occupation to begin to recognize the need to compensate the victims of Nazism and to make reparations for their sufferings and losses. Numerous international NGOs had begun to broker initial contacts between Germans and influential individuals from abroad. By 1946, NGOs had brought Germans and their former enemies, however reluctantly, into face-to-face dialogue. It was during the 1947–1949 period that many of these initial contacts developed into trustful relationships, which became the vehicles for cooperative peacebuilding in the years to come.

The significance of the occupation era has been sidelined in the study of the peaceful development of postwar Germany. Mostly, it has been treated as a transitional period during which everyone involved – the Germans, the Allies, and the broader world – prepared for the more significant drama of the Cold War. In contrast to the sorry record of the earlier experience in the wake of Germany's defeat in 1918, and to the ineffectual international peace movement of the interwar era, peace work during the post-1945 occupation era was crucial to the stabilization of Germany. This book examines how a wide variety of individuals and groups began the processes of reconciliation when Germans still had no access to conventional diplomacy. Remarkably, their work succeeded in all four zones of occupation, amid the hostile confrontation between two armed camps. Studying the work of NGOs and other groups involved in non-conventional forms of diplomacy reveals a broad scope of postwar German political developments, both Western democratization and Stalinization, and the significance that these groups can have in post-conflict reconstruction. Most surprising, perhaps, is the fact that the achievements of non-conventional diplomacy in postwar Germany did not rely solely on altruism or lofty ideas. Instead, idealism was only one part of a combination of outside pressure, German self-interest, and the participation of former victims that produced lasting results.

Scholarship

Scholarship pertaining to post–Second World War Germany has been largely concerned with how Germans have dealt with the crimes of Nazism, German democratization, and Germany's reintegration into international systems. The scholarship has often mirrored the broader contemporary interpretations of the Nazi era and has tended to proceed narrowly in its scope, focusing on one particular aspect of these developments.[3] Since 1990, concerns about contemporary German democracy and relations within the European Union have produced works that highlight the divergent Allied occupation policies over the East-West divide and investigate their effects on the German population.[4]

Similarly, when approaching reconciliation efforts between Germans and their wartime enemies – including personal indemnity payments, reparations, restitution, and international agreements – scholars have emphasized the pragmatic aspects of reparations in the respective occupation zones.[5] A broader view that includes NGO work is difficult to find. Like the low-profile work of NGOs themselves, scholarship on them has been neither well known nor widely circulated.[6] Scholarship on the German churches after 1945 has been excellent; however, it has tended to focus on internal church affairs and pays little heed to the churches' broader social and cultural engagement and impact.[7] A handful of works address directly the central questions posed in this book, but few assign significance to, or even mention, the grassroots work of NGOs, churches, and a variety of other organizations in the processes of reconciliation.[8]

The true test for German democratization involved reconciliation with Jews. Several works published in the past decade examine the interaction between Jewish communities and the broader German population, and how German-Jewish reconciliation has factored into Germany's integration into the family of nations.[9] Studies of Christian-Jewish relations have focused on programmatic aspects linked directly to German democratization and avoid use of the term 'reconciliation.'[10] In the German Democratic Republic (GDR), thinly veiled antisemitism, under the rubric of 'anti-capitalism,' curtailed the recognition of Jewish suffering under Nazism, which scholars have addressed in considerable detail.[11]

Competing with the focus on Jewish suffering has been the discourse that highlights, instead, the German people's suffering and misery, while simultaneously ignoring the enormous suffering that Germany wrought on its neighbours.[12] Issues of postwar justice have resurfaced in numerous works, which tend to expose the ongoing nature of the injustices suffered under Nazism, demonstrate the fact that victims continue to struggle with the atrocities committed over sixty years ago, and reveal that much is at stake in the manner by which these events are memorialized.[13]

Scholarly research on reconciliation addresses the questions in this book, but few works include detailed historical treatment of specific cases.[14] A recent wave of scholarship focuses on a broader range of approaches to post-conflict reconciliation, largely inspired by the hope of finding useful methods for application in today's world.[15] Scholars in this field have identified the central components of reconciliation that have achieved peace in Europe after 1945, which include justice, apologies, forgiveness, collective reconstruction, establishing shared institutions, and creating mutual understanding and trust.[16] Whereas some scholars avoid discussion of reconciliation's end point, the more compelling approach stems from scholars, like Yinan He, who identifies the differences between 'deep' and shallow' reconciliation,[17] and Lily Gardner Feldman, who rightly acknowledges that reconciliation 'involves ongoing, dynamic, long-term confrontation with a painful past.'[18]

This study incorporates the ongoing discussion of theories of reconciliation in the examination of postwar Germany. It casts the net broadly, examining numerous aspects of German integration internationally during the first decade after the murderous Nazi dictatorship. The goal is to show how this reconciliatory work contributed to the emergence of two stable states, which – despite their mutual hostility – recognized the need for a new beginning, which included a new approach towards the victims of the previous regime.

Approach and Organization

This book is organized chronologically, beginning with the initial stages of the Allied occupation of Germany in 1944 and concluding with the Allied High Commission's and the Soviet Control Commission's respective decisions in 1954 to grant sovereignty to the two Germanies. This end date also marks a watershed in East Germany as it began, along with the rest of the Soviet bloc, to reconfigure its political goals after the death of Joseph Stalin in 1953. The chronological approach facilitates well the introduction of this project's main topics, because the reconciliatory activities in occupied Germany developed and expanded from 1944 to 1954. Although the two main aspects of reconciliation highlighted in this book – coerced and pragmatic versus more altruistic – occurred simultaneously, a general expansion and deepening of reconciliatory activity was evident during 1947–1949, after Germans and international NGOs made direct contact. For this reason, I devote considerable attention to this two-year period.

The first chapter of the book examines processes by which the German people reconciled their actions to the kind of behaviour that the Allies demanded from them during the period immediately following the collapse of Nazism. Germans began, with varying degrees of reluctance, to acknowledge the misdeeds of the Nazi era and to pay reparations to the victims of German aggression. While learning the new rules of engagement and paying for some of the damages of war, Germans in all walks of life reflected on and interpreted the events that had landed them in their current situation, but they did not, for the most part, involve themselves in relational reconciliation with their wartime enemies and victims.

Chapter 2 addresses the development of a German discourse of victimhood during the first two years of occupation. This particular narrative allowed Germans to interpret their past – and present – misfortunes in a way that let them avoid taking personal responsibility for the evils of Nazism. Both of the first two chapters discuss the initial attempts that international NGOs, churches, and individuals made to contact Germans. These chapters show the mindset and activities of German personnel operating domestically in a variety of organizations without the direct interaction with, or scrutiny of, international onlookers. The deeper impact of collaborative work was yet to come.

During the Second World War, Germans and their collaborators in occupied territories murdered six million European Jews. After the war, gentiles as well as Jews in the international community demanded that Germans break their silence regarding the Holocaust and begin to address the antisemitism of the Nazi era. Chapter 3 deals with this topic and includes the first cases of international organizations making direct, face-to-face contact with Germans who were involved in gentile-Jewish reconciliation. Beginning in 1947, multiple forms of reconciliation projects began to emerge as Allied and German personnel coordinated their efforts.

The topic of Chapter 4 is the broadening of reconciliatory activity through increased personal contacts and dialogue between international organizations and Germans in many different groups and institutions. The efforts of numerous key reconciliatory elements converge as victims initiated forgiveness and dialogue, some Germans took responsibility for the past, and legal, financial, and political agreements were established between Germans and their wartime enemies and victims.

Finally, Chapter 5 gives an account of the state of affairs in the German Democratic Republic and the Federal Republic of Germany during the first six years of their existence, from 1949 to 1954. This chapter addresses in more detail the ongoing political developments introduced in the preceding chapter, examines the actions of the respective governments of the two Germanies under semi-sovereign status, and assesses the continuation and long-term effects of reconciliatory processes that had begun prior to statehood.

Taken together, the comparison of Eastern and Western Germany provides a treatment of issues of reconciliation that spans ideological and political motivations in a complex and politically volatile international context. Through transitional justice and various encounters between individuals and groups, rudimentary steps towards reconciliation were achieved throughout Germany. Although only a minority of Germans wanted to undertake the difficult work of reconciliation during the immediate postwar period, their work, and that of the majority who were motivated by pragmatic concerns, had considerable impact on the development of new relationships. Such relationships were of deep significance as they worked against the return to nationalism, militarism, and self-absorption characteristic of the interwar era. They marked the first steps towards new modes of European engagement and formed the foundation of European diplomacy and cooperation in the decades to come. In doing so, these relationships illuminate the unexpected: that amid the rubble and hatred in bombed-out Germany, concrete and lasting achievements were made in the realm of reconciliation between Germans and the victims of German wartime aggression.

Chapter One

The German People and Allied Demands: Pressures and Initiatives towards Reconciliation

When Marshall Knappen returned to the United States in 1947, after heading the Education and Religious Affairs Branch of the American Military Government for the previous two years, he offered a disheartening picture of the state of German reconstruction. In highlighting the disparity between the American military's priorities and the needs of the German people, Knappen recalled the creation of a new officers' club in Berlin in 1946. The club, which boasted the largest bar in Berlin at the time, was built to serve the personnel working at the neighbouring headquarters of the American Military Government. Adjacent to the club was the Jesus Christus Kirche, the church pastored by Martin Niemöller. At the time of the club's completion, the church remained exposed to the winter weather, a gaping hole still in its roof from a bomb in 1945.[1]

Knappen's dual image – the bar and the church – captures several aspects of the early Allied occupation of Germany. It points to the Nazi era and the enormous effort and cost in human lives and resources needed to destroy it. Accompanying the Allied invasion of Germany in 1944 was a great deal of mistrust for the German people, which was reflected in Allied occupation policies that made it illegal for occupation personnel to fraternize with the German people and forced Germans to address the crimes of Nazism in a variety of ways. This foundation of Allied-German relations – including the manner in which Germans addressed the Nazi past – would affect contemporary and future reconciliation between Germans and their wartime enemies.

Allied attitudes in the early stages of occupation are also indicated in the image Knappen described, including the prioritization of the Allies' goals and even comforts over German reconstruction. Furthermore, the image symbolizes how the Allies marginalized religion in occupied Germany, even while they considered German church leaders to be the most democratically minded Germans and intended to utilize them and their institutions in German democratization. These discrepancies led Knappen to lament that conditions in occupied Germany left 'little opportunity to develop the spirit which could have breathed into [Germans] the breath of life,' and to insist that the Allies needed to change their policies.[2]

Even Knappen's approach did not consider a broader range of possibilities when it came to the reconstruction and democratization of Germany. Both positions – the Allies' aloof policies steeped in self-interest and Knappen's goal of injecting the German people with new life – stemmed from external impositions concerning accountability that had little regard for German involvement in the development of trustful, cooperative relationships between the Allies and the German people. Moreover, they focused and relied on high-profile and influential people, who were to impose their values on the Germans and involved mainly the acceptance of those impositions by influential community leaders on the German side. In short, the first relationships between Allies and Germans did not mandate or even contemplate direct involvement of ordinary Germans in reconciliatory processes. Instead, the conditions of this early relationship led to communal reconciliation characterized by a one-way effort that involved Germans cooperating with and accepting Allied policies. In doing so, Germans hoped to build trust that they could utilize towards their main goal of sovereignty.

This chapter examines how, during the last months of the war and the immediate postwar period, the combination of Allied demands that Germans address the crimes of the Nazi era and the German response to those demands established a foundation for German-Allied communication and negotiation. For the Allies at this juncture, German accountability for the crimes of Nazism was paramount. Punishment – through denazification, prosecuting Nazis, restitution of stolen property, forced relocation, and reparations payments – superseded, and was a prerequisite for, the development of trust in relationships with the German people. At the Potsdam Conference held from 17 July to 2 August 1945, Allied leaders declared that their intent was 'to prepare for the eventual reconstruction of German political life on a democratic basis and for eventual peaceful cooperation in international life by Germany.'[3] However, the Allies were clear: part of German rehabilitation would be punishment 'by the peoples they have outraged,'[4] which provided the grounds for their statement at Potsdam: '[the Germans] cannot escape responsibility for what they have brought upon themselves, since their own ruthless warfare and the fanatical Nazi[sm] ... made chaos and suffering inevitable.'[5]

During the first two years of occupation, the Allied powers held disparate views on how to proceed in Germany, but they did agree on their respective, and collective, moral superiority vis-à-vis the Germans. The Allies incorporated their views into their occupation policies from the outset, with the intent to expunge Nazism and create a new Germany based on their understanding of sound morality. The Allies insisted that the German people align their conduct with Allied values as a starting point of the Germans' journey towards reconciling with their neighbours and regaining international standing.

To help facilitate the initial stages of democratization of Germany, the Allies, including the Soviets, began a complete overhaul of German society, introducing democratic practices in politics, the economy, culture, education, press and radio, and the legal system.[6] Even though democratization was interpreted differently within the four occupying powers, they proceeded along similar lines in their work to stabilize German society. However, the deep divide between the Western and Stalinist systems became evident during the establishment (in some cases, re-establishment) of democracy and democratic parties throughout the four zones, beginning in May 1945.[7] When the chief victims of Nazi political persecution (i.e., Communists and Social Democrats) began to engage in German politics after the end of the war, they were not always met with a warm welcome from the Allied powers.[8] In June 1945, the Soviets were quick to remove all leading German public figures from office and replace them with a mix of selected German Communist émigrés and Soviet administrators. Moreover, with the poor support for the German Communist Party in the 1946 Soviet zone elections, the Soviets forcibly created the Socialist Unity Party (SED), and enforced its governance.[9]

The Allies also guided German democratization through their respective cultural policies, seen in the Allied Control Authority's promotion of a free press in Germany. In addition to newspapers that were under the direct control and surveillance of the Allies – such as the *Neue Zeitung*, founded by the American Military Government in October 1945 – German newspapers, like the *Tagesspiegel*, were published as early as September 1945. Moreover, Allied cultural centres – the

Amerika Haus, the British Council, and the Maison de France – made available books, films, and periodicals for German consumption with the intent of infusing Western democratic values into German society. By 1948, the American Military Government had established a sizable cultural exchange program that allowed 'selected Germans' to visit 'free nations ... so that they [could] see democracy in action.'[10] In the Soviet zone, democratization efforts looked similar to those in the Western zones in form, but the message was one of alignment with Stalinist ideology. In April 1946, the SED founded the newspaper, *Neues Deutschland*, which, together with numerous other Soviet-controlled publications, informed Germans in the Soviet zone of how to interpret the Nazi past and life under occupation.

The German reaction to the introduction of foreign culture and Allied demands was varied. Some responses were cautious, even defensive, towards the alien cultural values that were being imposed on German people by their foreign occupiers. Many Germans found repulsive the films, music, and youth culture of the United States and Britain, warned their population of their dangers, and encouraged fellow Germans not to participate in certain activities that Allied personnel introduced into German society.[11]

Conversely, some Germans took the opportunity of Allied occupation and control of German society to express their anger towards the Nazi regime and to encourage self-reflection, self-criticism, and responsibility of all Germans for Nazi misdeeds. Numerous German periodicals that emerged in the first months after the collapse of Nazism voiced this type of criticism, including *Die Gegenwart*, and the *Frankfurter Hefte*, edited by Eugen Kogon. Neither periodical shied away from tough issues regarding the Nazi past. Similarly, the periodical *Neues Abendland* devoted its entire October 1946 edition to the issue of German guilt, complete with numerous pages of grotesque sketches of human suffering, intended to depict the horrors of Nazism.[12] These examples reveal that the creation of favourable conditions made possible public criticism of Nazism and illustrate how some Germans took advantage of these conditions to engender critical engagement with the Nazi past.

Although the majority of Germans did not share the views of these critical journalists, many conducted themselves, especially when in direct contact with foreigners, in a manner that reflected contrition in order to garner favour with the Allies. Indeed, Germans discovered very quickly that they would be required to reconcile many fractured relationships if they wished to achieve a wide variety of self-serving goals. Far from the ideal of the German people adopting a posture of widespread remorse and repentance, influential figures in German politics, churches, and NGOs found that they could further their goals of self-determination without altering their world-view. Through the use of appropriate language and actions, astute Germans discovered that they could appease the Allies even while they prioritized political and social autonomy and promoted an understanding of the recent past that absolved the majority of Germans from any specific responsibility. This mixed guidance from Allied and German sources encouraged Germans to ignore critical reflection on the Nazi past and perform in a manner that appeased foreign onlookers.

The Germans as Pariahs: Non-fraternization and Expulsion

At the Potsdam Conference in 1945, the Allied leaders declared their intention to disarm and democratize Germany. During the initial stage of the occupation of Germany, the Allies recognized that this project would be fraught with difficulties, because the German people did not view their Nazi past with the same disgust as their occupiers did. Contempt stretched beyond the past to the present, as the Allies viewed the German people as morally unclean and disseminated that view in literature and policy. Pamphlets and periodicals published in 1944 with the intent to guide Allied military personnel in Germany portrayed the German people as cunning, manipulative, untrustworthy, subservient, aggressive, and even demonic.[13] This widespread distrust of the German people was evident in President Harry Truman's 1945 policy directive for Germany, which delineated a 'just, firm, but aloof' administration of the occupied zones, and was to include denazification and reparations.[14]

In all four zones, the Allied non-fraternization law – introduced in 1944 to ensure that Nazi propaganda would not lure Allied personnel away from their duties – failed to produce positive developments and posed challenges to the broader program of democratization of Germany. How could the German people see 'democracy in action' if the Allied personnel could not have contact with them? Because of this obvious problem, the non-fraternization law in the American zone was officially dropped in September 1945 in favour of American-German fraternization. However, discouragement of contact between the two groups continued in the Western zones well into 1946.[15] The general attitude among the Western Allies remained clear: the German people were not to be trusted. In the Soviet zone during 1945–1946, Soviet soldiers engaged regularly in rape, murder, theft, and vandalism, and as a result, in mid-1947, the Soviet Military Administration in Germany (SMAD) mandated separation between Germans and Soviet personnel.[16] For the Soviets, their task was to mend the horrible wounds they had wrought on Germans during the first years of occupation. For all four Allied powers, the task was the same: to win over the German people to their respective way of thinking.

At the same time that the Allies were exacting this 'clean-up and pay-up' approach to the occupation of Germany, they were also pursuing their chief goal of integrating Germans into their respective social and political systems. This two-pronged approach sent a somewhat confusing message to the German people, who did not consider themselves to be morally deficient. Moreover, the Allies' interpretation of the German past countered the general idea among some or many Germans that a small clique had operated the Nazi regime, that no real Nazis could be found among the general population, and therefore, that it was preposterous to assign guilt to anyone – collectively or individually – for the misdeeds of a few wayward, high-ranking individuals. This view was to be reinforced by a series of trials of major war criminals at Nuremberg starting in late 1945, when attention was focused on a limited number of men, most of whom were found guilty. This led many Germans to regard themselves as being innocent. The die had been cast for the two dominant views of the past that would permeate dialogue between the Allies and the Germans throughout the occupation period.

The Allies' distrust of the German people extended beyond the borders of occupied Germany. In fact, the Allies decided at Potsdam to transfer the ethnic Germans from their homelands in Eastern Europe to occupied Germany, mainly because they considered that the presence of German government officials and, more generally, 'other obnoxious Germans and their families [would] constitute a danger in view of the possible future renewal of the German war effort.'[17] Whereas the expellees avoided moral and legal responsibility for the horrors Eastern Europeans experienced under German occupation, the Allies' handling of the expulsions contributed to the deepening of animosities between the two groups.

At the Potsdam Conference, the Allied Control Council provided numerous reasons for the expulsions and instructions regarding the manner in which they were to be conducted. The council's Coordinating Committee declared that ethnic Germans would be transferred in 'an orderly and humane manner,' and the committee promised to work in close consultation with the Polish, Hungarian, and Czech governments on an agreeable rate of transfer.[18] In fact, the Coordinating Committee proceeded with the population transfers in an unorganized fashion, admitting in September 1945 that it had not 'considered the question in all of its aspects,' as it had made 'no arrangements' in terms of the details of resettling these refugees.[19] An example of the council's lack of consideration is evident in its calculations, which concluded that a total of 4.3 million ethnic Germans would be transferred to occupied Germany, about eight million shy of the actual number.[20] Moreover, the swift decision in favour of the expulsions and the immediate commencement of them made it impossible for precautions to be made in all cases for the 'humane and orderly' component of the council's directive, resulting in some orderly but also some very violent and murderous encounters between the German expellees and their Eastern European neighbours.[21]

The rage Eastern Europeans had cultivated under German occupation permeated all discussion pertaining to the expulsions. Recognizing the moral significance attached to the treatment of the vanquished – and how that treatment would reflect on one's own people – in a radio interview in October 1945, Czech President Eduard Beneš took the opportunity of the expulsions to praise Czech morality and to expose the moral bankruptcy of the Germans. Beneš claimed that the expulsions were necessary, because over 90 per cent of Czech Germans had supported the rise of Nazism in Czechoslovakia and that it would be impossible for the two people to live next to one another in peace. These facts, as Beneš saw them, led him to take personal responsibility for the appropriate conduct of the expulsions: 'The Czechoslovakian Interior Ministry and its offices have been strictly instructed to handle the German population with strictness but in a humane manner. Even though we think back in horror at the unspeakable sufferings that many Czechs underwent in Gestapo prisons and torture chambers during the Nazi era, we still want to proceed justly in each situation.'[22]

According to a report in the American-German paper *Neue Zeitung*, 'the transport was done in a humane, decent, just, and moral way, organized well and took place under the approval of the Allies.'[23] Even though the Allies, and the Czechs, interpreted the expulsions in this way, the very act of forcibly transferring Germans, who had shared domicile with their Czech neighbours for centuries, could not be done without engendering and deepening bitterness on both sides. Indeed, regardless of this high-level concern for the humane treatment of the expellees, many Czechs, Hungarians, and Poles, who wanted to rid their lands of ethnic Germans, ensured that the expulsions were carried out as quickly as possible and proceeded to achieve this goal with cruelty and violence.[24]

Even though Beneš and the Allies were most probably correct in their assessment of postwar ethnic tensions in Eastern Europe – and in deeming the expulsion of Germans necessary to avert communal discord – the negative ramifications of the expulsions were considerable. The conditions in Europe left little room for reconciliation to succeed in these relationships, as the security and structural support necessary for all Eastern Europeans to begin the long process of cultivating new relationships of trust and cooperation were yet to be established. Of course, the most negatively affected were the expellees themselves, the majority of whom continued to harbour enormous resentment and bitterness towards the Allies and the Eastern Europeans who inherited their property. In turn, the expellees, and the Germans who took on their bitterness, would utilize their heightened sense of victimhood to blind themselves to the reasons for the expulsions. Ultimately, this bitterness served to complicate and make more difficult Allied efforts to democratize Germany, as these millions of homeless, embittered, and revenge-minded refugees struggled to find a new home in overpopulated and undernourished occupied Germany.[25]

Denazification

In addition to the expulsions during the first year of occupation, the Allies attempted to have Germans take direct ownership for the crimes of the Nazi era and to punish the guilty. Many methods were used to achieve this goal, which included forcing the German people to witness the carnage in the concentration camps.[26] The more thoroughgoing and problematic component was the denazification program, which attempted to assign the German people with a general responsibility for the misdeeds of the Nazi era, remove Nazis from leadership positions, hold numerous war crimes trials, and execute the guilty.

As part of its plan to democratize Germany, the Allied Control Authority removed all identifiable Nazis and their known collaborators from public service and from positions of influence in the private sector. The Allies intended to replace these people with individuals who, because of 'their political and moral qualities, [were] deemed capable of assisting in developing genuine democratic institutions in Germany.'[27] Trials and executions of Germans who were found guilty of numerous crimes of conduct began in the summer of 1945.[28] The Allied Control Council ensured that the denazification program went forward and drafted Law Number 10 in December 1945, which was used to prosecute German 'war criminals' who had committed 'crimes against humanity.'[29] Some have questioned the efficacy of the denazification process, as many people responsible for the Nazi catastrophe were never brought to justice, and could view themselves as exonerated after the completion of the program.[30] The validity of this concern notwithstanding, the process raised awareness of the need to deal with the Nazi past, and contributed significantly to the discourse on German atrocities and subsequent responsibility.

When implementing denazification procedures, the Control Council worked in concert with German political figures, who ensured that influential Germans adopted the Allies' way of thinking. The approach to denazification differed in each zone and proceeded according to the ideological and political goals of the occupiers.[31] For example, the Council of States (Länderrat) in the U.S. zone – a German political body that worked in concert with the Office of the Military Government, U.S. (OMGUS) – was very active in dealing with the Control Council and OMGUS in terms of their internal affairs, including denazification. The Council of States worked closely with the American Military Government in drafting the Law on Purging Bavaria of National Socialism and Militarism in the fall of 1945. This law anticipated the goals of the Control Council's 1946 Denazification Directive that sought to 'eliminate from public life [and] hold responsible for atonement' those who had openly supported Nazism, or who had 'selfishly availed themselves of the conditions created by [Nazism].'[32]

Once guilt was ascribed, atonement could be achieved via a wide range of services or payments, including work assignments, increased taxes, and contributions to an indemnification fund. But some members of the Council of States were outraged at some impositions, and German politician Dr Goetz claimed that the Law on Purging Bavaria of National Socialism and Militarism was useless because it merely satisfied the Allies' demands that the Germans pay reparations to victims of German aggression. Goetz predicted that denazification would fail in the American zone because of the widespread aversion that Germans had for it.[33] In the French zone, Protestant Bishop Theophil Wurm echoed Goetz's concerns in a letter to the American Military Government in April 1946, in which he expressed his 'grave concerns' on the law stating that it would bring new 'injustices' to Germany.[34]

In the Soviet zone, the Soviet Military Administration was more interested in expunging the sources of fascism from Germany than in punishing individuals. Thus, the focus was on distributing the property and assets of large estate holders and the owners of big business.[35] Of course, individuals were often targeted in this work. The Soviets found that many Germans were willing to cooperate in denazification proceedings, particularly German Communists and non-government organizations, such as Victims of Fascism (Opfer des Faschismus). In fact, German-led work, in targeting individual Nazis, complimented the Soviet approach of eradicating fascism collectively. In 1946, after the Soviets had forcibly retired nearly 400,000 Nazi party members and replaced them with more suitable workers, 262 German-led denazification commissions examined over 850,000 cases, from which more than 65,000 people were punished in some way.[36] Moreover, in May 1946, the administrators of the central office of Victims of Fascism – who wanted to highlight their anti-fascism – assumed some of the responsibility for denazification in the Soviet zone. The group's thoroughgoing investigation led to the conviction of 7,543 individuals of crimes during the Nazi era.[37] According to the leadership of this group, the swift success of the denazification program in the Soviet zone was the result, in part, of the 'earnest cooperation with the ministries of justice, the police, and political organizations throughout Germany.'[38] Through this experience, Germans living in the Soviet zone had learned for the first time that if they wanted to see justice served according to their criteria, they would have to take on the work themselves. Moreover, they learned that alignment with Soviet ideology and goals would lead to personal and group exoneration, a lesson that taught Germans how to conduct themselves in negotiations with the Soviets and with German Communist leaders.

Although the Allies considered denazification to be a necessary procedure in the democratization of Germany, its practice resulted in limited success, mostly because of the political agendas of those involved. The Allies' goal of installing politically and morally upright people in the seats left vacant by former Nazis did not succeed entirely, as many Nazis, sympathizers, and opportunists who abetted the Nazi government and war machine ended up in positions of power and influence throughout Germany. This failure taught the German people that pragmatic concerns could outweigh the desire to make a total break with the Nazi past and that favour could be found with the Allies – and German administrators – if one presented oneself in a manner that aligned with the political agenda of those in power.

Reparations

A central component of reconciliation that permeated all relations between the Allies and the German people was the need for the Germans to pay for the destruction of the recent past. During 1945–1946, the Allied Control Council established uniform guidelines for reparations, including the compensation of individual victims of Nazism, but the laws were implemented in a wide variety of ways. In all four zones, the priority for the Allies was to acquire German resources both to cover the costs of administering their respective zones and for their own purposes. In addition to utilizing what remained of German property and possessions at war's end, the Allied powers considered restitution and reparations payments to be an integral part of reconciliation, and they demanded that the German people compensate the other victims of German aggression, both inside occupied Germany and beyond its borders. The Allies' insistence that Germans consider the suffering of others and compensate them financially engendered the process of reconciliation but also exposed its limits. In fact, the German people learned that the Allies' view of reconciliation at the outset of occupation was limited to the legal realm and material compensation and that, in general, one-time payments would serve to absolve Germans of further responsibility towards the victims of German aggression.

Most German proponents of reparations viewed them as a one-time accomplishment – an end in themselves – and as a necessary and unwanted component of dealing with the Allies in moving towards the goal of German self-determination and sovereignty. Regardless of their motives, Germans who accepted the need for reparations had not necessarily engaged in any critical reflection on the Nazi era. Rather, they had chosen to adapt to their circumstances under occupation and gave lip-service to the rhetoric of guilt, responsibility, and even reconciliation, as they found in it significant diplomatic currency.

The process of compensation, and the actual garnering of German finances to distribute to foreign governments, was a cooperative legal effort between the Allies and German administrators. The guided ideological alignment on both sides of the East-West divide gave precedence to material compensation for victims of political persecution, which contributed to a schizophrenic development in restitution and reparations proceedings in Germany.[39] In spite of these different views and motivations – and often because of them – compensation became a central issue throughout occupied Germany.

Establishing an official forum for reparations discussion and compensation developed in all areas of Germany and involved both NGOs and government bodies. These groups attempted to acknowledge and compensate victims for their suffering and losses during the Nazi era and make amends for the widespread damage meted out in foreign lands in the name of the German nation. In the West, the first reparations office was opened in the U.S. zone in Stuttgart in June 1945. Dr Fischer of the Württemberg Reparations Office guaranteed that only anti-Nazi resisters ran the office, but he did not clarify who the office would compensate or on what grounds. Fischer's 21 June 1945 letter to the residents of Württemberg detailing the criteria for reparations was more of an invitation – especially to members of churches, unions, Freemasons, survivors of victim groups, political prisoners, and Jews – to report to the office for compensation, than a sophisticated document of reparations criteria.[40] By December 1945, the Württemberg Reparations Office had enacted a rather generous package that prioritized political prisoners and provided lump sums for clothes, household goods, and the like. Württemberg's Interior Ministry ensured that the following would receive compensation: former concentration camp prisoners who had returned home; those who had been imprisoned on racial, religious or political grounds; people who had fled Nazi Germany and who had continued in active resistance from abroad; and the widows, children, and parents of anti-fascists.[41]

The initial Allied demands that the German people pay for the widespread destruction that the Germans had wrought on Europe was followed through forcefully beginning in 1946. The procedure that ensued dealt exclusively with material loss, seen in the Control Council's 19 January 1946 Draft Reply to the Yugoslav Mission. This document detailed how victims' material losses were to be compensated, only mentioning in passing the Control Council's 'deepest sympathies' for the 'suffering and losses' incurred by Yugoslavs under Nazism.[42] Essentially, the Allies demanded that the Germans return stolen goods to the rightful owners and/or compensate victims of German military aggression financially, in order to help pay for the replacement of buildings and other materials damaged during the war.[43] The next step was to find the rightful owners of the property and determine other damages that would be compensated through German restitution payments. The evaluation procedure involved the solicitation of claims reports from countries that had been occupied and/or damaged as a result of German military aggression; these reports were gathered by the Western Allies beginning in August 1946. This Allied-imposed system was successful in returning at least some of the looted property to its rightful owners.[44]

However, the Allies failed to agree on a unified restitution law, and each military government developed its own law, respectively. The British and American Military Governments led the way in restitution proceedings with the promulgation of Law 59 in July 1947, which ensured that victims of Nazi persecution would be able to reclaim their property. The French and Soviets applied their restitution laws generally, in the context of war reparations, and prioritized their goals over the needs of the German population. This became evident in their exploitation and appropriation of German resources. The French occupation leadership, which joined the Allied Control Council after the Potsdam Conference, did not feel bound to the council's Potsdam Protocols and eagerly exploited German resources.[45] Similarly, the Soviets set out to take advantage of the people and resources in their zone, seen in the dismantling and shipping of Western German factories to the Soviet Union.

When it came to victim compensation, the Soviet Military Administration differed from their Western counterparts and took no responsibility during 1944–1946 for reparations for victims of Nazism in its zone. Instead, this task was left entirely to the German administrators and German People's Courts.[46] Grassroots groups took up the cause, led by Victims of Fascism, whose members were involved in drafting reparations laws – in Berlin (May 1945), Saxony (September 1945), and Thuringia (October 1945) – and were the sole advocates for victims of Nazism in the Soviet zone.

In Berlin, the Central Committee for Victims of Fascism initiated its activities as a non-government organization. It was comprised of four Communists, three individuals who had participated in the plot to assassinate Hitler in July 1944, one member representing Christian persecutees, and one Jew.[47] The committee's chief aim was the economic, medical, and social support of victims of Nazism, and it pursued its goals mostly through self-administration and with funds gathered at fundraisers and through donations.[48] Its members held influential positions throughout the Soviet zone, advocating for victims in a variety of ways. For example, after receiving considerable pressure from Berlin's Victims of Fascism chapter – most notably its founder Ottomar Geschke[49] – the Berlin City Council's inaugural meeting on 20 May 1945 resulted in a directive to evict Nazis from their apartments so that people they deemed to be 'victims of fascism' could have a place to live. Moreover, the council agreed that a one-time emergency sum of 450 German Marks was to be paid out to former political prisoners, and it encouraged donations of clothes, linens, blankets, housewares, and groceries to assist the victims.[50]

The public work of Victims of Fascism included mass rallies, which were intended to garner support for the victims of Nazism in the Soviet zone. The first mass rally was staged in Berlin on 9 September 1945, under the slogan, 'Die Toten – Den Lebenden' (the dead, for the living), and it focused on remembering and honouring the victims who had lost their lives to Nazi brutality and on continuing the struggle against fascism in Germany and the world. The rally's success was evident in the active role of Soviet occupation personnel, who attended in order to 'honour the German fighters against Hitler,' and in the participation of high-profile clergy such as Protestant Pastor Heinrich Grüber and Catholic Bishop Konrad von Preysing, who provided the historical and traditional sanction to the group and its work by leading religious services at the rally.[51]

Even though the group's leaders were much more diverse politically in the Western chapters than in the Soviet zone, where most members were Communists, all of the members of Victims of Fascism shared the common goal of eradicating Nazism from Germany. Group leaders who gave speeches at the rally attempted to distance themselves from Nazi Germany in every way and show victims as nothing but courageous heroes. Berlin Mayor Arthur Werner claimed that Nazism was not indigenous to Germany and that the demons of Nazism must be 'exorcised' in order for the rightful German heritage of thinkers and poets to emerge once again. Founder of Victims of Fascism, Ottomar Geschke – a Communist who was incarcerated in numerous camps throughout the entire Nazi era – pointed out how the resisters of Nazism were the 'really true Germans,' and he considered German anti-fascists to be part of an international brotherhood bound by blood. Geschke claimed that, although the Nazis had rendered Germany 'isolated, despised, and hated' by the rest of the world, the members of Victims of Fascism were washed by their blood sacrifices,[52] and they had salvaged Germany from 'total shame and disgrace.'[53] The 'other' or 'real' Germany, then, found representation among the resisters and victims of Nazism. Victims of Fascism attempted to utilize this interpretation as currency to shift the focus off Germany and onto the broader international struggle against fascism, and thus normalize contemporary domestic affairs and German involvement in international relations.

The acknowledgment that Germany had wrought horror on Europe and the broader world was not as readily accepted among Victims of Fascism members in the Western zones, who tended to internationalize the problem of fascism in a different way than Geschke had. In his speech at the rally, Berlin Social Democrat Gustav Dahrendorf claimed that German anti-fascists were willing to take on the 'entire responsibility of the German people and the responsibility for making things right,' particularly as German anti-fascists had 'failed to save Germany from the moral and political disaster of Hitler's fascism.'[54] Dahrendorf revealed the motive for this responsibility in claiming that Victims of Fascism members desired that Europe be united as a whole. In this manner, Dahrendorf, and other high-profile politicians such as Communist Party member Franz Dahlem, eclipsed the specifically German component of Nazism and focused, instead, on the duty of victims to carry Germany forward to its rightful membership in the family of nations.[55] Together these rudimentary but significant steps taken in the reconciliatory process throughout Germany set the stage for more thoroughgoing approaches, even while they largely ignored the Jews, the largest victims group in Europe. The arduous tasks involved in German-Jewish reconciliation exposed the deficits of dealing exclusively with material compensation and the need for a more comprehensive approach to reconciliation.

Reparations and the Jews in Occupied Germany, 1945–1946

For Jews, the reparations laws were the only assurance that they would receive some compensation and assistance for their suffering under Nazi rule. Moreover, the results of how the laws played out would have deep and long-lasting effects on the nature of gentile-Jewish relations in Germany and would determine whether there would be a Jewish community in Germany at all. Therefore, this legal point became one of high stakes for everyone involved: the Allies, who wanted to democratize Germany; gentile Germans, whose goal was to gain approval from the international community and sovereignty in their own affairs; and Jews, who were in desperate need of assistance.

The horrors of Nazism permeated the minds of Jews living in Germany, who considered themselves the *She'erit Hapletah*, or the 'spared remnant.' Of the nearly 525,000 German Jews in 1933, only a few thousand survived living in Germany during the Third Reich, either in mixed marriages to non-Jewish Germans or in hiding.[56] Added to their ranks were approximately 250,000 Eastern European Jews who ended up in Germany at the end of the war, most of them survivors of concentration camps, killing centres, and death marches. In 1945, approximately fifty thousand Jews inhabited Displaced Persons (DP) camps in the Western zones of occupation, and 4,600 found housing in the Soviet zone, over half in East Berlin.[57] Jews in immediate postwar Germany found themselves living an insecure, often transitory existence, in a place whose people had rejected and murdered millions of Jewish people throughout Central and Eastern Europe.

The Soviet 'liberation' of Eastern Germany ended the deportations and mass murder of Jews but it did not end Jewish suffering. Even though the Nazis had persecuted Jews and had marked them for annihilation based on Nazi racialism, Jews would not be recognized as a distinct category of victims in the Soviet zone due to Stalin's views, and concerns, regarding Jewish nationhood.[58] Therefore, when the Soviet Military Administration encouraged the re-establishment of Jewish communities in the Soviet zone, it was part of its attempt to end the myth of 'Judeo-Communism' and to be seen as morally and politically superior to the Nazis. However, the Soviets did not wish to level the victim hierarchy that rendered Communist 'anti-fascist fighters' superior to Jewish victims. This contradictory approach was evident when the Jewish community in the Soviet sector of Berlin applied for legal status as a religious organization. The Soviet Military Administration and the Berlin Magistrate, as well as Soviet General Nikolai Bersarin personally, responded favourably and the Jewish community (Gemeinde) of Berlin was formally re-established in July 1945.[59]

However, the situation for Jews living in the former Reich's capital was extremely difficult, particularly in terms of their sustenance and standard of living. When Jews applied for permission to function legally as a religious group, they were forced to explain how they had suffered under Nazism. This painful reiterating of the obvious is evident in Jewish correspondence with their Soviet occupiers. For example, in a January 1946 letter to the Magistrate of Berlin, the leaders of the Berlin

Gemeinde claimed that 'in the last twelve years it was particularly difficult for Jews to find food, much more difficult than for the rest of the population.'[60] The Soviet Military Administration approval of the re-establishment of a Jewish community in the Soviet sector of Berlin did not mean that the Soviets were sympathetic to Jewish suffering under Nazism, nor to Jews in general. The Jewish community's claim that the Nazis had treated Jews especially poorly, and that life for Jews was more difficult than for non-Jews, did not find accord with the Soviet Military Administration's hierarchy of suffering. Jews were officially deemed second-class victims of the Nazis, well behind more politically motivated Communist resisters.

The 1945 Berlin Reparations Law marginalized Jews, and no specific funds were designated to compensate Jewish suffering or losses. Because the Soviet Military Administration and German lawmakers had ignored Jewish suffering and compensation issues, the Berlin Jewish community was forced to look abroad for assistance, asking the Soviets for permission to receive aid from foreign sources. When doing so, the Jews attempted to convince the Soviet Military Administration that the aid organizations were 'apolitical.'[61] In July 1945, Berlin's Jewish community sent an urgent plea to international Jewish groups to recognize their plight as victims, and to offer aid:

> All these souly [sic throughout] and bodily sufferings with their terrible symptoms are *not enough to the authorities in Berlin to acknowledge these unhappy persons as victims of faschismo*. In contrast to the Allied Declaration of June 5, 45, article 6, part b, only those men are treated as victims who have been active politically and who, therefore, have been abducted in a concentration camp. By it bitter wrong is done to us. We who during 12 years have suffered grave damage to body and soul, heard under danger to life the foreign transmissions especially those of the ever memorable deceased president Roosevelt who promised us persecuted for race and religion full satisfaction, and now we are treated badly contrary to our expectations well promised. Therefore we beg our liberators to grant us the promised help. Especially we beg to induce that the Jews: a. having been in concentration camps; b. being hided from the persecutions of the Gestapo; c. being forced to wear the Jewish star, as well as their women and children *are recognized as victims of the National Socialism*. Furthermore they are equalized in the relation to the victims of fascism. Finally, we beg *all Jews* of German nationality and their families being always enemies of the Nazis and being treated as such to separate from the mass of the

German people, especially not to charge us the Nazis blame under which we have suffered and bleeded.[62]

During the first few months of occupation, some Jews in the Soviet zone enjoyed the same treatment as gentile victims, receiving compensation in monthly sums and funding to rebuild facilities, including synagogues. The roots of these initial and limited gestures towards the Jews, however, were soon to be exposed. In the first months during which compensation was paid to victims, Victims of Fascism began to differentiate between racial and political victims of fascism. In the summer of 1945, the group supported financially 'only active anti-fascist fighters, who were imprisoned for many years.' By September 1945, they recognized racial persecutees (mainly Jews) and Jehovah's Witnesses, who were forced out of work during the Third Reich, but only in creating a separate category of victimhood for them. These persecutees did not receive the one-time payment of 450 German Marks that the 'fighters' did, because of the 'financial burdens of the state.'[63] This discrimination against Jews escalated in the group's organizational meeting in Berlin in October 1945, where Heinz Brand, a founding member, suggested that Jews be separated into a different category from those who had participated actively in resistance against the Nazis.[64] With this position finding support, Jews and other victims of Nazi racial laws were lumped into the majority group, whom Victims of Fascism categorized as 'Victims of the Nuremberg Laws.'

The ranking of victims led to further problems. For example, 'fighters,' although clearly defined on some points, also included members of the Confessing Church and the 20 July 1944 plot, even though church resistance was limited to opposing government meddling in church affairs.[65] The problematic and presumptuous inclusion of these groups, particularly the church resistance, exposes the biases and assumptions of Victims of Fascism. This classification system that marginalized Jews was widespread. When Victims of Fascism launched its public campaign of accusations, at a rally on 16 December 1945, against the plaintiffs at the Nuremberg trials, they focused on how the Nazis had damaged Germany's reputation and vitality in the world and, when discussing Auschwitz, did not even mention Jewish victims as among the 'five million people' who they claimed had been murdered there.[66] Ottomar Geschke offered a rare reference to 'the most excessive pogrom in world history, the persecution of the Jews,' but the rest of his speech revealed that he supported the group's downgrading of Jewish suffering, and that his main goal was to highlight the 'crimes of the Nazis.'[67]

In the early months of 1946, questionnaires provided the standardization required to identify different victims in the Soviet zone. The categorization of victims and the accompanying hierarchy of suffering corresponded with a two-tiered compensation system. The hierarchy prioritized 'Fighters against Fascism' over 'Victims of Fascism.' The category of second-class victims was broken down into six sub-groups, highlighting the most numerous group of 'Victims of the Nuremberg Laws' and also including a wide range of others. Jewish and Roma and Sinti victims were relegated to the same status as those who, for example, uttered a bad word about the Nazis or had been imprisoned on religious grounds.[68] The ramifications of this split were disastrous, as it led to legislation barring certain victims from assistance. For example, on 6 February 1946, the Victims of Fascism administration at Halle sent out a circular on the 'Gypsy Question.' In it, the Halle office declared that 'because the Gypsies were imprisoned on grounds of their asocial behaviour, they cannot be recognized as political or racial victims. Each Gypsy who produces evidence that he was imprisoned for anti-fascist activity or for being a member of an anti-fascist organization can be recognized as a "victim of fascism."'[69]

By the end of 1946, there was grave concern among the leaders of Berlin's Jewish community concerning the failure of the Berlin Restitution Law to address Jewish issues. The other two reparations laws in the Soviet zone revealed the struggle that was emerging between the proponents of compensation for Jews and those who wished to marginalize the issue. For example, the Saxon law limited victims of Nazism to individuals who had been imprisoned for their political views and had continued their anti-Nazi struggle after release from prison.[70] Jews, or any other victims, were not mentioned. The Thuringian law, by contrast, not only mentioned Jews but included the only provision for Jews in the Soviet zone to gain material compensation, at least in the years 1945–1948.[71] However, most Jews in the Soviet zone continued to look beyond the Soviet authorities for assistance, sending urgent pleas to the American Jewish Joint Distribution Committee and other international Jewish groups to establish a liaison between the Berlin community and the Allied Control Council.[72] Whereas the Soviet Military Administration did not change its stance towards Jewish victims, in 1947 it allowed over a dozen foreign groups to assist Jews in the Soviet zone.[73]

Allied-German Reparations Negotiations and the Foundation for Reconciliation

Even though Victims of Fascism failed to recognize Jewish suffering, it appeared to all four occupying powers to have the ingredients of an ideal German organization: it was anti-Nazi; it wanted to reorganize and rebuild Germany democratically; it tied its activities to valued German traditions such as the German churches; and it seemed to be open to taking responsibility for the evils of the Nazi regime. Indeed, in some ways, Victims of Fascism was the most progressive association that lobbied for reparations in all of Germany, but it was also selective in doing so. For example, although the group ignored overt discussion of compensation for Jews, Gypsies, and homosexuals, it ensured that victims of forced sterilization were given official recognition and support in the Soviet zone, in February 1946, five years before the Federal Republic's related ministries of Health and Finance began to broach the subject (in 1951).[74] Similarly, victims of the Nazi 'Euthanasia' (T4) Program were recognized for their suffering in numerous press articles in the Soviet zone beginning in June 1945, long before victims of medical experimentation were compensated in the West.[75] The open engagement with these difficult issues reveals part of the ideological climate in the Soviet zone, where the Communist leadership wanted to emphasize their moral superiority vis-à-vis the 'fascists' and allowed Victims of Fascism to serve that purpose.[76]

For the Western Allies, concerns about the political foundation of Victims of Fascism took precedence over the positive results that the group was achieving in addressing the evils of the Nazi era. In fact, the Allied Control Council (and the Kommandatura in Berlin) liquidated the Victims of Fascism branch in the Western part of Berlin, even while the group continued to operate in the three Western zones. The Soviets responded differently. The SED had Victims of Fascism reorganize itself internally to align more directly with the party's platform and then incorporated it as a sub-section of the Social Welfare Office of the Soviet zone in August 1946. Throughout that year, a small group of people within the SED championed reparations for the victims of Nazism. These advocates consisted of Helmut Lehmann and Leo Zuckermann of the SED's Central Committee, Karl Raddatz and Heinrich Grüber of the Victims of Fascism leadership, and Julius Meyer and Leo Löwenkopf, who were high-profile Jewish community leaders in the Soviet zone. Together, these men advanced the Jewish cause in restitution discussions and lawmaking, albeit with limited success. It was the former Social Democratic Party (SPD) member Helmut Lehmann who ran the German Administration for Work and Social Welfare after being elected to the SED's Central Committee in April 1946. Prior to the election, Lehmann had been involved in lobbying for Jewish compensation and in dealing with reparations. When he was appointed to the Welfare Office by the Soviet Administration, it was due to the Soviets' acknowledgment that victims of Nazism needed to be recognized and compensated, particularly if the Soviets were to succeed in bringing about a 'democratic stabilization' in Germany in conjunction with the other Allied powers.[77]

Ultimately, the Allies' meddling with Victims of Fascism in all four occupation zones interfered with the possibility of cross-zonal developments in reconciliation work. To be sure, the ban on the Victims of Fascism group in West Berlin and its incorporation into the SED apparatus did not stop its members from meeting, even in an inter-zonal conference titled 'International Reconciliation,' in Frankfurt from 20 to 22 July 1946.[78] Rather than supporting these German initiatives, the Allies prioritized their respective political agendas, thus thwarting German steps towards dealing with their troubled past in potentially constructive ways.

The reparations criteria in the Soviet zone were, in some ways, more progressive than in the Western zones during the early stages of occupation, especially after they were assumed by the government and became legislation in 1948, and adopted by the Soviet Military Administration in 1949.[79] Such a uniform approach to the evaluation and compensation of victims was non-existent in the Western zones during this period, where each jurisdiction had its own guidelines. The lack of German contrition towards the victims of Nazism factored significantly in the slow development of reparations laws; it also affected reconciliation in Allied-German affairs generally, which became evident in numerous other realms in occupied Germany.

The Allies and the German Churches

The Allies, including the Soviets during 1945–1949, considered religion to be one of the most significant elements to be employed in the denazification, re-education, and general reorientation of the German people after the Second World War. Moreover, the Western Allies believed that religion had inherent, positive effects on the individual, and in its affinity to democracy. This view was met with both positive and negative responses from the German side because the vast majority of German churchmen were not yet interested in reconciliation, especially if it meant having to engage in self-criticism.

Many on the Allied side had a difficult time embracing the German church leaders, believing that Germans were inherently evil and were not interested in peaceful coexistence with their European neighbours, a view that found some credence because of the overtly pro-Nazi elements that remained within the German churches.[80] To be sure, a significant contingent held that the majority of Germans had been seduced by Nazism and forced into following its leaders and that Germans simply required kindness and assistance in order to reawaken the good elements within them. British Bishop George Bell of Chichester, for example, claimed in 1945 that Nazism was not particularly German but a product of unbelief, and extolled Christian resistance heroes in Germany, such as Dietrich Bonhoeffer.[81] However, the majority of German churchmen refused to honour Bonhoeffer, and viewed his actions as traitorous. With these competing notions at work, the Allies assigned the German church leadership a significant role in German democratization on the basis of their 'respectable anti-Nazi record.'[82]

In the Soviet zone, the SED claimed in its July 1946 statement, titled 'Our Position towards the Churches,' that the 'democratic construction of Germany includes the freedom of thought and religion' and that 'the Christian religion is a welcome ally in the construction of the new Germany ... and is a natural partner of socialism.'[83] Protestants in the Soviet zone replied to the SED statement in their document 'Christianity and Socialism Are in No Way at Odds,' in which they claimed solidarity with the new regime, particularly in establishing 'social justice and free thought among our people.'[84] Although the respective agendas of the SED and the German Protestant leadership differed on many points, they both worked successfully to establish an educational curriculum in the Soviet zone that imbued students with socialist ideology and provided students in 1946 with the option to have religious instruction in school.[85]

Similarly, U.S. general and zonal commander Lucius Clay stated clearly the role that religious institutions were to play in the American zone and how they were to complement the broader work of the American Military Government. Clay considered the churches to be crucial to the 'building of a peaceful and democratic Germany' and insisted that the Germans do this work themselves.[86] Specifically, Clay stressed three aspects of German reorientation that related directly to religion: denazification; the revitalization of religious life (primarily Jewish and Christian) in Germany; and interaction between German church leaders and international religious leaders, which would foster the democratization of Germany.[87]

The Allied view of religion and its usefulness in German democratization led Allied personnel to support the German churches unabated, even when questions emerged regarding the 'anti-Nazi record' of the German church leadership after the Allies gained more information on church affairs. For example, Protestant Pastor Martin Niemöller's legacy was contested in 1947 on both sides of the East-West ideological divide in Germany, where he was seen as a 'National Socialist with a clean conscience' in the Soviet zone and hailed as a 'martyr to the cause of democracy' in the U.S. zone.[88] Upon closer inspection, the Americans also recognized that Niemöller held a 'highly skeptical ... attitude toward democracy' but that he 'may be counted upon to be an effective ally of Military Government in its opposition to totalitarianism from the left.'[89] By adopting the mistaken view that German Protestants and Catholics had opposed Nazism outright, the Allied Control Council utilized the churches for its purposes and continued to view religion as central to Allied interests in Germany.

The Allies' pragmatic usage of the churches sent contradictory messages to the German people during the first two years of occupation: that the Allies prioritized results in the democratization of Germany over remorse and genuine change and that, by focusing on spiritual institutions, they cared about inner change and personal renewal. This confusing approach became evident when the American Military Government employed an ad hoc policy of denazification in its zone, which included soft measures for German religious institutions. Marshall Knappen reported how the Americans gave the German clergy time to 'clean house' before returning their denazification questionnaires, unlike any other German institutional employees, including school personnel.[90] Moreover, the American Military Government senior leadership instructed Religious Affairs officers not to interfere in ecclesiastical matters during denazification. In all, German tribunals removed a considerable number, albeit a minority, of German clergy from their posts because of their Nazi affiliation, but left senior leadership intact.[91]

While the Allies continued to view religion as important in the democratization of German society throughout 1945–1946, it became evident that three important components of German religious life were in need of immediate attention: the repair of church buildings; the availability of clergy; and religious education in the schools. The disparate views that the Allies held towards Germans became evident in the Control Council meetings, particularly when discussing the fact that most churches – like the Jesus Christus Kirche in Berlin – were in poor condition, and clergy were hard to find. This latter point led the British delegation to suggest, in October 1945, that German clergy be released from prisoner-of-war (POW) camps in order to 'reinforce the insufficient religious personnel.'[92] Moreover, the Bishop of Winchester and a Roman Catholic delegation visited the British zone to ensure the spiritual care of POWs, that interzonal travel permits were issued for ecclesiastical authorities, and that church seminaries were reopened.

It was evident at this early stage of occupation that the Allies viewed religious education as a primary tool in the democratization of Germany. The American member of the Control Council recognized the need to reopen Catholic schools, but only after the 'individual examination of all clerics,' and the French stressed the need for religious education, noting that its effects could include bolstering the trend of younger pastors, who were joining progressive movements that opposed nationalism.[93] The British considered the reopening of denominational schools to be 'an urgent matter,' whereas the American member also stressed its significance, suggesting a number of options.[94] The main objection to standardized religious instruction came from the Soviet delegate, who revealed that the Soviet position towards religious education was less enthusiastic than previously indicated. He encouraged the Control Council to consider passing a directive that would have religious instruction held outside of normal school hours, a practice already in place in the Soviet zone.[95] The three Western Allied representatives refused, revealing their insistence on the centrality of religious instruction in democratization, but ended up compromising with the Soviet delegate. The four powers agreed that 'religious instruction in schools in so far as there are children whose parents desire it, must be given in the normal school hours on the same footing as the other subjects.'[96]

The message to the German people, if mixed, was that the Allies favoured German religious traditions and Germans participation in them. Although those who attended religious services were likely to be seeking comfort in tradition and community, the messages they heard from clergy instructed them about how to interpret their national and personal past, and how to do so within the context of occupation, which often contradicted the interpretation offered by the Allies. By the end of the first year of occupation, the German church leadership had proven its general disdain for the Allies and continued to quarrel with occupation personnel over personal freedoms, such as refugee issues, cross-zonal travel, and attendance at church conferences.[97]

These problems led the Allies to shift towards delegating ecclesiastical concerns to religiously affiliated NGOs. Thereafter, NGOs played a major role in postwar relief and aid in Germany, with organizations under the auspices of the Council of Relief Agencies Licensed for Operation in Germany (CRALOG), in addition to numerous volunteer personnel, contributing millions of dollars in aid to the U.S. zone alone.[98] Beginning in 1946, these groups began to play a central role in the relief and recovery of the German people, and they also began working to restore relationships between Germans and their wartime enemies, often using religion in that process. In short, these groups – and the grassroots initiatives that accompanied them – were becoming a crucial component in the democratization of Germany and an aid to the achievement of Allied goals in Germany.

The Allies, Religiously Affiliated Organizations, and the Germans

Numerous international, religiously affiliated organizations – including ecumenical groups and other NGOs – were eager to make contact with the German people after the end of the Second World War. These groups included the International Fellowship of Reconciliation (IFOR), Moral Re-Armament (MRA), Pax Christi, the International Council of Christians and Jews (ICCJ), and the World Council of Churches (WCC). Whereas the other groups will be examined in other chapters, the World Council merits discussion here. Although the WCC was not officially established until 1948, its Provisional Council was the most organized of the groups mentioned above, and its members had extensive dealings with the Allies during the first stages of their occupation of Germany.

The Provisional Council had as one of its chief goals the reinvigoration of the interwar ecumenical movement in order to promote the peaceful and Christian reconstruction of Europe. In November 1945, the Provisional Council's leaders from the organization's Department of Reconstruction and Inter-Church Aid sent a letter to General Eisenhower, detailing the purpose of the council in Europe, and in Germany in particular. The leaders were clear: 'the World Council of Churches... considers the spiritual reconstruction of Germany to be a matter of highest priority [and] a promising instrument for national regeneration on both

Christian and democratic lines.'⁹⁹ German Protestant clergy applauded the council's initiative and gained membership in the organization in October 1945. Moreover, German clergy participated in the council's leadership meetings in Switzerland in 1946 and secured an invitation to the inaugural WCC conference held in Amsterdam in 1948.¹⁰⁰

For the most part, the Allies supported the Provisional Council's assertiveness in religious affairs, believing that international contacts by religious organizations would benefit the German people. However, the Western Allies favoured a cautious approach that continued to restrict interzonal and international travel for Germans, and the Soviets continued to harbour concerns about the westernization of Germany.¹⁰¹ This disagreement hindered the work of the WCC in Germany at a crucial time in the development of German attitudes towards their recent past.

In contrast to the Allies' politically motivated curtailment of reconciliatory work within Germany between Protestants in Germany and the outside world, in 1946 WCC Provisional Council members in Poland laboured towards German-Polish reconciliation from within their own country. Polish Protestant clergy had refused to support Nazism while forced to endure German occupation during the Second World War and emerged in 1945 to rebuild their lives and, in many cases, to make amends with the German people. Two Polish Provisional Council members – Lutheran Pastor Michelis and Methodist Pastor Najder, both of Warsaw, together with Pastor Niemczyk of Silesia – worked together to reconcile their relationships with German Protestants in the aftermath of the forced population transfers. Through his correspondence with council liaison Stewart Herman, Pastor Michelis told the German people that the 'Polish Lutheran Church made no effort to take unfair advantage of the weakness of the German church in order to appropriate its properties or to alienate its people.'¹⁰² After the German population left the country, the number of Protestants in Poland dropped from 1.5 million to 600,000. This situation led to insecurity for Polish Protestants, who claimed that 'the Roman Catholic Church took advantage of its opportunity to insinuate that all Protestants were Germans because Lutheranism originated in Germany,' and by mid-1946 the Catholic Church in Poland had confiscated over 75 per cent of Protestant property.¹⁰³ Thereafter, Polish Protestants laboured to protect German Protestants, often interceding on behalf of German political prisoners.¹⁰⁴

In a letter to Pastor Michelis, Pastor Najder explained the reasons behind the generosity of the Polish Protestants. In his view, the brutality of the Nazis – and he did acknowledge that 'most Germans in Poland were awful' – did not in any way justify the Polish government's brutality towards ethnic Germans after the war. Instead, Najder called on Poles to empathize with the German people and to treat them as Jesus treated his accusers – with mercy and kindness: 'In spite [of the Nazi crimes] we come to the foot of the cross of our crucified Christ and look to his example: "Forgive them, Father, for they know not what they do." And we say to you, "judge not if you wish not to be judged."'[105]

In Silesia, Pastor Niemczyk laboured against the Allied-sanctioned expulsion of ethnic Germans from Poland, assisting German Protestants as they attempted to maintain their homes in Poland.[106] In doing so, Niemczyk put his entire church in jeopardy, as he and fellow parishioners often travelled into Germany illegally to support their German co-religionists.[107] These examples of solidarity and self-sacrifice provide a glimpse into the effectiveness of religiously affiliated NGOs in the first stages of reconciliation between Polish and German Protestants, which stand in stark contrast to the widespread animosity that most Germans in Poland experienced during the transfers.

This shift towards organic, indigenous involvement in religious affairs was not entirely new but part of what General Clay had been thinking about from the first days of Allied occupation. Already by October 1945, Clay had recognized the need for international contact for the democratization of the German churches, claiming that 'German Protestant leaders ... are anxious to purge the German church of pro-Nazi elements,' and maintaining it was 'of utmost importance to bring democratic and well-disposed religious leaders in Germany into close and early contact with colleagues in democratic countries.'[108] By 1946, Clay, with President Truman's approval, had succeeded in establishing a liaison program between American denominational affiliates to the German churches and other German religious and social groups.[109]

From 1946 on, the American Military Government sought and acquired liaisons from numerous Christian denominations and social groups, believing that their combined work would encourage the democratization of Germany.[110] Numerous American religious and communal representatives functioned as liaisons, including Jews, Roman Catholics, Lutherans, Methodists, Baptists, Mennonites, Mormons, Quakers, and others.[111] Although intended to operate outside the official parameters of Allied operations, the liaisons were the harbingers of German participation in international conferences, beginning in 1946, and educational exchange programs, beginning in 1948.

Initial Lessons

Allied efforts to stabilize Germany during the first year of occupation met with mixed results. The imposition of democratic values – both Western and Soviet-style – forced the German people to re-evaluate their past and their present, which led to positive developments – albeit incomprehensive and inadequate – in victim recognition and compensation and legal accountability for some of the leaders of Nazi Germany. The external introduction of democratization measures obliged the German people to see that a new change of heart was part of the punishment for losing the war and that they would be required to address the crimes of Nazism if they intended to gain the favour of the Allies.

Given the magnitude of problems that the Allies faced, it is remarkable that democratization, in any form, took place in occupied Germany. But it did. With the tensions of the Cold War beginning to take shape, Germans struggled to come to terms with their place in domestic affairs and the broader geopolitical battle. For the most part, Germans engaged in this struggle through indigenous, religiously affiliated organizations whose main concern was to alleviate German suffering and to wrest control of German affairs from the Allies. Germans, operating in a variety of organizations, proceeded to realize these goals with the lessons learned from the Allies during the first year of occupation: that they would be required to repudiate the evils of Nazism, and pay – in many ways – for the past. Any preoccupation Germans held towards their own suffering would postpone the realization of both their short- and long-term goals.

Chapter Two

German Church and Political Groups

The Allies' utilization of the German churches as a central component in German democratization included direct exchanges between influential figures on both sides. This approach established a modus operandi that was steeped in pragmatism. In January 1946, German Protestant Pastor Hans Asmussen, head of the Protestant Church Chancellery, wrote a letter to the Allied Control Council to express his irritation about how the Allies continued to demand that Germans take responsibility for the Nazi past.[1] Claiming astonishment that the Nazi legacy had not faded away outside Germany, Asmussen lamented, 'It is a terrible thing that we cannot drown the question of guilt; we should like to forget it all and begin anew ... but the world will not leave us alone and keeps on bringing up the question.'[2] This foreign pressure and the continuous 'cries for justice and atonement' necessitated a German response. Asmussen concluded that the Germans must, in some way, pay for the misdeeds of the past, because 'all unatoned injustice drags on through the centuries.'[3]

Asmussen's comments typify pragmatic reconciliation in the immediate postwar era. His letter revealed two realities that came to characterize Allied-German relations: that Germans would have to submit to the Allies if they wished to engage in international relations and garner more control of their domestic affairs, and that foreign pressure led even Germans who were keen to avoid the Nazi past into reconciliatory dialogue and action. Imposition of the Allies' demands for reconciliation led Asmussen to perform accordingly. Indeed, in the same letter he adopted a submissive stance towards the Allies, admitting that the Germans had 'no valid excuse ... for [their] evil deeds' and declaring that Germans should not attempt to keep themselves from the 'arm of justice [because] it has pleased God ... to [use the Allies] as our judges.'[4] Similar half-hearted admissions of guilt and the impotent response to it characterized the way that leaders of the German churches, and their affiliated relief organizations, dealt with the Nazi past immediately after the war.

For foreign reconstruction workers in Germany, including Allied occupation personnel and international NGOs, the priority was to stabilize Germany. Doing so required meeting the enormous material needs of the German people. The central role of relief work in this project is evident in the labours of Stewart Herman, who had pastored the American Church in Berlin prior to the war and returned to Germany in 1945 under the auspices of the Provisional Council of the World Council of Churches to aid refugees and help reconstruct the German Protestant Church. Herman recognized, in 1946, the threat of renewed hostilities if German suffering was not adequately addressed: 'The 1945 winter was over ... the problem of feeding and clothing the ex-Reich still remained unsolved in the laps of Allied authority and provincial German governments. As long as it was unsolved, the whole so-called "German problem" would remain unsolved, and as long as no real efforts were made to solve that, there would be no peace in Central Europe. Without the hope of peace in Central Europe, there would be no possibility of an enduring peace in the Western world.'[5] Asmussen's and Herman's views provide a window into the respective mindsets of the German people and the Allies and the nature of relations between the two during the first two years of occupation. In short, the attempt to realize their respective goals resulted in the Allies charging the German churches and their affiliated groups with central reconstructive work, and in Germans supporting, at least in practice, Allied goals.

This chapter explores the pragmatic attitudes and actions of Germans involved in a variety of organizations that both hindered and advanced reconciliatory work in occupied Germany. On the one hand, Germans focused on their own postwar suffering and on creating self-serving interpretations of the Nazi era. On the other hand, many Allied-German encounters, like the one between Asmussen and the Allied Control Council, witnessed the positive effects of Allied policies, seen in German admissions of responsibility and actions that moved forward reconciliatory dialogue and relationships.

After German religious and political leaders reinforced for the German people a whitewashed rendition of the recent past, they undertook proactive approaches to realize their goals of gaining more control of German affairs. Clergy and laity from both official churches in Germany taught their co-religionists to prioritize developmental projects over critical reflection on the Nazi past. In 1945, both churches established organizations whose sole purpose was relief work: the Catholic Church's Aid Society (Kirchliche Hilfsstelle) and Protestant Relief Work (Das Hilfswerk der Evangelischen Kirche in Deutschland). These groups, along with other domestic and international aid organizations, laboured to relieve German suffering, but they also served to reinforce in Germans the notion that they were victims of Allied injustice.

The goals of the church groups corresponded with those of German politicians, who were vying for control over German reconstruction in new, or refounded, political parties and political groups. Like all Western German politicians at this time, the members of three political groups – the German Office for Peace Questions (Deutsches Büro für Friedensfragen, established in 1947), the Institute for Occupation Issues (Institut für Besatzungsfragen, established in 1947), and the Association for Expellees (Bundesministerium für Heimatvertriebene, established in 1949) – focused on establishing political alignment with the Western powers while, at the same time, achieving more control of German affairs. In 1947, when Cold War demarcation lines deepened, these political groups attempted to influence foreign powers in their decisions concerning Germany's borders, and economic aid to Germany. In their efforts to make their case to the Allies, personnel from all three German political groups often employed reconciliatory language when addressing their occupiers. In doing so, they revealed their submission to the Allies' values, and advanced reconciliatory dialogue in occupied Germany.

In the Soviet zone, religion, relief work, and political motives were much more tightly intertwined, at least officially, because the Soviet occupiers and German Communists claimed Nazism was foreign to international socialism, and to life in the zone. Victims of Fascism and People's Solidarity (Volkssolidarität) adopted the official political interpretation of the recent past in claiming that Germans in the zone were victims of Nazism, and proceeded both to relieve and to indoctrinate the German population. Communist ideology claimed to bring food, clothing, and housing to people who had been assaulted by the evils of Nazism and who, according the Soviets, did not need to look to the

United States for sustenance. Together, all of the groups operating in the four zones of occupation contributed to establishment of interpretations of the Nazi past that ignored German responsibility and guided discourse in the Germanies for decades to come.

The German Protestant Church in Occupied Germany

During the first year of occupation, the leadership of the German Protestant Church (Evangelische Kirche in Deutschland, EKD) strove to rebuild its church buildings, and to re-establish its central place in German society. It also sought to contribute to the reconstruction of Germany and to participate in international ecumenical dialogue. Matthew Hockenos has detailed the fragmentation among German Protestants both during the Second World War and in the immediate postwar era. The groupings fall under two headings: the pro-Nazi German Christians and the Council of the German Protestant Church. After the war, the sub-groups competed for power in the Protestant Church and favour from the occupiers, who, initially, treated German Protestants monolithically as resisters of Nazism even though the Allies knew that many German Protestants – most notably the German Christians – had supported and continued to support Nazism. Ignoring the German Christian movement, which the Allies banned in September 1946, Hockenos places Protestants into three categories: Reformers, composed of members of the Protestant Church Council such as Otto Dibelius, Martin Niemöller, and Hans Iwand; Conservatives, who shared an ideological border with the German Christians, such as Hans Asmussen; and Moderate Conservatives like Theophil Wurm, who were somewhere in between the two views.[6]

Using this categorical approach, it would seem most probable that critical reflection vis-à-vis Nazism and reconciliatory dialogue would emerge from the Reformers, but this was not necessarily the case. The evidence suggests that the Reformers held their own politically conservative views and agendas and viewed guilt and reconciliation as strictly religious and personal issues. Under occupation, these pastors denied the right of the Allies to impose any form of collective guilt on the German people. For Reformers, reconciliation, if addressed at all, was an entirely personal matter centring on God's mercy in relation to guilt and suffering.[7]

The Protestant Church Council, created at the foundational meeting of the German Protestant Church at Treysa in August 1945, was determined to reinstate the German Protestant Church's structure without the pro-Nazi German Christians. To that end, the council distanced itself from Nazism, even though many of its members continued to sympathize with some aspects of Nazi ideology. It also ignored the zonal partition of Germany, viewing the establishment of the Soviet zone with particular disgust. The council continued to operate as a united church throughout Germany with limited support, as the Allies granted cross-zonal travel to Protestant Church leaders and supported a unified Protestant Church, at least until the early 1950s. Berlin pastor and Protestant Church Superintendent Otto Dibelius, a Reformer, desired to eliminate these restrictions and to stave off Communist influence in the Protestant Church and in Germany in general. Dibelius promoted himself to the title of bishop in mid-1945, hoping that the title would give him an advanced status in the eyes of the Russians, who knew nothing about Church superintendents.

The Protestant Church leadership's interpretation of the Nazi era did not align with the Allied version of events and served to deepen the divide between Germans and their occupiers. This interpretation taught that German Protestants had been faithful both to God and to their cherished traditions throughout the Nazi era. Church leaders preached that God had spared them from death in the war in order to give them the privilege to rebuild Germany in a new, more Christian, way. By 1946, the Protestant Church leaders were irritated by the fact that the Nazi past would not simply fade away. In response, Protestant pastors preached sermons that denounced collective guilt and called on Germans to forgive their ungodly occupiers, in an attempt to highlight the Allies' misdeeds and eclipse their own.

The campaign to instruct the German people in this manner began immediately after the end of the Second World War, as Protestant pastors distanced German Protestants from Nazism. In a June 1945 sermon titled 'A New Beginning,' Otto Dibelius claimed that Protestants in Germany had been victims of Nazism and lauded Confessing Church members for maintaining their allegiance to God and proper theology throughout the Nazi era: 'Behind us lies a decade in which some sought to make our Protestant church the handmaid of political ideals ... [but] the church [remained] faithful [and] defended itself ... after a short time of being bewildered by such a distortion of the gospel.'[8]

Dibelius appropriated the Jewish concept of *She'erit Hapletah* when he disseminated the view that Protestants in occupied Germany were a spared remnant, a minority of true believers in Germany. According to Dibelius, the glowing example of right-mindedness that set these Protestants apart from the Nazis resulted in them being chosen by God to represent the German nation after the Second World War.[9] In his June 1945 sermon, titled 'The Representative Minority,' Dibelius explained his position: 'The faithful church community is a minority among our people ... and what does God say about such a minority? ... God takes that minority as the representative of the whole ... and ... in the last years hundreds of our pastors were in prisons, because they believed and chose to say no to [National Socialism] ... and these survivors, who saved our people, are the essence of our church today.'[10]

The core message of Dibelius' sermons also appeared in the Protestant Church's collective declaration, given at the Protestant Church Synod at Stuttgart during 18–19 October 1945. The declaration, which avoided direct responsibility for the evils of Nazism, was more of a reiteration of basic Christian devotion to God and the Christian religion. Before stressing that devotion and admitting any guilt, the Protestant Church leadership made sure to emphasize German suffering alongside the suffering of Germany's wartime enemies.[11] After praising Protestants for having 'fought in the name of Jesus Christ against the spirit ... of National Socialism,' the Stuttgart Declaration called for a revitalization of Christian devotion, to make a 'fresh start in our churches' and to 'purge [them] of influences hostile to the faith.'[12] The reason for this revitalization became clear, as the Protestant Church, in its hour of weakness and great need, sought to receive better treatment from the Allies and utilized the threat of renewed German radicalization to encourage the Allies in the right direction: 'We feel deeply, that in this new beginning, we be in communion with the other churches; in an Ecumenical Congregation ... we hope to God that through the common effort of the churches the spirit of force and revenge ... will be banned from the world and the spirit of peace and love will [bring] healing.'[13]

The need for the Germans to appeal to the Allies' interest in having Germany integrate peacefully into the international community became evident in the correspondence between German Protestants and Allied personnel. Indeed, the Allied Control Council claimed that it continued to distrust German institutions but maintained it was 'satisfied with the work of re-establishing the church on a sound and healthy basis' and promised that the churches would continue to receive Allied support, so long as they 'concentrate on ecclesiastical affairs.'[14] It became evident to both sides that the Germans were required to find Allied approval before gaining any degree of self-determination, a realization that, by early 1946, came to involve a direct treatment of German guilt and responsibility for the Nazi past.

The Stuttgart Declaration did not acknowledge the crimes of the Nazi era and – as Asmussen revealed – left the question of German guilt at the forefront of German-Allied relations. In part, Protestants dealt with this problem by highlighting particular cases of German heroism and innocence and pointing to wartime atrocities committed by the Allies, in order to shift the onus of blame onto the Allies and absolve the Germans of guilt and responsibility. In a December 1945 letter, titled 'To the Christians of England,' Bishop Wurm celebrated the fact that the Archbishop of Canterbury had taken the right step in addressing the German people in brotherly terms. Wurm then used the primate's reconciliatory gesture as an opportunity to whitewash German misdeeds and condemn Allied practices.

Wurm began his letter by claiming that German Protestants had been victimized by both the Nazis and the Allies. The Nazis, he maintained, had 'hated [the Protestant Church] ... particularly because they were aware of our condemnation of their misdeeds.'[15] As for the Allies, Wurm contended that Allied victory in the war was 'not simply the victory of good over evil.' Instead, to Wurm, Allied actions were comparable to the Nazi attack on the Jews: 'To pack the German people into a still more narrow space, to cut off as far as possible the material basis of their very existence is no different, in its essentials, from Hitler's plan to stamp out the existence of the Jewish race.'[16]

Wurm's intent was clear: he wanted to vent his anger towards the Allies, and at the same time, manipulate them into softening their stance towards the German people. To achieve these seemingly incompatible goals, Wurm again highlighted the potential negative ramifications of the Allies' policies in Germany: 'If the political authorities today act according to the same recipe, and seek to make Germany as small and weak as possible, and its neighbours as great and strong as possible, then the evil spirits of revenge and retribution will not be banished from the world.'[17] Wurm's criticism of the Allies led him to revise the historical record on at least two counts. His comments on Nazi-Protestant antagonism did not hold up to the record of the Protestant Church's actions in the Nazi era, and his equating of Allied practices with German misdeeds during the Second World War was also unfounded.

Fuelled by this dubious historical interpretation, German Protestants attempted to manipulate the Allies by appealing to their shared Christian values. In August 1945, Heinrich Grüber wrote a letter to Bishop Bell of Chichester claiming that the atrocities of the Allies went far beyond those committed by the Germans during wartime. For Grüber, the solution was for churchmen of all nations to ask for forgiveness from each other and from God.[18] Similarly, Wurm's letter encouraged Britons to join Germans in practising forgiveness throughout the world and closed with a manipulative plea: 'Nothing could help the German people more ... than an object lesson in the behaviour of the victor powers in the administration of justice.'[19]

Throughout the spring of 1946, representatives of the Protestant Church in Germany continued to express their irritation towards the Allies' approach to the Nazi past. On 9 May 1946, one week after gathering for their annual meeting at Treysa, the Protestant Church leadership drafted a letter to the Allied Control Council in which it vehemently opposed the Allies' denazification program on moral grounds. Although the clergy conceded the 'necessity of such a purge' in Germany, it absolved itself – and the Protestant Church – of responsibility for Nazi crimes and entrenched further its interpretation of the Church's actions in the past: 'The Protestant Church carried on the struggle against [Nazism, and] ... did not have the power to overcome these influences; these *facts* and the responsibility devolving on the Church before God give it the right and freedom to express its serious misgiving against the procedure followed today.'[20] The authors concluded the letter boldly: 'to the churches alone belongs the decision of saying who shall exercise the spiritual office and from whom it shall be withheld.'[21]

The Church's letter also claimed that the end of denazification would serve both Allied and German goals, because it would expedite German integration internationally and foster reconciliation with Germany's wartime enemies: 'Our people can only come to a really new beginning when they are able to hear the message and the word of God ... only when the necessary measures are taken with obvious justice and responsibility before God will the way be made clear for the German people to find a new relationship to the peoples of the earth.'[22] For Protestants, the 'responsibility before God' did not include the notion of collective guilt, and Protestant teaching opposed the charge as it did war-related guilt in general. In his 2 June 1946 sermon, titled 'Guilt and Forgiveness,' Otto Dibelius invoked the biblical story of Job, who had suffered terribly in a faith-testing duel between God and Satan. For Dibelius, the example of Job, who refused to curse God and die, was akin to the experiences of the German people. According to Dibelius, the German people were undergoing a test of faith, and the proper response was for Germans to become better Christians. The 'guilt' in this equation was the guilt of personal sin, which belonged to all humans, rather than any specific guilt related to Nazism.

In relation to personal guilt, Dibelius utilized the Christian teaching of sin and forgiveness for the absolution of personal and communal responsibility. When he did so, he made sure to depict the Germans as morally superior to the Allies. In the same sermon, Dibelius declared that it was not the Christian's responsibility to admit personal guilt – the guilt of sin – to anyone who did not know or experience God's forgiveness.[23] Dibelius was referring to the Soviet occupiers who laid claim to the city of his home, Berlin. He mused, 'I don't understand how people who do not know God and who embrace a so-called materialistic world-view can call one to the seat of judgment and reproach them for their guilt.'[24] Instead of placating Allied demands, Dibelius admonished his congregation to stop 'whining,' stop participating in the Allies' 'self-righteous' accusations about collective guilt, and move on to address the only issue that should concern them: seeking personal forgiveness for their sins before God.[25] For Dibelius, the Allies would only have the right to talk about German guilt if they had first forgiven their enemies, the Germans. Because the Allies had not done so – and continued to harbour hatred towards the German people – Dibelius admonished his parishioners to focus on their own personal lives and assist their fellow Germans physically and spiritually wherever possible.[26]

Taken together, these teachings encouraged German Protestants to face their own, personal, sins in conventional ways, by attending church more often, praying more, and being more devoted to God. Returning to or reviving Christian devotion in Germany allowed Protestants to avoid facing German crimes during the Nazi era and to focus, instead, on their own suffering. This work, and the related discourse on German suffering and victimhood, was developed by the German Protestant Church's chief relief organization, Protestant Relief Work.

Church-Affiliated Relief Organizations

Like Stewart Herman and the leaders of the German Protestant Church, many others recognized the latent dangers that ongoing suffering in

Germany posed to German and European stability and the central role that religious and relief organizations could play in staving off a resurgence of political radicalism.[27] Realizing the gravity of the situation, both mainline churches in Germany established relief organizations in 1945: Protestant Relief Work (Das Hilfswerk der EKD) and the Catholic Church's Aid Society (Kirchliche Hilfsstelle). These groups, together with the German Red Cross, were the sole German agencies responsible for relief work in the Western zones at that time.[28] Together these groups laboured to supply the German population with food, shelter, and clothing, and at the same time, they circulated their respective church's teaching vis-à-vis the Nazi past.

Protestant Relief Work

Protestant Relief Work was officially established at the Protestant Church's founding conference at Treysa in August 1945.[29] With its headquarters in Stuttgart, Protestant Relief Work was intended to further the German Protestant Church's vision and role in the reconstruction of German society. The organization communicated this intent to the Allies in October 1945, claiming that it desired to get on with its 'most pressing tasks,' including the 'Re-Christianization of the German people ... [and the] Christian education of German youth.'[30] Bishop Wurm's presidency ensured that the organization's activities would reflect the Protestant Church's conservative agenda.

Akin to the Protestant Church leadership's approach to the past, Protestant Relief Work took great pains to dissociate itself from Nazism, while aligning itself with a different or 'other' Germany. Eugen Gerstenmaier, the organization's head of operations, had been part of the 20 July 1944 plot to assassinate Adolf Hitler, and he utilized his legacy to promote the innocence of Protestants in Germany. When Gerstenmaier addressed the Protestant Church leadership and Protestant Relief Work workers in a New Year's Day sermon, on 1 January 1946, he claimed – as had Dibelius – that German Protestants had resisted the Nazis and he expressed gratitude for the fact that God had spared the Church from the Nazis' 'violent Satanic leadership.'[31] He then acknowledged the 'great guilt' of the German people for not resisting the Nazis as they rose to power. It was this oversight alone that had turned the Germans into the 'pariahs of world history.'[32] Gerstenmaier was convinced that religious devotion and hard work could overcome this stigma, because, 'the churches had already breached the rejection of the German people by enacting the message of reconciliation in relief work.'[33]

Protestant Relief Work proceeded on the assumption that its work in the recovery and reconstruction of Germany would suffice to reconcile the people within Germany and Germans with the broader world. In speaking of German guilt and responsibility in this way, Gerstenmaier addressed simultaneously what the Germans and the Allies wanted to hear. Regarding the Germans, Gerstenmaier's rendition of the past freed the German people from collective guilt; instead, he put the German people in a favourable light, separate from the Nazis, and he deemed the work of relieving German suffering to be their highest calling. For the Allies, Gerstenmaier's embrace of moral responsibility, 'in relationships between German citizens and a German government, and ... in the affairs of the church both inside and outside of Germany's borders,'[34] gained him certain favours. For example, he established a good working relationship with Mr Ohlsson, head of the American occupation forces' Religious Affairs Branch, who agreed in January 1946 to grant Gerstenmaier's request to allow foreign aid into Germany and to permit Gerstenmaier to travel to Switzerland to attend organizational meetings of the World Council of Churches.[35]

Engendering favourable relations with the Soviet occupation personnel and German Communists proved more challenging. Protestant Relief Work had been involved in the politically charged task of distributing illegally foreign aid in the Soviet zone, because until 1947 it remained impossible for foreign aid workers to operate there directly.[36] Keen to counter the image of Eastern Germany relying on the West for its reconstruction, German Communists resented the infiltration of this anti-Communist Protestant relief organization in the zone and pointed to what they considered the dubious anti-Nazi record of the organization's leadership.[37] Tensions and travel restrictions led the Protestant Relief Work leadership to establish a second office in Berlin in 1946 to oversee operations in the Soviet zone. Led by Erich Tillmanns and Christian Berg, Berlin's Protestant Relief Work office brought Protestants into direct contact – and confrontation – with German and Soviet Communists during a volatile period of the emerging Cold War.

The political views and agenda of Protestant and Catholic relief organizations largely countered the Allies' goal of the German people taking responsibility for the Nazi past. Indeed, the relief organizations utilized the conditions of bombed-out Germany and the expulsions to avoid taking responsibility for the crimes of Nazism in two ways: in establishing a deep sense of German victimhood that exceeded that of Jews and Eastern Europeans during the Second World War, and in claiming moral superiority vis-à-vis the Allies. Rather than encouraging the German people to reflect critically on their past, German relief workers admonished their co-religionists to take the lead in forgiving the Allies for their misdeeds and to continue to strive towards personal and institutional holiness. These tactics deepened a sense of victimhood not only among the expellees but also among the people who worked with them and among the German people in general.

In all four occupation zones, when Protestant Relief Work personnel addressed the crimes of Nazism and the responsibility of the German people, they did so for political purposes. Often, conceding some German wrongdoing proved an effective way to highlight the offences of the Allies and Germany's wartime victims while claiming the moral high ground. For example, in January 1947, after the completion of the expulsions of ethnic Germans from Eastern Europe, Protestant Church pastor and Protestant Relief Work officer Siegfried Preuss wrote an internal memo to Eugen Gerstenmaier, in which he stated, 'the Protestant Church cannot observe passively the loss of the Province of Silesia.'[38] Preuss wanted to utilize ecclesiastical influence in Germany and abroad to persuade the delegates to the Foreign Ministers Conference in Moscow – who planned to meet in spring 1947 – to have Silesia remain within Germany, rather than become part of Poland. Preuss stressed the urgency of the situation and called on Gerstenmaier to use his influence in whatever way possible, because 'the Moscow Conference, where the difference between the life and death of our people will be decided, is upon us.'[39]

Preuss suggested the manner by which Gerstenmaier could achieve the desired result, which centred on garnering the support of influential co-religionists in Switzerland, the Netherlands, Scandinavia, and North America.[40] In doing so, Preuss stressed that Germans should take on a posture of forgiveness when relating to the Allies and their Eastern European neighbours. Preuss appended a flyer in his letter to Gerstenmaier, titled 'The Refugee Crisis and the People: Forgiveness or Retaliation?' which he intended to send to church leaders abroad. Hoping to garner the support of foreign church leaders for his goal of saving Silesia, Preuss' flyer was full of references to German guilt and responsibility for Nazi crimes.

Preuss's flyer admonished Germans to forgive rather than harbour thoughts of retaliation because of the 'injustices that had been practised in the name of the German people' during the Nazi era, including the attack on Jews during the 'Night of Broken Glass' in 1938.[41] Preuss went on, referring to the miseries of the Poles, Jews, and Britons – to name a few – who were on the receiving end of German bombs and the horrors of German occupation and asked: 'what will happen when the pendulum swings back in our direction?'[42] Penitence filled the second half of the document, which pointed out how the German people had provoked the wrath of foreigners but also acknowledged – and highlighted – the extent of German suffering: 'What we began with the Poles and the Jews has now come back to us in increased measure, which is in keeping with the law of retaliation, which we set in motion. And now the guilty and the innocent members of our people have to suffer unspeakably.'[43] Pointing to the example of Jesus, who forgave and prayed for his persecutors rather than using his power to smite down them down, Preuss called on Germans to end the cycle of violence between Germans and the rest of Europe.[44] For Preuss, taking the moral high road would mean winning the sympathies of foreign governments.

An example from the Soviet zone also depicts the connection between admitting the evils of Nazism and achieving political goals. In order to be allowed to operate freely in the Soviet zone, Protestant Relief Work had to find favour with the Soviet occupiers. To that end, in August 1945, the organization's leaders drafted a letter to the head of the Soviet Administration in Germany, Marshal Zhukov. The Protestant Relief Work spokesman acknowledged that Nazi Germany had included the 'greatest criminals of all time' and expressed gratitude to Stalin for sparing the German people from annihilation.[45] Like his counterparts in Stuttgart, Christian Berg also proclaimed, in October 1945, that German suffering originated in German sins during the Nazi era. Like Preuss, Berg claimed that the Germans were forced to endure more than those they had victimized during the war: 'So it is said straight out: German suffering is above all entirely clearly fruit and consequence – the final result and heritage – of the Third Reich and its lost war ... before we will be allowed to make someone responsible somewhere else in the world, we have to take responsibility for it ourselves ... it is in our memory ... how in the years 1939–1942 the Polish villages ... were depolonized and Germanized by our SS or regional leadership ... now it is all coming back to us in a way that is much worse.'⁴⁶

Berg's and Preuss' historical interpretation – of the Germans losing the war, but winning the comparative victimhood contest after 1945 – became common currency among the expellees in the immediate postwar period. Comparing postwar German suffering to that of East Europeans during the war became a tool for Protestant Relief Work personnel in evaluating both eras and for highlighting German morale and courage. In July 1946, Berg asserted, much as Dibelius, Gerstenmaier, and Preuss had done, that God had given the Germans the burden of suffering to bear. Postwar German suffering, he maintained, gave Germans an opportunity to rebuild their country, physically and morally. Indeed, this latter point was important for Berg, who warned of the alternative: a resurgence of political radicalization among German youth.⁴⁷

By focusing on their own suffering and pointing out the dangers of a resurgence of German radicalism, Protestant Relief Work workers in all four zones were able to twist historical facts for their own purposes. To be sure, Protestants were not alone in this regard, as Catholics employed a similar approach to the Nazi past. Like their Protestant neighbours, Catholic clergy and relief workers found that speaking openly about German guilt was a useful tactic in both appeasing and accusing the Allies. In the process, they contributed to the emerging discourse of German victimhood that eclipsed honest reflection on the Nazi era.

The Catholic Church in Occupied Germany

In the period immediately following the Second World War, Catholics in Germany dealt with the recent past by retreating into religious tradition. This retreat found support in papal and episcopal teachings, and the Vatican stayed the course it had set during the later stages of the Second World War, which was vehemently anti-Communist and supportive of a strong Catholic Europe. Pope Pius XII welcomed the anti-Communist Western powers that occupied Germany while, at the same time, he continued to hold the German nation in high regard, seeing it as a crucial component in the realization of Vatican interests. For Pius XII, the priority was to stabilize and Christianize Europe in the wake of total war and stave off the further spread of Communism. In the service of these goals, the Vatican wished to free Europeans – Germans, in particular – of the responsibility for Nazi crimes, a burden that would only hinder progress in the Vatican's stabilization program. This goal would best be served through Catholic teachings of forgiveness and grace, not through acts of revenge, such as the expulsion of ethnic Germans from Eastern Europe.[48]

The pontiff did not shy away from addressing the evils of Nazism, but he made sure to accompany such references with praise for the rectitude of German Catholics. For instance, in a November 1945 letter to German bishops, he lauded the valiant actions of Catholics who had opposed the Nazis' 'false teaching [that] attempted to supersede Jesus.'[49] Moreover, he instructed Bavarian bishops – who he claimed had been victims of National Socialism[50] – on how to interpret the recent past: 'Brave heroes have given their lives for the true Christian faith. These heroes were from among you; there were also a great number who perpetrated violence and fear, but they were not among you, but under you and against you, just as they were against the Bavarian people ... they have endured many sufferings on account of their terrible sacrilege, and they will suffer more.'[51]

In aligning the Catholics of postwar Germany with the martyrs of the faith who had defended heroically Christian values under Nazi rule, Pius XII promoted the notion of German victimhood both during the Nazi era and in occupied Germany. The pontiff embedded this belief in his letter to all German bishops, where he claimed that Catholics had been victimized by the Nazis and 'dragged through an insidious and severe persecution.'[52] The pontiff concluded, much as German Protestants had, that those who had survived the fires of persecution were a noble lot: 'The best from among [the German Catholic] people have made an impression in Our favour.'[53]

Pius XII was deeply disturbed by the fact that millions of Catholics in Eastern Europe faced the imminent establishment of Communist states in their countries. To stave off the spread of Communism and further the goal of establishing a Christian Europe, the Pope encouraged German bishops to restrain German expellees from meting out revenge on their Eastern European neighbours and lobbied the Allies for their assistance. In general, he encouraged the people of Central and Eastern Europe to create 'an atmosphere of friendship and love' based on their mutual Catholic faith that 'overrides the terrible and consuming fires of hatred.'[54]

German bishops found accord with the Pope's views and wove them skilfully into their sermons throughout 1945–1946, as they attempted both to underscore the notion of German victimhood and impress their Allied occupiers. For example, Bishop Michael Buchberger of Regensburg's 1945 year's end sermon reinforced the notion of German victimhood. Ignoring the horrors that Germany had wrought upon its neighbours in the preceding six years, the bishop claimed that 1945 had been the 'worst year in human history,' because Germans in Eastern Europe were forced to flee the 'apocalyptic horseman with the plagues of the end times.'[55] Buchberger considered the war trials to be a divine invitation to renewal rather than a punishment. 'We are Christians,' he claimed, 'and we view the hard life also as a gift from God; a difficult time as a time of mercy, and collapse as a commission from God for rebuilding.'[56]

German bishops also echoed the pontiff's view that Nazism was alien to their fold. The Bishop of Regensburg called Nazism 'un-Christian, unspiritual, and at base un-German' and concluded that it was doomed to fail, 'due to its spiritual, moral, and emotional degeneration.'[57] He blamed the Nazis for bringing misery instead of the Paradise they had promised, and claimed that the Allies continued the unjust punishment of the German people after the war.[58] In doing so, he revealed his belief in the inherent superiority of the Germans and, with a dig at both the Nazis and the Allies, he thanked God that there 'is an eternal home no one can take away from us.'[59]

Buchberger concluded his letter with reference to God's suffering on behalf of humanity. He quoted Jesus' anguished words from the Garden of Gethsemane, just before his crucifixion: 'Father if it is your will, take this yoke from me; if not, your will be done.'[60] In doing so, the bishop compared the German nation to the sacrificial Christ and lauded German Catholics as a group that God had chosen for a special purpose and tested with persecution. He signed off with a call to godly living and encouraged Catholics to be proud of their 'heroic deeds' in resisting Nazism and in their 'heroic suffering' thereafter.[61]

Developments in the British zone reveal the same defensive posture among German Catholic clergy. In the immediate aftermath of the war, Cardinal Joseph Frings, Archbishop of Cologne, wrote a 'Defeat Letter,' in which he claimed that the Catholic Church in Germany had mounted a significant campaign 'against the heresy of National Socialism,' pointing particularly to the anti-Euthanasia efforts led by Bishop Clemens August Graf von Galen in Münster. Frings maintained that 'the atrocities had been hidden' and that it was 'common knowledge under this menace that speaking out would bring terrible punishment.'[62] Building on this reflection was a joint statement, issued in January 1946, by Frings and his counterparts in Paderborn, Osnabrück, Münster, Hildesheim, and Aachen that aligned the archbishops with the notion of German innocence. In this letter, the archbishops, who wished to influence Catholic clergy in Eastern Europe, decried the 'revenge through criminality' that had been meted out on 'innocent [ethnic Germans] in order to atone [for the past]' and called for 'those who are truly guilty to give an answer.'[63]

This theme of differentiating Germans from Nazis became a common interpretive tool among Catholic clergy. In the French zone, Freiburg Archbishop Conrad Gröber's December 1945 address claimed, like Frings' letter, that German atrocities had been hidden from the public, and that those who had committed terrible deeds comprised a small minority.[64] The conclusion was that punishing the entire German nation – and ethnic Germans in Eastern Europe – was unjust, and 'comes close to the [Nazi] system of criminal forced population transfer.'[65] However, just two months later, in February 1946, Gröber's efforts to garner sympathies from the Allies for Germans living in Poland included reluctant admissions of German crimes in Poland. In his Lenten sermon, Gröber contributed to the discourse that acknowledged German responsibility, stating that 'the horrible nature of the crimes that Germans meted out in Poland goes far beyond what the Germans have to go through now in Poland. Unfortunately, we cannot deny that ... but all people will recall that it is not raw force that triumphs, but humaneness, reconciliatory action, and Christian love.'[66]

According to the November 1945 reflections of the Bishop of Ermland, East Prussia, the Devil was to blame for the misfortune of the German people, including the bishop's fellow-expellees. Only God could rescue the expellees from the Communists, the bishop concluded, and he pleaded with God to do so: 'The Devil has dashed us into misfortune; come Father, King, without hesitation, come raise up Your kingdom under us, do not let us fall, do not allow us to sink into financial or spiritual poverty.'[67] Retreating from the physical world, the bishop, like his counterparts in occupied Germany, used Scripture to give weight and credence to his claims and to situate the German people within the history of salvation. Armed with this teaching about past and present events in Germany, the Catholic Church's Aid Society set out to assist the spiritual and physical suffering of Catholics in occupied Germany.

The Church's Aid Society

After the defeat of Nazi Germany, the Catholic Church leadership rekindled the Church's organizational model of Catholic Action of the 1920s, which centred on the renewal of Catholic traditions and practice in Germany, and it intended to utilize existing and new lay organizations to further that cause.[68] Accordingly, in October 1945, at their annual conference at Fulda, Catholic bishops founded the Church's Aid Society to address the specific needs of Catholic expellees, and appointed Bishop Hermann Wilhelm Berning of Osnabrück to oversee its operations. The Aid Society headquarters were located in Frankfurt am Main, but the chief centre of operations was in Munich, where Richard May, Paulus Sladek, and Hans Schutz, all expellees, formed its operative head. The central goals of the Aid Society were to give material assistance to Catholic expellees, to provide pastoral care and maintain Catholic culture and traditions among the expellees, and to help integrate the expellees into the economy of occupied Germany. From its founding in 1945 until its dissolution in 1950, the Church's Aid Society contributed significantly to the material and spiritual well-being of millions of German Catholics and to the collective memory that Christian Germans developed about the Second World War.

Catholic relief workers frequently compared the expellees' flight from the east to the plight of Jesus Christ, who was born during a family pilgrimage and lived a life of holy pilgrimage thereafter.[69] The Free Association for Pastoral Care in Freiburg selected the occasions when Catholic leadership opposed Nazi practices and published their findings in a pamphlet, 'What Have We Learned over the Last Twelve Years?' This essay called on Catholics to practise the piety of these heroic men and focus on the renewal of Catholic youth education. Fuelling this action was a deeper calling to follow Jesus' example of forgiveness and sacrifice. To that end, the Aid Society aligned German Catholic expellees with the martyred Christ, claiming that even though one 'cannot and should not forget' the brutal expulsions, the expellees must forgive, 'just as Christ forgave his murderers on the cross with the words, "Forgive them Father for they know not what they do."'[70]

Utilizing these motifs, and bolstered by Allied support and papal and episcopal teachings, the Church's Aid Society succeeded in rationalizing the deep sense of victimhood and injustice among ethnic German expellees.[71] And there was ample material with which to work. Aid Society reports between the summers of 1945 and 1946 revealed that the Potsdam decree to expel all ethnic Germans from Eastern Europe merely gave official sanction to the ill-treatment that ethnic Germans were already receiving for their non-German neighbours in Poland, Hungary, and Czechoslovakia.[72] Although in isolated cases Eastern European clergy treated Germans with kindness, as seen in the Polish Protestant case earlier, the Aid Society's correspondence reveals that, in early 1946, relations between Polish and German Catholics were anything but reconciliatory. Germans expressed their astonishment at how brutally the Poles treated them before and during the expulsion and how German areas of Silesia were forcibly Polonized.[73] One German Catholic man expressed to a Polish soldier that the SS were heathens – and, therefore, it was understandable that they had brutalized the Poles as they had – but he was shocked to see Poles, who were fellow Catholics, treat Germans so terribly.[74]

The Polish clergy's response to such accusations was mixed, with some observing that the Germans were reaping what they had sown during the war. Priests of this persuasion participated in the widespread practice of restricting the use of the German language in religious and primary schools. Other Polish clergy, however, like Father Karol Milik of Silesia, called on both Germans and Poles to leave their racial and ethnic hatred behind and follow the merciful teachings of God and the Pope in building a new peaceful relationship.[75] These conciliatory voices were in the minority, but their legacy was significant in creating possibilities for future cooperation.

On the German side, both types of approaches can be found. A letter sent from General Vicar Richard Popp of the Sudetenland to the bishops in Bavaria, in 1946, revealed that German priests who reflected critically on the Nazi past could expect severe criticism. The letter details how Popp reprimanded a priest who had concluded that the plight of Eastern European Germans was a natural consequence of having supported Hitler's war aims. According to Popp, such damaging words should not come from a man of God, and Christians needed more understanding and love from their priests than the man in question had displayed.[76]

Similar views were evident among ethnic Germans expelled from Czech-German borderlands in 1945–1946. A number of Aid Society workers were in this group, including Aid Society co-founder Hans Schutz. Like the Protestant writings discussed above, Aid Society publications acknowledged German war crimes in order to contend that the Czechs had done even worse after the war. In one flyer, the Aid Society used the massacre at Lidice as a springboard to express the organization's views on injustice. However, the injustice spoken of here was not the murder by the SS of all of Lidice's men in response to the assassination of Reinhard Heydrich in Prague in 1942 but the expulsion of Germans from Czech lands after the war. From the perspective of the Church's Aid Society, Czech postwar violence towards Germans eclipsed the SS actions in Lidice, in terms of the total number of people affected and the number of missing children.[77] The flyer concluded with a lengthy reminder that many Czechs had supported Heydrich and had opposed his assassination, which was intended to heighten the sense of injustice in the expulsion of the Sudeten Germans. Moreover, many expellees claimed that the Sudeten Germans had not been supporters of the Nazis, a stark contrast to accounts that reveal that the opposite was true.[78]

Other Aid Society circulars also admitted German misdeeds in the attempt to normalize Nazi terror in the context of twentieth-century brutality and highlight the crimes of their Eastern European neighbours. In doing so, the Church's Aid Society pointed out the absurdity of the claim that justice was being served at the trials of leading Nazis at Nuremberg and of the German Death Squads (Einsatzgruppen). When referring to the Nuremberg trial results in November 1947, one writer stated outright that the victims of Nazism should be compensated and that the 'guilty should be punished.' The reason for this admission became clear, as the writer went on to claim that the expulsion of ethnic Germans from Eastern Europe was far more horrendous than any German wartime deed.[79]

Similarly, the Church's Aid Society utilized the 1947 trial of the Death Squads to point out how, in their view, the Allies had surpassed the Germans in brutalizing their wartime enemies. Rather than addressing the mass murders carried out by the SS and auxiliary forces during the war, the Aid Society circular, titled 'An Orgy of Murder,' focused, instead, on Soviets and Eastern Europeans. The flyer claimed that the only thing that had changed from the Nazi era was that the 'the perpetrators shifted from the SS to Eastern Europeans,' with the 'undesirable elements' shifting from Jews to Germans. The circular concluded that the 'bearers of the Hammer and Sickle have the same verdict of guilty as the bearers of the Swastika.'[80] In the end, the attempts of the Church's Aid Society to minimize and defray responsibility for Nazi crimes led its leaders to acknowledge that those crimes had occurred, contributing thereby to the discourse on Nazism that was necessary for reconciliatory work to proceed.

Admissions of guilt and references to German responsibility in Aid Society correspondence served to gain the sympathies and assistance of the Allies and Germans who received the expellees in their towns and homes. After attempting to prove that Allied atrocities outdid those of the Germans, the Aid Society moved to distance itself and the expellees from the Nazis and from the German people in general. In a sermon penned by Aid Society leaders Sladek and Naj, the authors claimed that the Sudeten Germans had not lost the war but were forced to atone for the evil deeds of a 'conscienceless group among our people who inflicted wanton criminal acts on us and other nations.'[81] In highlighting German guilt, Sladek and Naj attempted to arouse the German nation's sense of responsibility towards the expellees rather than towards victims of German wartime aggression. According to Sladek and Naj, '[The expellees'] suffering and fate begins with all of us ... in some way we all need to perform atonement for the sins that were begun in the name of our German people, and our atonement lies in our assistance to those who lost their homes ... and God has spared us, not because we were better, but because he wanted to give us the opportunity to become better.'[82] This plea for forgiveness might appear in hindsight to be manipulative, but it, nevertheless, included an acknowledgment that all Germans somehow had a share in the crimes of the war and needed to turn away from the path of Nazism.

In the Soviet zone, Church's Aid Society workers were even more overt in highlighting German suffering in order to garner sympathy from the Western Allies. The March 1946 Aid Society report, titled 'The Suffering of German Catholics in the Russian Zone,' claimed the central role of NGOs in relief work in the zone, stating that they 'alone ha[ve] the power and the strength to make public and to inform the world of the suffering and misery.'[83] The Aid Society detailed the horrific experiences of the nearly two million Catholic expellees in the Soviet zone, in what was called the German Communist 'Rule of Terror.' The organization's complaints were levelled at both German Communists and the Soviet occupiers, who did nothing to alleviate the suffering of expellees and even contributed to it by looting German goods and raping German girls and women.[84] The priority of the Church's Aid Society was to promote Catholic goals, and its work was particularly challenging in the Soviet zone, where no significant Catholic infrastructure existed. Indeed, the report highlighted the greatest areas of need in the Soviet zone, namely, that over a hundred priests were required to provide for a dignified death and proper burial for expellees.[85] The Aid Society complained that Protestant expellees were receiving a great deal of aid from German and international sources, compared with the meagre 'one wagonload' of goods that had arrived, to date, for Catholics in the Soviet zone.[86] The lack of Catholic educational material was of particular concern because Catholics viewed the Soviet zone as the front line of the spiritual battle for Europe. 'The refugees ... in the Russian zone,' the report stated, 'are waiting for the Church ... Here lies the battle of deciding between Christendom and Bolshevism ... We need your assistance!'[87]

According to the Church's Aid Society, effective religious education would set Germany back on the proper moral path. It worked in tandem with its youth group, the Ackermann-Gemeinde – and the German Catholic Youth – towards relief of expellee suffering and rebuilding of Catholic traditions in Germany. Catholic Youth was pragmatic in its treatment of the Nazi past, which was evident in its 1947 letter-writing campaign for the release of German prisoners of war. In the campaign, the group offered different interpretations of the past to different audiences. When appealing to international groups, such as the Allied Control Council and international youth organizations, the group claimed that Catholic youths had experienced 'pain and shuddering' upon realization of the 'enormous guilt' of the German people, and that they were willing, even as the 'least guilty' among the German people, to 'atone for these sins.'[88] In contrast, when writing directly to the POWs, Catholic Youth referred proudly to their appeal to the Allied Control Council and reported that they had made reference to the 'unlawful and unjust' incarceration of German soldiers without alluding to German guilt or responsibility.[89] Meanwhile, the Ackermann-Gemeinde tried throughout the occupation era to gain the right for expellees to return to their homelands;[90] marshalled by Aid Society leaders Sladek and Schutz, the group's efforts were cloaked consistently in the language of reconciliation.[91]

Bolstering these initiatives was a broader Church's Aid Society effort to lobby the international community on behalf of the Sudeten Germans. In a 1950 joint letter, titled 'The Sudeten German in a Federated Europe,' a number of Sudeten Germans who held public positions backed the Aid Society in stating that the expulsions of ethnic Germans were wrong and that expellees should have the right of return. This group both revealed its pragmatic interest in reconciliation, and voiced an important truth about the postwar world when it claimed that 'reconciliation between France and Germany is necessary for the salvation of Europe.'[92] For Sudeten Germans, a continent-wide reconciliation between Germany and its wartime enemies would occur only after expellees were allowed to return to their homes in Eastern Europe.

These tactics found accord with, and were bolstered by, direct teachings from Catholic educators who fused conservatism, tradition, and progressive approaches in their efforts to revitalize German educational institutions in the immediate postwar era. For example, the celebration of the opening of the Munich Volkshochschule, in July 1946, included repeated references to the significance of re-education and moral development of the German people after Nazism. At the opening of the Volkshochschule in Munich, the city's mayor, Karl Scharnagl, said the event proved there were Germans who were willing to 'contribute towards the reconciliation and redress of split and divergent personal convictions [which would] achieve practical success in forming our people into a nation with sound democratic principles.'[93] Scharnagl admitted the wrongs of the past, which served as 'a sufficient warning to all,' in order to highlight his solution: the renewal of German Catholic traditions. 'German reflection,' he announced, *should mean nothing else*, but to [awaken] in German consciousness the best and lasting achievements of the German mind and spirit, achievements which have been universally appreciated by humanity.'[94]

Mayor Scharnagl also took the opportunity of the school's opening to address the Allies and their politics. Much as Asmussen had done, Scharnagl took a posture that combined refuting the notion of collective guilt and expressing German hubris with submission to the Allies' view of Nazism. At the same time, he claimed that the German people had been victimized by Nazism and, therefore, did not need to be 'denazified': 'Active participation in the cooperative course of the Volkshochschule is, therefore, the best denazification work we can do ... It is not only capable of completely eliminating evil mental attitudes; it replaces them by sound democratic conception and ways of thinking that are based on old and tested truths.'[95] To Scharnagl the evil deeds of the recent German past, perpetrated by a few people, could be expunged via Catholic education, which would 'achieve the spiritual recovery of our people [and] stimulate ... its most noble qualities and powers.' Moreover, he reasoned, this simple cleansing process would further the ultimate goal of the German people, as schools, like the Volkshochsschule, would 'assist in leading [Germany] back into the community of magnanimous nations.'[96]

Karl Vossler, Rector of the University of Munich, offered the parting words at the end of the inaugural meeting of the Volkshochschule. Vossler echoed Mayor Scharnagl's praise of religious education and went further, pointing to the crucial elements of self-criticism and reconciliation that are inherent in proper education. He considered these aspects to be key in the development and maintenance of future relationships, proclaiming, 'The Volkshochschule is destined especially as a sanctuary of free thought to fulfil compensatory, reconciliatory, and invigorating functions ... and ... to develop the critical faculties and the faculty of self-reflection.'[97]

Although based on a selective view of the past, the Catholic retreat into religious traditions and practices during the first two years after the Second World War yielded some significant results in the realm of reconciliation. Whereas the defensiveness of Catholics permeated all discussions of the past, the dire situation prompted churchmen and relief workers to open up about Nazi crimes, even if their intention was to garner more sympathies for their own plight. These early utterances on German crimes during the Nazi era constructed a discourse that would develop further and, ironically, serve processes of reconciliation in the years to come.

Politics, Racism, and Relief

The general claim of German victimhood among German churchmen and relief workers found widespread acceptance among the German population, and it was evident in the work of German political bodies in all four zones of occupation. Two significant political groups formed in the British and American zones in 1947: the German Office for Peace Questions and the Institute for Occupation Issues. Acting as the predecessor to the Federal Republic's Foreign Ministry, the German Office for Peace Question's chief goal was to broker a peace treaty with the Allies, whereas the Institute for Occupation Issues served as a watchdog of occupation practices and costs. Both institutions wished to press the Allies in their decisions regarding Germany's future, particularly – as the Protestant Relief Work had done – through influencing the outcome of the Foreign Ministers Conferences held in London and Moscow during 1947.[98] In November 1946, Victims of Fascism was dissolved in the Soviet zone to re-emerge in February 1947 as the Association of Victims of Nazism (Vereinigung der Verfolgten Naziregimes, VVN). The VVN and People's Solidarity – together with the Social Assistance arm of the

SED's Central Committee – guided all assistance programs for Nazi victims in the Soviet zone. By 1947, these four groups were negotiating regularly with the Allies.

During 1945–1947, in the Western zones, many figures in German public life introduced democratic initiatives, often for opportunistic reasons. The defensiveness typical of German churchmen and relief workers was also evident in the work of German political groups, who tried to win international recognition for their suffering and promote German self-determination. In all cases, it was the terms of their Allied occupiers that led Germans to admit certain aspects of German guilt and responsibility for actions during the war. Nevertheless, such admissions, however insincere or coerced, contributed to reconciliatory work.

An excellent example of this interplay is seen in the Office for Peace Question's endorsement of Bremen Senator Gustav Harmssen's 1947 book, *Reparations, Social Productivity, and Living Standards: An Essay on Balancing the Economy*, which was intended to serve the organization in its negotiations with the Allies.[99] Harmssen detailed the dismal situation in occupied Germany in the hope of garnering Allied leniency in economic affairs. In the process of describing conditions in Germany, Harmssen admitted German guilt and acknowledged a moral responsibility for making reparations, but only after he had stressed the victimhood and continued suffering of the German people. 'Even though the German people had suffered awfully as victims of the war,' he wrote, Germans recognized the need to move forward with a 'new ideological foundation.' Harmssen did not explain this new ideology, but he did highlight German suffering, and presented an economic plan to solve it. His approach resulted in enormous outcry and condemnation from abroad, seen in one *Economist* reviewer's reference to the book as a new *Mein Kampf*.[100] In the setting of 1947 – in marked contrast to the climate after the First World War – even a German conservative like Harmssen voiced acceptance of German reparations, albeit in order to gain hearing from the Allies. In doing so, he advanced the process of reconciliation by broadening British-German communication following the publication of his book.[101]

The Office for Peace Questions coordinated its efforts with the Institute for Occupation Issues in working towards maintaining German territory and challenging Allied occupation policies. When it came to dealing with Germany's Nazi past, both agencies insisted that there were very few 'real' Nazis and that Allied denazification efforts were a joke.[102] Similarly, the Association for Expellees – a political organization in the Western zones that sought the right of return for expellees – mocked the French for not being able to find any German war criminals in the late 1940s and chastised them for punishing innocent Germans for Nazi crimes.[103] Instead of encouraging the ownership of German wartime violence, the Association for Expellees focused entirely on the suffering of German refugees.[104]

By contrast, Soviet occupation personnel and German Communists in the Soviet zone focused on uniting Germans in an 'anti-fascist front.' This effort was led by the amalgamation of the German Communist Party and the Social Democratic Party of Germany (SPD) into what became the ruling Socialist Unity Party of Germany (SED) in 1946. The dictatorship that emerged under Soviet and German Communist domination left little room for dissent or democratization. Rather, the priority was to incorporate the zone into the Soviet bloc, which meant distancing Germans from the Nazi past.

In the Soviet zone, People's Solidarity – a politically aligned, state-sponsored, relief organization – worked in tandem with Victims of Fascism on behalf of the victims of Nazism. For Victims of Fascism, aligning itself with international Communism was a priority. To that end, it made repeated mention of Nazi atrocities in order to distance itself from Nazism and fuse it with Communists abroad who had been victimized under German occupation. In the 1945 pamphlet, titled 'To all Women and Families in Germany: Where Are the Children from Lidice?' Victims of Fascism attempted, like the Church's Aid Society, to raise awareness of missing family members from the Czech town. However, unlike the Aid Society, it ignored German suffering and highlighted only the Czech victims who had been forcibly displaced and separated after the 1942 massacre of Lidice's men.[105] The efforts of Victims of Fascism proved successful, and by February 1946, at least a few children were able to find, and reunite with, their mothers.[106]

The work of People's Solidarity followed the party line of the SED, which announced that it intended to use the association as a 'pure propagandistic instrument ... in order to mobilize the population for reconstruction.'[107] To that end, People's Solidarity accepted Western donations via the International Red Cross. This pragmatic cooperation with the West also led the SED to court Protestant Relief Work,[108] the Church's Aid Society, and other NGOs, and to allow these groups to do the grunt work of reconstruction. In doing so, the SED hoped to stave off the advance of capitalism.[109] To ensure that things were proceeding appropriately in the political realm, People's Solidarity provided moral and political instruction for the people.¹¹⁰ In short, the SED and the relief organizations used each other to realize their respective objectives of influencing the German population in the Soviet zone on the proper path.

When it came to dealing with the genocide of the Jews, German NGOs in all four zones failed to overcome the antisemitic beliefs that shaped their perception of responsibilty towards their Jewish neighbours. For example, Protestant pastor Heinrich Grüber, one of the founding members of Victims of Fascism, had laboured to save Christians of Jewish descent from the Nazi death machine. After the war, he exaggerated gentile protection of Jews during the Nazi era. In 1945, a letter was sent from Grüber's office to Swedish, British, and American religious groups who wanted to support 'non-Aryan Christians.' Grüber's associate, Curt Radlauer – a Jew who had converted to Christianity – drafted the letter, which claimed that when the Nazis attacked the Jews, the Confessing Church branch of the Protestant Church had sought to protect the Jews as best it could. Because of this model of sacrifice, the letter asserted, foreigners should offer their moral and financial support to converted Jews living in occupied Germany.¹¹¹

Indeed, when German NGOs addressed the suffering of Jews, they limited their focus to Jews who had converted to Christianity and often showcased converts like Radlauer to bolster their campaigns. Grüber, and other like-minded Christians in all four zones who wanted to help Jewish converts, established the Consortium of Christian Aid Societies for Racial Persecutees of Non-Jewish Faith in Germany (Arbeitsgemeinschaft christlicher Hilfsstellen für Rassenverfolgte nichtjüdischen Glaubens in Deutschland). The consortium limited its focus to assisting Christians who were of Jewish descent, and did not offer assistance to Jews.¹¹²

The very existence of a consortium to aid 'racial persecutees of non-Jewish faith' revealed the continuation of racial categories and religious division in the first year after the war. The Catholic welfare organization Caritas published a flyer that offered a reason for the divisive support structure, stating that Jewish relief organizations only compensated religious Jews so that 'racial persecutees of the Christian faith are not supported at all.'¹¹³ Even though Jews who remained in the Jewish faith and in Jewish communities in occupied Germany were desperate for food and clothing – and established a consortium to lobby international groups for assistance¹¹⁴ – Protestant Relief Work leader Eugen Gerstenmaier claimed that Jews were being supported very well by the

United Nations Relief and Rehabilitation Administration (UNRRA), and therefore the 'Jewish Welfare organizations are not interested in [Protestant Relief Work].'[115]

Members of all German relief organizations continued to use Nazi racial categories and terms when talking about Jews. For example, the Consortium's very title differentiated between Christian and Jew, even after a Jew had converted to Christianity. Even the correspondence of the well-intentioned consortium was rife with references to 'non-Aryan Christians,' 'Jewish Christians,' and 'Hebrew Christians.'[116] Meanwhile, Protestant Relief Work referred to the Central Association erroneously as the 'Association of Non-Aryan Christians,'[117] and Gerstenmaier used Nazi terminology to describe the wife of a Protestant man as a 'full Jew.'[118] Nazi categories did not emerge from thin air in 1933, nor did they dissolve in 1945. Instead, they remained embedded in the vocabulary of Germans as obstructions to the process of reconciliation.

Pragmatic Relations

During the first two years of occupation, the Allies and the Germans considered each other to be responsible for the disastrous situation in postwar Germany. Both groups upheld religion as useful in the reconstruction process. The Allies relied on the notion that the churches had resisted Nazism when they decided to utilize the German churches in the democratization of Germany. However, the attitudes and actions of German churches and their affiliated NGOs cast doubt on this interpretation of the past. Instead, German churchmen attempted to extend the need for moral awakening to all of humanity, including the Allies, who, according to the Germans, had committed war crimes of their own.

The development of a discourse of victimhood allowed the German people to avoid the task of reconciling with their wartime enemies beyond vague admissions of German misdeeds that were intended to mollify Allied onlookers. Notions of victimhood emerged along ideological lines in Eastern and Western Germany. Together, ideology and admissions of German guilt played an important, and ironic, role in the establishment of another discourse – one of reconciliation – in occupied Germany. This discourse of reconciliation became a significant factor in encounters between Germans and their wartime victims. Although these encounters were of a very different nature in Eastern and Western Germany, Germans in all zones considered them to be highly disagreeable, even if, because of outside pressures, they came to regard them as necessary.

Chapter Three

Steps towards Christian-Jewish Reconciliation

During the months leading up to the founding of the Federal Republic of Germany, in May 1949, the Western Allies revealed the propensity to distance themselves from direct involvement in Jewish affairs while focusing on German democratization. This trend concerned Jews like Harry Greenstein, who was Adviser on Jewish Affairs to the U.S. High Commissioner for Bavaria. With Allied support, Greenstein organized the Conference on the Future of Jews in Germany, held in Heidelberg in July 1949. At the Heidelberg Conference, Jews living in Germany, representatives of international Jewish organizations, Germans, and Allied personnel gathered to discuss the dire situation that Jews faced in the new Federal Republic of Germany. Although Greenstein had the support of U.S. High Commissioner John J. McCloy, he represented a minority viewpoint at the conference that wished to establish permanent Jewish communities in Germany and utilize Jewish victims' assets for that cause.[1]

Most Jewish participants echoed the majority view of all Jews in Germany, who opposed the establishment of permanent Jewish communities, pointing to the Holocaust and continued antisemitism in Germany as grounds for Jews to emigrate.[2] The debate revealed participants' different positions and highlighted the persistence of antisemitism, not only in the West but throughout Germany. As serious as the situation was in the West, it was obvious to everyone involved that, in 1949, a similar conference on the allocation of Jewish assets in the Soviet zone was out of the question.

At the Heidelberg Conference, the most enthusiastic support for the establishment of permanent Jewish communities in Germany came from gentiles, who revealed both self-serving and altruistic motives.

For McCloy, the success of the Allies' democratization program included religious pluralism, which he considered inextricably linked to the establishment of Jewish communities in Germany. McCloy intended to achieve this goal with little concern for the Jewish people or their preferences. That there were only five gentiles at the conference did not dissuade McCloy but seemed to embolden his claim of the 'world significance of the relationship of the new Germany and the Jew.' To McCloy, the emigration of Jews from Germany would be 'an acknowledgment of failure.'[3] He suggested that it was the responsibility of Jews to curb German antisemitism and called on Jews to assimilate: 'The attitude of the Jew who remains in Germany [will determine] the extent to which [the Jewish] community becomes less of a community in itself and merges with the general [German] society.'[4]

Following McCloy's pragmatic proposal, Eugen Kogon, chief editor of *Frankfurter Hefte* and a gentile survivor of Buchenwald, expressed grave concerns regarding Jewish emigration and offered moral and altruistic reasons for wanting Jews to remain in Germany. Kogon painted an optimistic picture, claiming that 'all decent Germans will surely take the opportunity to live normally with fewer than twenty thousand Jews.'[5] Kogon, an active participant in Frankfurt's Society for Christian-Jewish Cooperation (Gesellschaft für Christlich-Jüdische Zusammenarbeit), after its establishment in February 1949, highlighted recent developments in interfaith dialogue in which, he felt, the seeds of new relationships between Germans and Jews were being planted: 'Everywhere, also in Germany, a very promising discussion has been going on about what the Jewish and the Christian religion have in common, as both of them stem from the same root of the Old Testament ... We are gradually beginning to recognize that what we share in common is more important than what differentiates us. Surely there is still some hope for reawakening among an increasingly large number of Germans.'[6] McCloy's practical goals and Kogon's idealistic approach to interfaith dialogue became the two primary forms of gentile-Jewish reconciliation practised by non-Jews.

The Zionists at the conference responded negatively to these gestures, whereas Jews who wanted to re-establish permanent communities in Germany were cautiously optimistic. Philipp Auerbach, a survivor of numerous concentration camps, became one of the first Jews to hold a government position in postwar Germany. As State Commissioner of Bavaria, his tasks included identifying and compensating victims of Nazism. Auerbach's negative experiences with German gentiles over the years led to conflicted feelings regarding Jewish life in Germany: 'The German people have no sense of guilt and are not held culpable by others... There is no inclination on the part of the German people to restitute what they acquired illegally... [Moreover] antisemitism will continue to exist in Germany. It is, perhaps, even stronger now than it was during the Hitler regime.'[7] As for Kogon's optimism regarding interfaith dialogue and the possibilities it offered for German-Jewish reconciliation, Auerbach highlighted numerous problems, including school curricula. He also offered a starting point for solving that problem: 'The hatred the Germans have for the Jew is partially explained by the indoctrination the Germans received in the Catholic schools that Jews are a cursed people. If the relationship between Jew and gentile is to be improved, the religious texts and other books must be revised.'[8]

Peisach Piekatasch, a Displaced Person (DP) from Poland involved in assisting Jewish emigration, echoed Auerbach's views and those of most DPs, asserting that 'to remain [in Germany] is to die.' Piekatasch also agreed with Auerbach that the German people failed to acknowledge their crimes against the Jews. In his assessment, 'the initiative for the rapport between the Jews and Germans [should] come from the Germans, and let it be reflected not in words but in deeds.'[9] Auerbach's and Piekatasch's comments addressed two central components of German-Jewish relations in occupied Germany. On the one hand, they highlighted the widespread disinterest Christian Germans showed in reconciling with Jews. On the other hand, they pointed towards concrete ways to improve relations, such as revising the education curriculum.

The few Jews who shared the optimism of McCloy and Kogon recognized the necessity of a joint Jewish-gentile effort in the reconciliatory process. German Jews – notably, Norbert Wollheim, Benno Ostertag, Max Cahn, and Philipp Auerbach – were the most supportive of establishing permanent communities in Germany, even though many in this camp were not optimistic about the success of such an endeavour. Regardless of the tempered optimism at the conference, they set up the Central Council for Jews in Germany to represent their collective interests.[10] Max Cahn closed the debate by supporting McCloy's notion of a combined Jewish-gentile effort to build a new Germany. He put the onus on gentile initiatives: 'We cannot ignore the demand of those Germans who have asked us to join in the common fight for the moral reconstruction of the German people.'[11] For all present, it became evident that for German-Jewish reconciliation to begin, non-Jewish Germans would have to start the process and convince Jews of their good will.

This chapter explores the first steps of gentile-Jewish reconciliation in occupied Germany that began immediately after the collapse of Nazism. Even though much of the reconciliatory work was motivated by narrow self-interest and tainted by antisemitism, it yielded remarkable results. Just a few months after Allied armies ended the Nazis' campaign of mass murder, Jews began to receive compensation for their suffering, and occupied Germany became a relatively safe haven for Jews who fled persecution in Eastern Europe. Through a combination of self-serving and idealistic reconciliatory gestures from gentiles, and with the partnership of some engaged Jews, personal and communal processes of reconciliation were advanced.

During the initial stages of occupation, the German people had successfully combined submission and defiance in their relations with the Allies. After state formation in 1949, however, the defensive component became untenable. When the Allies, representatives of world Jewry, and the international community in general demanded that Germans make tangible, significant amends for the destruction of European Jewry, the Germans were forced to take action. The Allies, however, had not modelled a form of reconciliation that extended beyond pragmatic and often superficial results. German gentiles mimicked this approach and employed the conventional method of material compensation. Most expressed little concern for the communal or personal well-being of Jews. Nevertheless, a few diligent Germans, like Kogon, laboured, with Allied support but against German public opinion, to include Germans in international Christian-Jewish dialogue and to develop Societies for Christian-Jewish Cooperation in Germany.

In the Soviet zone, Stalinism, although officially repudiating antisemitism, encouraged antisemitic practices in government and NGO work. A 1948 law rendered impossible the restitution of Jewish property, and official policies sidelined German-Jewish reconciliation throughout the zone. These diverging approaches to the Jews in occupied Germany – and to the Nazi past – affected the governance of the four zones, the decisions of Jews to leave or stay in Germany, and the reconciliatory discourses that imbued the foundation of the two Germanies.

Jews in the Soviet Zone

By 1947, the majority of the roughly 200,000 Jews in occupied Germany had established social, cultural, and political organizations, but the divide between Eastern European DPs and German Jews remained marked.¹² Jews continued to endure antisemitism, which, coupled with the horrific memories of the Nazi era, led most Jews to oppose the establishment of permanent communities in Germany. With the support and assistance of international Jewish organizations, most Jews in Germany emigrated during 1947–1949.¹³ In 1949, in the U.S. zone, the total number of Jews dropped from 64,329 in January to 15,000 in November. In 1946, excluding Berlin, there were 2,094 Jews in the Soviet zone. By 1949, the number had dropped to 1,149, and most of these people were elderly, sick, or both. East Berlin's Jewish population also diminished during the late 1940s, from 2,535 in 1946 to a few hundred by 1953.¹⁴ It was obvious to all – including the participants at the Heidelberg Conference – that if Jews were to establish permanent communities in Germany, they would require assistance from their German neighbours. Indeed, during Allied occupation, the few Jews who attempted to found permanent communities in Germany had no choice but to rely on the black market for sustenance and on Allied Military Police – and in some cases, German police – for protection against violent attacks from their German neighbours.¹⁵

In 1947, the frail and underpopulated Jewish community in the Soviet zone was barely holding onto its existence, dependent on the labours of Victims of Fascism and assistance from international organizations. A 1947 report commissioned by Paul Merker, an SED member employed in the Office of Labour and Social Welfare in East Berlin, revealed that the Jewish community's chief frustrations had not changed since the summer of 1945. Jews continued to seek recognition as a national minority in Germany to get back the property that had been stolen from them. Whereas most Jews had embraced Zionism, others, to the surprise of Merker, aimed 'to overcome the difficulties and adversity in the rebuilding of a democratic Germany.'¹⁶ Indeed, throughout 1947–1948, Jewish communities in the Soviet zone persisted in promoting their interests to repeated frustration. For example, when Paul Merker and prominent Dresden Jew Leon Löwenkopf appealed to the Allies for recognition of Jewish victims and restitution of Jewish property, they were ignored.¹⁷ Appeals to People's Solidarity and to the Victims of Fascism's Reparations Committee also went unheard.¹⁸ Clearly, outside help was necessary. However, those who supported Jews discovered the depth of antisemitism in the Soviet zone.

The few gentiles who devoted themselves to assist Jews in the Soviet zone faced significant resistance from antisemitic Soviet administrators and German Communists. Historian Jeffrey Herf illustrates this tendency in his discussion of Paul Merker's work in the Office of Labour and Social Welfare, which was under the leadership of Secretary Helmut Lehmann.[19] Merker and Lehmann worked in tandem with the founder of Victims of Fascism, Heinrich Grüber, and Jewish members Julius Meyer and Heinz Galinski to include the recognition of Jews as victims of Nazism in the Reparations Law. These efforts coincided with a volatile period in the Soviet zone, when denazification and reparations legislation shifted from concerted Allied policy to laws that developed along ideological lines in each respective zone of occupation. To be sure, Merker and Lehmann had a difficult task, as Victims of Fascism, re-established in 1947 as the Association of Victims of Nazism (VVN),[20] had already relegated Jews to second-class victim status below the 'anti-fascist resistance fighters.' Merker and Lehmann presented their draft of a restitution law to the SED leadership, which operated under the close supervision of the Soviets. The law levelled the distinctions between racial and political victims and supported the return of stolen property. To realize their goal, they proposed a VVN-staffed government committee that would oversee implementation of the law.[21]

Ultimately, all of these efforts failed because of the promulgation of the Soviet Military Administration's Order 82 on 29 April 1948, which restricted restitution of stolen property. Order 82 put into force the restitution of property to organizations that were recognized in the Soviet zone and set deadlines for submission of claims one month after its introduction. The impossible task of proving the pre-1945 ownership of buildings and property in the loosely organized Jewish communities throughout the zone resulted in very few successful claims.[22] The law drew sharp criticism from Jews, who were supported by Merker. Jewish SED Central Sekretariat member Leo Zuckermann expressed his shock and disappointment in a controversial article, 'Restitution and Reparations,' in the April 1948 edition of the *Weltbühne*. Zuckermann tackled the Stalinist negation of Jewish nationhood, stating 'the Jewish people have the same claim to restitution as the other assailed nations.'[23] Zuckermann appealed to Merker, in a 30 April 1948 letter, and Merker vented his anger towards Wilhelm Pieck, co-chairman of the SED. Merker demanded that Jews be recognized as a national minority and that restitution reflect the scale of Jewish suffering under Nazism, but to no avail.[24]

Concerted gentile-Jewish attempts to gain appropriate recognition of Jewish suffering resulted in no improvement for Jews in the Soviet zone.

In fact, things got worse.[25] Part of the political restructuring of the zone included closure of the SED's Executive Committee in September 1948 and the subsequent creation of the Central Party Control Commission.[26] One of the SED Control Commission's main tasks was to weed out 'saboteurs' within the divisions of the SED apparatus. Among the accused were Merker and Lehmann in Labour and Social Welfare and other like-minded individuals. Merker, who was imprisoned from 1952 to 1956, recalled after his release the accusations that his interrogators and prosecutors had levied against him for his reparations work during the late 1940s. Based on false evidence, he had been accused of 'selling the GDR to the Jews' and 'defending the interests of Zionist monopolist capitalists.' He discussed how a team comprised of Soviets and East German secret police (Stasi) jeered him as 'king of the Jews': 'The Soviet and German interrogators repeatedly commented on how they could in no way understand how I, as a non-Jew – if I was not receiving pay from the Jews or from Jewish organizations – would advocate on behalf of the Jews ... [unless] I was an agent of imperialism.'[27] For Merker, it was simple: guided by 'humane motives,' he believed that it was the 'duty of non-Jews to oppose antisemitism.'[28]

Although the Communist foundation of the new East German state, in October 1949, officially repudiated antisemitism, its anti-capitalism employed familiar antisemitic motifs that deemed Jews as greedy entrepreneurs.[29] In this light, coupled with the extremely rare gestures of empathy from gentiles,[30] it is astonishing to find the perseverance of Jews to establish permanent communities in the German Democratic Republic. To be sure, the government did fund the re-establishment of some Jewish institutions, for example, in Thuringia's state-funded rebuilding of synagogues and the protection of Jewish cemeteries, even while it refused to return property to Jewish individuals.[31]

Jews in the Western Zones

Although the Americans were most active in addressing the plight of Jews in Germany, all three Western Allies supported the American promotion of gentile-Jewish reconciliation, and they worked in tandem to address issues of reparations. The shift from denazification to reconstruction in Western Germany in 1947 was accompanied by changes in the Restitution Law, which focused on property return, individual monetary compensation, and more general compensation schemes involving international Jewish organizations and, after 1948, the state of

Israel.[32] Unlike the situation in the Soviet zone, where reparations and restitution debates were closed and unfavourable for Jews, Western German newspapers continued to discuss openly the 'next phase' of reparations in spring 1948, which specifically addressed compensation of Jews.[33]

Attitudes towards Jewish suffering and compensation, however, were not much better in the Western zones than in the East. Even though the Office for Peace Questions endorsed the basic rights of Jews in Germany, it levelled all suffering under Nazism and downplayed Jewish compensation, asserting that specific categories for Jews would be 'food for antisemitism.'[34] Moreover, the tenuous situation of the Jewish communities in Western Germany, a subject broached by Benno Ostertag at the Heidelberg Conference, meant that Jews who wished to remain in Germany would have to rely on gentile support.[35]

The ongoing discussion of Jewish compensation in the West was due, at least in part, to the Allies' continued control of reparations proceedings. The Western Allies used that control to try to lead Germans to recognize and atone for the crimes of the Nazi era themselves. To that end, the Allies ensured the creation of German political bodies that dealt with restitution. Noteworthy results came from those efforts, particularly in the American zone. In Baden-Württemberg, Karl Hauff led the provincial committee that dealt with the recognition and compensation of racial, political, and religious persecutees. Beginning in 1947, Hauff embarked on a public campaign supporting the persecutees, as did his successor Otto Küster after 1948.[36] Moreover, during the months before the introduction of the Occupation Statute and the onset of semi-sovereign status in Western Germany, the Allies emphasized repeatedly the importance of disarmament, demilitarization, restitution, reparations, and the practice of civil rights in Germany.[37] The Western Allies also reminded the Germans of Allied power, noting that after the creation of the Federal Republic of Germany, the respective Allied High Commissioners would have veto rights in each of the three Western zones.[38]

Together, the Allies and the Western press – and the emerging liberal free press in Germany – exerted pressure on the German governing bodies in Western Germany to pay for the evils of Nazism. Moreover, the United States government made it abundantly clear that the future political and social course of Western Germany was to follow direct American guidance. To that end, in February 1947, the American Military Government passed the first uniform laws – applicable to all

Länder in the zone – guaranteeing property restitution. The French did the same later that year, and the British in 1949.[39] Starting on 1 September 1949, the first restitution payments to individuals were to be paid out, including 5 German Marks (DM) for every day that an individual had been incarcerated in a Nazi concentration camp. Moreover, the zonal Restitution Office and the religious tax funded Jewish communities.[40]

By 1949, it was clear that the Jews would require some assurance from their German neighbours in order to feel secure in their communities, especially with plans for full German sovereignty in the works. Germans like Eugen Kogon provided some promise, if his words at the 1949 Heidelberg Conference were to be taken seriously. Kogon had responded to the demands from Jewish participants that Germans initiate reconciliation by stating that he was 'convinced that the battle in Germany is not lost.' 'I prefer to remain [in Germany],' Kogon said, 'because I want to make my contribution in that fight ... It is our duty to strengthen the minority [of "good" Germans] and not to abandon it.'[41] Kogon left the conference early in order to address fifty thousand Catholic youths at a nearby gathering. He promised the Jewish delegates that he would pass along their words and concerns to those young people.[42] For Kogon and other members of the 'minority' he called upon in 1949, it was interfaith dialogue that was key to gentile-Jewish reconciliation. Such efforts proved productive, but they, too, were fraught with difficulties that ranged from Christian philosemitism, which was steeped in ulterior motives, to Jewish reluctance to engage in these projects.

Christian-Jewish Reconciliation, 1947–1949

In the wake of the Holocaust, many people saw the need for a new approach to gentile-Jewish relations, but it took the efforts of a few courageous individuals to spearhead its formulation and implementation in occupied Germany. Initiatives towards that end came from German gentiles, Jews, Allied personnel, and international NGO workers. Akin to the central role of the German churches and their affiliated relief organizations in material aid and reconstruction, the churches – and the struggling Jewish communities in Germany – were to play a crucial role in the first stages of German-Jewish reconciliation. The Western Allies, Germans, and Jews all recognized that the shared elements in the Christian and Jewish religions could provide a basis for intercommunal relations. Accordingly, in 1947, the Western Allies increased their support for interfaith dialogue via their Religious Affairs branches.

The rare initiatives of Christian-Jewish reconciliation in the first years after the Holocaust came from a wide variety of individuals, whose motives were equally varied. The majority of Christians throughout Germany either ignored Jewish suffering and discouraged dialogue with Jews or rekindled their pre-war efforts to convert Jews to Christianity. In the Soviet zone, Stalinist ideology dispelled the notion that Nazi ideology, persecution, and mass murder had targeted Jews in particular ways, and gentile Communist 'anti-fascists' eclipsed Jews in political consideration and material compensation. This ideological setting – and the small number of Jews in the Soviet zone – allowed Christians there to ignore the topic of Christian-Jewish reconciliation. Meanwhile, a small group of Christians and Jews laboured individually and in concert, most notably in the Societies for Christians-Jewish Cooperation, to expunge antisemitism from the Western zones of occupation and to secure compensation for Jews.

The road to Christian-Jewish dialogue was exceedingly difficult. Even while Kogon encouraged the Jews at Heidelberg to 'give the German people [a] new chance [to] repair the wrongs' of the past, he acknowledged Jewish concerns as 'justifiable.' Warning against an 'overdose of criticism,' Kogon encouraged a 'joint gentile-Jewish enterprise,' claiming that 'ours is a common cause [and] we, the minority, must insist that [the West German government] take the initiative [in the] moral reconstruction of Germany.'[43] Kogon's call for mutual gentile-Jewish acceptance and cooperation in Germany was rare, but he provided the much-needed encouragement for Jews to consider the possibility of entering into dialogue with Christian Germans and to contribute to the establishment of a democratic Germany.[44]

By the end of the conference, the Jewish delegates had not fundamentally altered their prior views, but many participants voiced appreciation of Kogon's approach and acknowledged, with much hesitation, the merits of his position. Harry Greenstein reiterated the fundamental problem of German antisemitism, explaining that 'no one can work in Germany for even a brief period without being conscious of the deep, underlying hatred and hostility against the Jews which exists on all levels of life.'[45] At the same time, however, Greenstein conceded that he, too, believed more was at stake than the opinions of the participants: 'Regardless of our personal feelings, I am convinced that there will continue to be a Jewish community in Germany ... From the long range point of view, it is of the utmost importance to encourage a positive, democratic program that will reach into government circles, into the church, the family, and into the daily lives of the German people.'[46] Rabbi Isaac Klein, Adviser on Jewish Affairs in the American Military Government, also recognized the absence of German support for the Jewish communities but stressed the broader network of support that Jews in Germany could develop in the future. Like Greenstein, he pointed to the bigger picture, calling it the Jews' 'sacred duty to help [Jews] establish [themselves in Germany] and live a Jewish life.'[47]

The few Jews and gentiles who laboured against the majority viewpoint of their co-religionists would bring about significant results in Christian-Jewish reconciliation in Western Germany. In many cases, German initiatives preceded the introduction of formal Allied material and institutional support, even though they came to rely on that support for their sustenance. Regardless of their motives, which were various, such efforts improved relations between Jews and Christians in a number of ways.

Protestants

At the outset of Allied occupation, there were no extant groups that fostered Christian-Jewish dialogue in Germany. The German Protestant mission groups established during the nineteenth century had been disbanded by the Gestapo in the late 1930s and early 1940s.[48] Of the few international church-based groups that addressed Christian-Jewish relations in the mid- to late 1940s, the vast majority were mission organizations established in the nineteenth century, such as the International Missionary Council's Committee on the Christian Approach to the Jews, and the Hebrew Christian Alliance. After the Second World War, these groups renewed their commitment to the traditional Christian goal of converting Jews to Christianity. At its inaugural meeting, in 1948, in Amsterdam, even the World Council of Churches stated its intent to missionize Jews.[49]

German Protestants did not show much change in their views and actions towards Jews after the Second World War. When German Protestants issued their well-known statements at Stuttgart in 1945 and at Darmstadt in 1948, they refrained from spelling out the responsibility Germans held for the crimes of the Nazi era, particularly in regard to the Jews. Instead, the German Protestant Church focused on proselytizing Jews and supporting Christians of Jewish descent, whom they continued to categorize racially, as 'non-Aryan' Christians.[50] To realize these goals, in 1946, German Protestants spearheaded creation of the interconfessional Consortium of Christian Aid Societies for Racial Persecutees of Non-Jewish Faith in Germany, and in 1947, the German Protestant Committee for Service towards Israel (Deutsche evangelische Ausschuss für Dienst an Israel).

The failure of the German Protestant Church to reconfigure its stance towards the Nazi past and towards the Jewish people had considerable consequences in the realm of gentile-Jewish reconciliation. The few explicit admissions of guilt and responsibility from German Protestants came at the local level, in Provincial Church statements and, in one case, from the Ecclesiastical-Theological Society of Württemberg, established by Hermann Diem. An outspoken critic of Nazism, Diem had offered a critical appraisal of German Protestantism under Nazi rule, which resulted in his marginalization within the Church. In April 1946, he issued the most direct and hard-hitting statement to date on the issues of German guilt and responsibility towards the Jews, stating, 'We succumbed despondently and idly as the members of the people of Israel among us were dishonoured, robbed, tortured, and killed ... we encouraged racial arrogance ... and thus impaired our service to the Word of the Gospel.'[51] A similar stance was taken by the Westphalian Synod, expressed in its declaration of July 1946.[52]

In the Soviet zone, the most far-reaching statement in the realm of Protestant-Jewish reconciliation came from Pastor Albrecht Oepke in Saxony. In April 1948, Oepke issued a declaration on behalf of the Protestant Church in Saxony that implicated all German Protestants, and indeed, all Germans, in the Holocaust.[53] The 'Declaration of Guilt towards the Jewish People' – the first of its kind in the Soviet zone – admitted the 'deep shame' of the German people for having murdered 'millions of Jews' and begged God to forgive the German people for their 'sins against the Jewish people.' Moreover, it promised an ongoing commitment of the Protestant Church in Saxony to the welfare of the Jewish people, beginning with seeking justice for and extending compassion to the Jews of Saxony.[54]

The vast majority of Protestants in all four occupation zones avoided making such statements and distanced themselves from those who did. German Protestants continued to grapple with what they called the 'Jewish Question,' and in Darmstadt, in April 1948, the Council of Brethren of the Protestant Church issued a declaration called 'Word on the Jewish Question.' In contrast to the exceptional statements outlined above, the declaration reiterated the charge of deicide against the Jews, contending that, 'since Israel crucified the Messiah, it has rejected its election and destiny' and asserting that Jews could only regain a right relationship with God through conversion to Christianity.[55] Instead of finding common ground between the two faiths, the German Protestant Church continued to focus on promoting its interests through conversion and increased church membership. When Protestants approached Jews in the first years after the Second World War, they did so most often through mission groups that were established during the nineteenth century, shut down during the Nazi era, and re-established in 1945.

PROTESTANT MISSIONS

It was external pressure that compelled the German Protestant Church, in limited ways, to confront the Nazi past and reassess its view of the Jewish people. In a November 1947 letter addressed to all German Protesant pastors, Pastor Hans Asmussen revealed that there was 'great concern' among those in ecumenical circles abroad over the 'Jewish Question' and that 'people look directly to Germany for an essential contribution towards the position of Christianity towards this problem, and wait for Germany's response.'[56] Asmussen suggested that the Protestant Church Council respond to this foreign imposition by developing clarity on the 'Jewish Question,' particularly as to what responsibilities German Protestants should assume in their relations to Jews.[57] Outside pressures prompted German Protestants to elucidate their position vis-à-vis the Jews, which resulted in a reaffirmation of Christian supersessionism and resumed efforts to proselytize Jews.[58]

In October 1947, guided by the majority opinion and official statements of the German Protestant Church, the Protestant Church Council met to discuss the Church's 'service towards Israel.' The council recognized the need to instruct pastors and theological students in matters related to the Church's 'obligation towards Israel.' The council encouraged Protestants to pray for Israel, stressed that 'the church would like to recognize [in annual church services] the connection between the path of God and Israel in light of Holy Scripture,' and urged Protestants to teach that antisemitism was an aberration of Christianity.[59]

The limits of Protestant philosemitism soon became evident, as the Protestant Church Council supported material assistance for 'Jewish-Christians,' revealing that it was not interested in recognizing Jews as Jews.[60] One of the Protestants who openly advocated conversion of Jews to Christianity as the solution to the 'Jewish Question' was Pastor

Gunter Harder, who considered Zionism to be a 'misunderstanding of Jewry' and laboured to convert Jews and have them assimilate into Christian German society. To that end, Harder and like-minded Protestants targeted Jews in DP camps, reporting in November 1947, that missionaries had 'success with the inmates' at Labertheim Camp. Success was defined as conducting Bible studies with Jews and converting some of the twelve thousand Jewish DPs in the camp.[61]

These efforts to convert Jews were part of a broader missions program that emerged in occupied Germany during the fall of 1945. To realize their goal of contacting Jews, the German Protestant Church established a missions organization, the German Protestant Committee for Israel, which was affiliated with the International Missionary Council's Committee on the Christian Approach to the Jews.[62] The Committee for Israel's work echoed the international group's aims of converting Jews and was akin to that of the Mission to Israel and the Jewish Institute, both of which were reconstituted, in October 1945, by Karl Rengstorf.[63] Serving as an arm of the Protestant Church, these groups sought to convert Jews to Christianity and thereby eliminate antisemitism in Germany. Beginning in 1948, the Committee for Israel launched a series of annual meetings for these purposes.

At the first conference of the Committee for Israel, a student gathering called 'The Church and Judaism' held at Düsseldorf in October 1948, Rengstorf gave a speech full of convoluted language that revealed the problematic nature of his attempt to fuse philosemitism with proselytization. According to Rengstorf, 'the Jews no longer have any special position, neither through righteousness nor through membership in the Jewish nation. This does not indicate any renunciation, however, because the Messiah of Israel is the head of the Church. This means that for the church, where it excludes the members of Israel, it loses their share of the love of Christ.'[64] Rengstorf failed to address Jews on their own terms. In his attempt to appear philosemitic by including Jews in the life of the Church, he revealed that his sole concern had nothing to do with Jews as Jews. Instead, he longed to incorporate Jewish converts into the Christian fold and expunge their 'Jewishness' altogether.

Forced to endure this mixed message of dialogue and proselytization at the Düsseldorf Conference were three leaders of the Jewish community in Germany: Rabbi Leo Baeck, Rabbi Wilhelm Weinberg, and Rabbi Max Wolf. Baeck, who participated in the same forum where Rengstorf gave his speech, provided a stark contrast to Rengstorf's convoluted embrace of Christian supersessionism. In his speech, Baeck focused on how Jews and Christians were inextricably tied to each other, both historically and in the contemporary world. Christianity required Judaism for its survival, he asserted; Jews and Christians shared in the mystery and sovereignty of God; and the primary task of Christians and Jews was to love and understand each other.[65] This fundamental difference of approach – Christian insistence on proselytizing Jews, and Jewish focus on mutual acceptance and peaceful, even cooperative coexistence – was evident in all of the annual Committee for Israel meetings during the late 1940s and early 1950s, and in the meetings of the International Missionary Council's Committee on the Christian Approach to the Jews.[66]

Protestant efforts to convert Jews and address antisemitism were also evident in the late 1940s in the Soviet zone, even though very few Protestants there attempted Christian-Jewish dialogue. The few who did, included East Berlin's Protestant Superintendent Heinrich Grüber, Pastor Albrecht Oepke of Leipzig, and Pastor Karl Kleinschmidt of Mecklenburg.[67] Grüber, who had laboured under Nazism to save Christians of Jewish descent from murder, worked after the war to secure compensation for these 'Jewish-Christian' survivors, but did not extend his work to Jews and maintained the charge of deicide against the Jews for the rest of his life.[68] Oepke and Kleinschmidt attempted to engender Christian-Jewish dialogue in the Soviet zone, which was much more challenging than in the Western zones. Oepke's efforts included rebuilding the former headquarters of German Protestant Missions to the Jews in Saxony, and he remained in close contact with the like-minded Kleinschmidt. Both men experienced little success in their efforts to dialogue with and proselytize Jews, partly because there were so few Jews in Saxony, and even fewer in Mecklenburg.[69]

In short, Protestant-led meetings – which consisted mostly of proselytizing Christians, a handful of more progressive-minded Protestants, and a few Jews – did not bear much fruit in terms of reconciliation. They did see Jews and Christians begin to sit down and discuss their relations, but for the most part, Protestants in all four zones were unable to abandon their view that Jews were first and foremost objects of proselytization. In the Western zones, a few more progressive individuals found they needed to break away from these groups in order to realize their goals of Protestant-Jewish cooperation with the maintenance of each group on its own terms.

Catholics

In the immediate postwar period, Catholics in Germany, led by the teachings of Pope Pius XII and German bishops, prioritized the construction of a Christian Europe that would serve as a bastion against the spread of Communism in a continent ravaged by war. When it came to Nazism and Christian-Jewish reconciliation, the Vatican and the German bishops were silent. Similar to their Protestant neighbours, some Catholic leaders addressed, vaguely, the evils of the Nazi era, but generally they focused on the goals of spiritual and social renewal that were common foci in Catholic discourse during the late 1940s.[70] On the few occasions when the Catholic hierarchy addressed Catholic-Jewish relations during the late 1940s – save the one-time admission of German crimes against Jews at the Mainz Catholic Conference in 1948[71] – it sought to quell the warming of relations between the two faiths on the grounds that open-ended dialogue implied the Church's acceptance of indifferentism, which claims that all religions are equally valid paths to salvation.[72] Much like their Protestant counterparts, it became clear that German Catholics required a new approach and support from outside of their tradition and faith community if reconciliation with the Jews was to take place.

To be sure, some individual Catholics did strive towards reconciliation with Jews. Freiburg psychologist Michael Müller-Claudius, who had founded the journal *Der Morgen* in 1925 to counter German antisemitism, resumed his work in the immediate postwar period and established the German Institute of Psychology and Overcoming Antisemitism in Freiburg in 1945.[73] The institute laboured to expose how 'religious instruction of all confessions is an ongoing source of antisemitic hatred' and encouraged Protestant and Catholic theologians to examine church dogma and curricula in German schools.[74] Given the ubiquity of antisemitism in Germany, Müller-Claudius viewed ad hoc attempts to address it as inadequate and created the institute to tackle the problem.

In 1948, the institute published numerous books and pamphlets, including Müller-Claudius' book, *Der Antisemitismus und das deutsche Verhängnis* (Antisemitism and German Fate), which he claimed was 'the first comprehensive psychological, ethical, and religious treatment of antisemitism.'[75] The book was an exposé of Christian anti-Judaism and its ties to modern antisemitism, and it opposed those who denied a link between Christian teaching and antisemitism. 'Men forget the motive of hatred,' Müller-Claudius wrote, 'but hatred does not forget the men.'[76]

This radical approach, advanced at a time when most Christians claimed innocence for the murderous racism of the Nazi era, aimed to have Christians take responsibility for the past by changing their views in the present. Müller-Claudius put it this way: 'The individual must view individual freedom as the highest good and he must also feel personally responsible for the German community ... from there he cannot ever [claim that] the state [was] disconnected from the German people, [or] claim innocence with the excuse that [Germans] were only following orders.'[77]

In a letter to Sterling Brown, secretary of the American Military's Religious Affairs Branch, Müller-Claudius urged the Americans to address the problem of antisemitism in Germany. He asserted that the German people – starting with the youth – needed to be re-educated with democratic values and acceptance of others. This approach not only indicted Christian teaching as connected to the development of modern antisemitism but called it one of the main sources feeding antisemitism in occupied Germany.[78] Müller-Claudius offered Brown a bold assessment of the link between ending antisemitism and fostering democracy: 'As long as the masses are not freed from the hate-complex and intolerance of exalted antisemitism ... understanding between peoples cannot be revived as the moral grounds for democracy ... The re-instatement of German respect in the world depends upon whether our people can bring about institutions to show the world that there is a will here in Germany to carve out a new way.'[79] The impulses behind Müller-Claudius' work fit well with the goals of the Allies, as he recognized how the problem of antisemitism hampered the democratization of Germany. They also found accord with some like-minded Germans, who were labouring towards similar goals of tackling antisemitism in occupied Germany.

Müller-Claudius's work found support from Gertrud Luckner and the members of the predominantly Catholic Freiburg Circle she founded after the war. Luckner, who had attended the German Evangelical Church's 'Church and Judaism' conferences, did not seek to convert Jews to Christianity, like Rengstorf, nor did she limit her service to Jews who had converted to her religion, like Grüber. Rather, akin to Müller-Claudius, Luckner devoted her life – before, during, and after the Nazi era – to Christian-Jewish reconciliation. For these efforts she spent two years in the concentration camp at Ravensbrück.

Luckner returned to Freiburg, in 1945, to become a leading proponent of Christian-Jewish reconciliation in the French zone of occupation.

In 1947, she formed the Working Group of Christians and Jews, which grew out of the Freiburg Circle.[80] Realizing that 'silence, indifference, and lack of understanding accounted for the murder of millions,' the group's objective was to begin 'building bridges and healthy relationships with our Jewish fellow-man.'[81] Beginning in August 1948, the Working Group of Christians and Jews spread its pioneering interfaith work in its periodical, the *Freiburger Rundbrief*, calling on Christians to fulfil their obligation of 'overcoming prejudice' and to 'begin dialogue ... with our Jewish brothers.'[82] Members of the group wrote letters to international figures who were sympathetic to its mission, and interested in engendering Christian-Jewish reconciliation in Germany. In January 1949, Luckner invited Pierre Visseur, a leading organizer of the budding International Council of Christians and Jews (ICCJ), and Reverend Carl Zietlow, whom the American Military Government had commissioned to establish Societies for Christian-Jewish Cooperation in Germany, to visit the Freiburg group. Neither did so at the time. Instead, Zietlow hired Freiburg Circle member Karl Thieme as his assistant and, in 1950, incorporated the Freiburg Working Group into the Freiburg Society for Christian-Jewish Cooperation.[83]

The Formation of the Societies for Christian-Jewish Cooperation

The shift in Allied policy in 1947 to more direct involvement in German democratization in the Western zones included the conviction that interfaith dialogue would play a crucial role in that process. To that end, the American Military Government's Religious Affairs Branch liaised with international groups of Christian-Jewish cooperation and with Protestants, Catholics, and Jews in Germany. Between 1948 and 1953, Germans and the Religious Affairs Branch established thirteen Societies for Christian-Jewish Cooperation in the three Western zones.[84] When establishing the societies, the Allies worked in concert with Germans who were already labouring towards Christian-Jewish reconciliation. The Germans could not have done it alone. Steering the societies' establishment were Pierre Visseur of the emerging ICCJ; Everett Clinchy, president of the American National Council of Christians and Jews; the American Council's liaison Carl Zietlow; and Sterling Brown. Backed by the governments of the Western Allies, occupation personnel provided the organization, structure, vision, much-needed finances, and general support as foreign workers and Germans laboured together to engender new relationships between Christians and Jews.[85]

The establishment of the Societies for Christian-Jewish Cooperation occurred in the context of international efforts to improve relations between Christians and Jews in wake of the Holocaust, and stemmed from efforts by members of the National Council of Christians and Jews in the United States, and the emerging International Council of Christians and Jews. The origins of the ICCJ can be traced to a meeting of twenty representatives from their respective national councils in four European nations, Australia, and the United States. Even though these visionaries called the group the ICCJ during 1946–1948, theological concerns and denominational differences postponed the formal establishment of the ICCJ until 1974.[86] Nevertheless, representatives from nations that had suffered from German aggression either at home, on the battlefield, or both, invited German pastor Herman Maas to the ICCJ's inaugural meeting at Oxford, England, in August 1946, where they laid the foundation for international Christian-Jewish cooperation.

Sterling Brown attended the second ICCJ meeting at Seelisberg, Switzerland, in July 1947, together with two German representatives: Wilhelm Neuss and Curt Radlauer. Jacques Maritain, the French ambassador to the Vatican, conveyed a bold message to the gentile participants at the conference that began with the recognition that Christians had 'an enormous task of contemplation, and inner renewal' before them. He beckoned Christians to search deeper into Paul's teaching, in order to discover 'the deeper meaning of antisemitism' in light of the close relationship between Jews and Christians in the Bible.[87] The official report of the Seelisberg meeting lauded the 'personal ... basis for participation in the Council,' which included 'removing the causes and remedying the effects of antisemitism.'[88] The recommendations for this remedial work were published in a series of Commissions after the 1947 conference, including the 'Ten Points of Seelisberg,' which stressed the Jewish origins of both religions, the dangers of the charge of deicide, and Jesus' command to love.[89] Another part of the report chastised Germans for not compensating Jewish victims of Nazi crimes and called on Germans to address 'at least material[ly] ... some of the wrongs committed under the Nazi rule.'[90] Finally, the report praised the success of the conference, claiming that 'members learned to know and to respect each other' as they contributed to a 'new spirit of understanding and cooperation ... and a true and lasting peace.'[91] Lucius Clay endorsed Sterling Brown's recommendations for the establishment of a German branch of the ICCJ, and the first Societies for Christian-Jewish Cooperation were founded the next year.[92]

Both altruistic and pragmatic motives drove the establishment of the societies in Germany. The American Military Government's political objectives in establishing the societies were delineated in Sterling Brown's 1951 report. He claimed: 'Democracy can function effectively only when the body politic rests upon attitudes of amity, mutual respect and good will. For this reason OMGUS and HICOG rightly included interfaith and intergroup relations as an essential area of the re-education program for Germany [through which] ... the moral and spiritual resources of the German people are being stimulated and utilized in establishing the foundations of a free society.'[93] Brown also acknowledged the considerable encouragement that Germans expressed towards the Allies' initiatives and lauded the organic work that Germans had already done in the realm of gentile-Jewish reconciliation. Clay and Brown decided to support a joint German-Allied effort of establishing the societies and found that 'enough encouragement was forthcoming from German churchmen, educators and civic leaders to make firm the decision to proceed with the project.'[94] Following this cooperative approach, Carl Zietlow and Everett Clinchy laboured with the three German leaders – Munich's mayor, the Catholic Karl Scharnagl; a Protestant, Ernst Lichtenstein; and a Jew, Julius Spanier – to establish the first Society for Christian-Jewish Cooperation in Germany in Munich. It opened formally in July 1948.[95] Later that same year, societies were founded in Wiesbaden in November and in Stuttgart in December.[96]

Together, the three societies drafted a constitution, which revealed that the groups intended to take seriously the eradication of antisemitism from Germany. The constitution stipulated that 'a special responsibility must be taken on to tackle and defeat racial, social, national and religious prejudice in increasingly more areas of spiritual and public life,' and proclaimed that Christians and Jews in the group had 'joined in a path of belief based on the creator God the Father and [were] bonded in the belief in the brotherhood of all people.'[97] In contrast to the efforts of many Protestants to proselytize Jews, the societies' focus on shared aspects of the Judeo-Christian tradition was meant to unite the groups' members. Society members claimed to have no interest in 'the questions of cooperative worship, nor in the watering down of theological and religious foundations.' They were not concerned with 'unifying religious bodies nor in fusing the different beliefs of the members.'[98]

Rather than attempting to change members of the other religious tradition through conversion, the goal of society members was to change

German society through education. The constitution stated that the groups 'encouraged the development of a feeling of personal and public responsibility.'[99] Each society was organized into numerous committees that would ensure its presence and influence in all areas of German life. Each committee had three members, one from each faith group, and included a wide range of people, including business people, schoolteachers, university professors, journalists, filmmakers, actors, and others.[100]

By November 1949, four societies had been established throughout the American zone and the American sector in Berlin, and general participation in them was on the rise. To administer the groups, the Coordinating Council of the Societies for Christian-Jewish Cooperation was formed in March 1949, composed of people who were familiar with the work of Christian-Jewish reconciliation. Among them were German Catholics Anton Fingerle and Karl Thieme; German Protestant Ernst Lichtenstein; Berlin publisher Knud Knudsen; German Jews Benno Ostertag and Alfred Mayer; and American Pastor Carl Zietlow.[101] Carl Zietlow and Dr Ohlson, of the American Military Government's Religious Affairs Branch, presided over the planning meeting and made sure to remind everyone present that it was the Allies who had introduced the societies into Germany. This format, and the atmosphere of the meeting, left no doubt to participants and onlookers that the German people required foreign intervention if they were to cure their antisemitism.

Although outside impulses were crucial, interest and participation in the founding of the societies was widespread among German gentiles and Jews. German support was evident in the overwhelmingly positive response to Knud Knudsen's invitations to the inaugural meeting of the first German society, held in Munich, in May 1949.[102] Many high-profile people attended, including Pierre Visseur, Gertrud Luckner, and Protestant Church Council member Otto von Harling, along with over a hundred others from all three Western occupation zones.[103] The response from the Jewish side was positive as well. Hans-Joachim Schoeps and Hugo Lang gave addresses, and one representative of the Central Committee of Liberated Jews in the British Zone, Norbert Wollheim, who had survived the horrors of the concentration camp at Bergen Belsen, extended, in absentia, his sincere joy at the fact that new societies would soon emerge in the British zone. He had been 'impressed' with the Coordinating Council's efforts, and he wrote, he was 'sure that [the participants'] motives in this meeting are noble and ethical.'[104]

Christian efforts to gain the trust of their Jewish counterparts in the groups centred on their approach to antisemitism. At the May meeting, the Protestant leader of the Munich society, Ernst Lichtenstein, offered a hard-hitting address, titled 'Antisemitism: A Question for Us.' In it, Lichtenstein countered directly the Christian teaching of Jewish deicide and asserted that one should eradicate 'racial hatred ... [which is] the sickness of social life.'[105] Although Lichtenstein submerged the specific aspects of German antisemitism into a human problem, calling it a 'homo sapien catastrophe' and insisting that 'in no way is it only a German sickness,' he went much further than most Germans to embrace Judaism as a close relative of Christianity. He declared, '[Judaism] will always be the mother religion of Christianity,' admitting that Christians had a great deal for which to answer after the Holocaust: 'The situation of Jews ... has not been created by Jews but only triggered by [their presence]. It became our deepest concern, and now it is our deepest matter of conscience. These problems have emerged not only due to our lack of courage and general fears of the world, but also due to our lack of reverence and lack of holiness.'[106] Based on these beliefs and the conscious weight of the recent past, Lichtenstein celebrated the budding reconciliation work of the societies, which he claimed would demonstrate justice to a 'godless world.'[107]

One courageous Jew who engaged in gentile-Jewish dialogue in the immediate aftermath of the Holocaust was Hans-Joachim Schoeps. Schoeps had lost nearly all of his immediate and extended family in the Nazi death camps. At the inaugural meeting of Munich's Society for Christian-Jewish Cooperation, in 1949, Schoeps used the first quarter of his speech to show, as other Jews who addressed the audience at the conference had done, that the Holocaust would form one of the bases for contemporary Christian-Jewish dialogue.[108] He told the audience that only 3 per cent of German Jewry survived the 'concentration camps and the gas chambers of the Third Reich,' that 'the murdered will not come back to life through well-intended proclamations,' and that these catastrophes occurred, in part, due to the failure of prewar Christian-Jewish dialogue.[109] After this hard-hitting introduction, Schoeps's address took a positive course, declaring, 'I approve of and welcome your work ... I only fear that it comes too late.'[110]

Schoeps acknowledged that most Jews living in occupied Germany planned to emigrate as soon as possible. But, he also pointed to the significant number of Jews who had chosen to make Germany their home indefinitely, and who wished to forge new relationships with gentile Germans. In doing so, he demonstrated to the mixed audience the reconciliatory initiative that some Jews had begun, and the cost and courage that it took for them to do so: 'There are a few Jewish Germans [who] have chosen to return to Germany, and they believe that they are free of all feelings of resentment. There are, however, very few Jewish partners who desire to cooperate with you and to face you. In any case, we are prepared to do so ... As a German Jew I stand in unlimited solidarity with all other Germans, so long as they are decent people.'[111]

Schoeps, like Leo Baeck and many others, viewed theology as a starting point for Christian-Jewish reconciliation.[112] Already in 1937, Schoeps had identified shared theological tenets between Judaism and Christianity when he wrote that 'the absolute in religious history is the one unchangeable God, who has revealed His truth in diverse ways ... to Israel upon Sinai, and to the world upon Golgotha ... [Both are] absolutely valid.'[113] At Munich, with the horrors of the Holocaust still fresh in his memory, Schoeps reiterated this belief and asserted the validity, and vitality, of the Jewish faith. On that basis, he posed a radical challenge to Christians: '[Jesus] has nothing to do with breaking the covenant from Sinai, which has only to do with Israel ... Judaism remains: from our side there is certainly the possibility for harmony with Christianity. Is there also on the Christian side the possibility to discover and accept our knowledge of God and His covenant with us as truth – and God's work with us as not only religated to the Old Testament and in the past – but also in the post-biblical Synagogue, that is, in Israel today?'[114] Schoeps' approach left Christians bearing the ultimate responsibility for any progress towards Christian-Jewish reconciliation.

Schoeps' speech, and those of other Jews at the conference, contributed to the societies' discourse on the Nazi era and established the modus operandi between Christians and Jews in society work. After responding to Schoeps with 'tremendous applause,' the Christians involved turned to acknowledge Jewish suffering and began or continued to dialogue with Jews. One conference report, written by Dr. Traub von Grolman, lauded 'the magnanimous attitude of the Jewish representatives whose closest relatives had died in the gas chambers or through imprisonment' and expressed amazement at the fact that Jews, like Schoeps, still considered themselves to be Germans.[115] The Allied report on the conference credited the society for the actions of the Hessian education minister, who began immediately to incorporate society recommendations into a new education curriculum that expunged antisemitic material. The report also pointed to the hundreds of businessmen, government leaders, and participants from women's groups who were now expressing concerns over pervasive antisemitism in Germany and continuing to discuss the issues.[116] 'People left with the conviction there were important leaders in Germany concerned with developing a practical program for overcoming intolerance,' the report concluded. 'They left with the feeling that this movement already has a good beginning.'[117]

According to Allied and German reports on the conference in Munich, the society's approach balanced idealistic exchanges between Christians with an emphasis on the link between Christian-Jewish reconciliation and German democratization. The American High Commissioner's report summed up the religious commitments of the Christians involved in this way: 'There was agreement among the Christians that the problem of antisemitism and of Christian-Jewish relations would still be a problem in Germany, which the churches must be concerned with, even though there were few Jews remaining in Germany. The problem is one that has to do with the recognition of the dignity and worth of the human being which is far deeper than antisemitism.'[118] Still, pragmatism was also apparent in these interfaith meetings, evidenced by von Grolman's report. Like other Germans, von Grolman's ultimate aim was German self-determination in German affairs. She expressed this goal in her reference to German guilt in the past and its tie to Christian-Jewish relations in the present: 'It is our common guilt that we did not oppose Hitler more than we did. But true democracy can only grow from religious foundations. We Germans do not want to become beggars ... we want to become economically and politically free, in order to create a true democracy, for a dictated democracy has doubtful value.'[119] This ongoing struggle towards democracy and pluralism was also reflected in the official conference reports. One reporter, who was proud of the societies' contribution towards intercommunal understanding and peace, used Nazi terminology to describe the gathering as a meeting between 'Aryan and non-Aryan people.'[120]

The societies launched Christian-Jewish reconciliatory work into the public sphere. It became part of the official agenda of the Federal Republic of Germany in 1949. At the December 1949 inaugural meeting of the Wiesbaden society, West German President Theodore Heuss gave the keynote address, which reached an estimated 3.5 million Germans via radio.[121] Heuss' speech, titled 'Courage to Love,' exemplified courage, but not before blaming

Hitler for the calamity of the German people. 'The worst thing Hitler did to us,' Heuss proclaimed, 'was to force us into the shameful position of having to call ourselves Germans, just as he and his accomplices did.'[122] Heuss recognized that a root of German racism could be found in German biological materialism, 'which knew no moral categories, but wished to propagate [racism by] not making allowance for the fact that there are certain ethical values that govern relations between one human being and another.'[123] Heuss urged the audience, and Germans in general, to accept the burden of responsibility for Germany's manifold crimes against the Jews: 'We should not forget the Nuremberg Laws, the Jewish Star, the burning synagogues, the deportation of Jewish people to foreign lands, to misery, to their death. These are facts we should not forget, we must not forget, for we must not make things too easy for ourselves.'[124]

In 1949, Jews who lived in occupied Germany had other priorities than working with Christian Germans in the reconciliatory process, but favourable Jewish reception to gentile initiatives was necessary if reconciliation was to occur. Mixed Jewish responses to the societies' efforts rendered their success tenuous. Some Jews, including Norbert Wollheim, expressed enthusiasm for working alongside sincere Christians like Eugen Kogon, for whom he declared his 'profound respect.' At the same time, however, Wollheim 'seriously question[ed] [Kogon's] hypothesis that there are [Germans] who would fight against the rejuvenation of Nazi practices.' In the early 1950s, Wollheim decided to emigrate to the United States.[125]

A few Jews shared Schoeps' determination to remain in Germany and work towards gentile-Jewish reconciliation. Nathan Levinson, a German-Jewish survivor of the Nazi era who returned from the death camps to Germany, described his response to a Protestant pastor's claim that religious brotherhood, in the true sense, was reserved for those of the same faith. 'I was so furious,' Levinson recalled, 'that I got up and left ... at that time I was against such dialogues [because] there weren't yet any theologians who were in it with all of their soul.'[126] Eventually, Levinson saw the societies as providing a positive vehicle for German-Jewish dialogue, and he became involved in their work. During the 1970s, he chaired the Coordinating Committee of the Societies for Christian-Jewish Cooperation.

Generally, gentile Germans on both sides of the East-West divide were more interested in their own plight than in reconciling with Jews.[127]

Nevertheless, numerous accomplishments in gentile-Jewish reconciliation occurred in spite of this fact. In Western Germany, the accomplishments of gathering thousands of Catholics, Protestants, and Jews in open dialogue just a few years after the Holocaust was amplified by the societies' success in propelling Christian-Jewish reconciliation into the public sphere. Indeed, the list of successes of the societies at this early stage, in late 1949, are remarkable: There were over three hundred members in each emerging council, with several hundred more who had shown interest in the societies; German professors had drafted society pamphlets for use in university curricula, and university convocations were incorporating society themes; and over 500,000 society handbooks had been printed for distribution in Western Germany, including such titles as 'Overcoming Prejudice' and 'The Foundation of Our Civilization,' along with thousands of copies of the bi-monthly periodical of the societies, *Zusammenarbeit* (Working Together).[128]

In the Soviet zone and East Germany, by contrast, the work of the Societies for Christian-Jewish Cooperation was barred from taking root, and gentile-Jewish contacts were essentially non-existent. After the promulgation of the new Restitution Law of 1948, Jews were unable to reclaim the property stolen from them. Instead, Jews were left to the graces of the Association of Victims of Nazism (VVN), which considered them as second-class victims compared with the 'anti-fascist' resistance fighters, both socially and with regard to compensation. This absence of gentile-Jewish reconciliatory work, and specifically Christian-Jewish dialogue, in the Soviet zone and the GDR had enormous, negative, long-term ramifications for Jews in Eastern Germany. Indeed, those repercussions exploded in the late 1940s. Between 1948 and 1952, Jews were again forced to endure a wave of antisemitism that spread throughout the Soviet bloc via government purges and attacks on citizens deemed to be 'American-Zionist' agents.[129] After the founding of the German Democratic Republic, in 1949, the GDR government refused to recognize the state of Israel or to enter into diplomatic relations with it. The churches also lost the spark of rejuvenation that questioning old teaching brought, and missed out on the fruitful challenges of engaging with Jews and adapting to a religiously pluralistic context.

Limited Success

In the Western zones and, after 1949, in the Federal Republic of Germany, emergence of an open-ended, ongoing approach to Jewish suffering in the past, compensation, and dialogue facilitated the first steps towards gentile-Jewish reconciliation. By the end of 1949, the combined efforts of the Allies, gentile and Jewish Germans, and international NGO workers witnessed the successful establishment of numerous Societies for Christian-Jewish Cooperation. Although the labour of the societies was difficult, and participants often revealed less than ideal attitudes towards that work, the societies' method, based on mutual acceptance of the other group, succeeded in ways that traditional forms of Christian-Jewish interaction could not. Conversely, the approach in the Soviet zone and the German Democratic Republic – which ignored the depths of Jewish suffering under Nazism and the urgent needs of Jews thereafter – formed a toxic foundation for future relations between Jews and Christians and, more generally, between Jews and gentiles in Germany.

The contrast between outcomes in the West and East points to the massive influence wielded by the Allies in shaping occupied Germany. Participation of Germans of good will – gentiles and Jews – was essential to the success of reconciliation efforts, but without support from outside they could make but little progress. Allied policies and practices set the terms and limits within which reconciliation work could or could not develop. Foreign NGOs, as the next chapter shows, provided much of the day-to-day impetus.

Chapter Four

Broadening International Contacts and Reconciliation Work

When Peter Peterson and Irene Laure attended the Moral Re-Armament (MRA) Conference at Caux, Switzerland, in July 1947, they harboured attitudes that were anything but conducive to reconciliation. Peterson was part of a group of 150 Germans whom Frank Buchman, founder of MRA, had invited to Caux. Buchman intended to incorporate Germans into the reconstruction of postwar Europe. Peterson had been in the Hitler Youth and continued to sympathize with Nazi ideology after the war. The majority of Germans, he admitted, including the ones present at Caux, had become 'masters at defending [them]selves when ... accused.'[1]

Laure, a French Socialist member of the Marseilles parliament, had been active in the French resistance during the war. Her son was tortured by the Gestapo, and she admitted at Caux that she 'so hated Germany that [she] wanted to see her erased from the map of Europe.'[2] Realizing after her arrival at the conference centre that Germans would be participating, Laure decided to return to France. Adding to her reasoning was the suspicion that big business had financed the gathering, an insult to her socialist sensibilities.

The gathering of wartime enemies at Caux revealed seemingly insurmountable barriers to reconciliation, but surprisingly, the meetings yielded positive results. German and French delegates listened to one another's personal accounts, and French attitudes and actions even opened the possibility of forgiveness. Peterson attributed the success to the way that Germans were treated at Caux. He recalled, 'We were met by a French chorus with a German song, a song that foretold the true destiny of Germany ... Here the doors were wide open for us and we were completely disarmed.'[3] After some convincing from Buchman, Laure decided to stay for the conference, a decision that transformed her life. When she took the podium during a plenary session, she offered her part in the renewal of peaceful relations between the French and German people. She confessed, 'I have seen here that my hatred was wrong and I wish to ask the forgiveness of all the Germans present.'[4] This speech dumbfounded Peterson who, in turn, began to challenge his own views along with his anger. He concluded that if Germany were to regain its place in the civilized world, Germans would have to engage in the difficult work of confession and forgiveness. At Caux, Franco-German reconciliation had begun.

Both Peterson and Laure went on to devote much of their lives to Franco-German reconciliation. The encounter between them was soon replicated in all areas of French and German society as the work of Moral Re-Armament became well known. The following year, in 1948, Konrad Adenauer attended the Caux meetings along with numerous other influential Germans in politics, industry, trade, and labour. Similarly, French Foreign Minister Robert Schuman also attended Caux conferences and, like Adenauer, developed a personal friendship with Frank Buchman. Years later, both men attributed a good portion of the success of postwar Franco-German reconciliation to Moral Re-Armament. Indeed, Schuman credited Buchman's labours for having 'provid[ed] teams of trained men, ready for the service of the state, apostles of reconciliation and builders of a new world, [which was] the beginning of a far-reaching transformation of society.'[5] Similarly, Adenauer claimed, in 1960, that 'MRA has given the most valuable stimulation to the great work of uniting Europe.'[6]

This chapter focuses on the cooperative efforts of international and German organizations to establish peace and security in Germany and Europe. In the two years preceding formation of the German states in 1949, church groups, NGOs, and even Communist organizations played a central role in reconciling Germans with their wartime enemies abroad. Occupation policies provided the much needed stability and generally favourable environment required for German democratization in the Western zones, and for the integration of Eastern Germany into the Soviet bloc. However, the Allies could achieve only limited success in moving forward the processes of reconciliation in occupied Germany. During the late 1940s, foreign individuals and groups rose to the occasion and initiated contacts between Germans and the outside world. These initiatives forged key relationships of international cooperation when the economic, military, and official international agreements of the 1950s were still a long way off. In 1948, one Swiss observer noted the significance of this grassroots diplomacy at a time when the 'doors of [Allied government] ministries remained closed,' and the Allies refused to engage Germans in any 'discussion of foreign policy.'[7] German and international personnel involved in the organizations took to heart what that commentator called the 'vital importance' of their efforts. Through hard work and unconventional diplomatic encounters, they contributed to the stabilization of Germany while simultaneously bolstering the ideological foundations of both West and East.

A variety of motives drove the work of international organizations as they brokered reconciliation between Germans and their wartime enemies during 1947–1949. The effectiveness of all of the organizations depended on their ideological alignment with the guiding politics in their sphere of operation and on their ability to work with existing German bodies. Given these criteria, it is not surprising that the labours of pacifist groups like the International Fellowship of Reconciliation, and groups limited primarily to confessional concerns, like the World Council of Churches (WCC), yielded meagre results.[8] NGOs that incorporated a more overt political agenda that meshed with the dominant ideology of their zone experienced more success, as seen in the work of Pax Christi and in the NGO with the widest impact in Europe during the late 1940s, Moral Re-Armament (MRA). In the Soviet zone, the most effective groups in fostering international stabilization were the Office for International Cooperation, the Society for German-Soviet Friendship (Gesellschaft für Deutsch-Sowjetische Freundschaft), and the Association of Victims of Nazism (VVN), all of which were guided directly by Soviet authorities.

Western Church Organizations and NGOs in Occupied Germany

The church groups and NGOs in this study can be traced to the international peace movement of the interwar period, but their impact after the Second World War was much more widespread than it was during the 1920s and 1930s. On the eve of the outbreak of the First World War, those who sought a peaceful solution to the rising international tensions extended beyond government officials to the laity, especially German and British Protestants.[9] Because most groups worked against the majority opinion and widespread nationalism during the interwar era, they had little effect. Moreover, German peace advocates were muzzled after 1933. Despite the horrors of the Second World War and the hostile environment in Europe thereafter, many of these NGOs rekindled their efforts and helped broker the peaceful incorporation of Germany into postwar Europe.

International Fellowship of Reconciliation (IFOR)

The international pacifist organization, Fellowship of Reconciliation, was co-founded by British Quaker Henry Hodgkin and German Protestant Friedrich Siegmund-Schultze at Cambridge in December 1914, with the intention of fostering peaceful relations between nations. The fellowship continued this work in the decades to come despite ongoing international hostilities. Thirty years later, with the end of the Second World War in sight, British members of the fellowship convened to discuss the same issue, in particular the daunting topic of postwar British-German relations. British fellowship member Marian Parmoor revealed in November 1944 her belief that Germans 'had proven themselves to be...abnormal criminals.'[10] Echoing the predominant view among Allied personnel, Parmoor wished to embark on 'a redemptive mission' in Germany, which she felt should be directed by 'a band of saints, acting perhaps with medical experts [whose] fiery love towards God and Man [would] burn out the evil thing' that had influenced the German people during the Nazi era.[11]

Parmoor offered a distinct alternative to the heavy-handed treatment of the German people exercised by the Allies. She was dismayed with how international political leaders approached German reconstruction, lamenting that 'instead [of a spiritual approach] Roosevelt, Stalin and Churchill declared at Moscow that those criminals "will be taken back to the scene of their crimes and judged on the spot by the peoples whom they have outraged." '[12] Parmoor pointed to the problems of this approach, and reiterated her proposed solution: 'If World War III is to be prevented it is clear that all Christian opinion must unite to secure impartial justice between victor and vanquished and the whole problem of such crimes must be raised to a higher level.'[13] For Parmoor, the fellowship's spiritual foundation and interwar contacts with Germans could serve to realize the Allies' goal of German integration in a deeper, more relationally based form of reconciliation.

Most fellowship members did not demonize the German people but proceeded with the spiritual focus that Parmoor and Siegmund-Schultze had advocated: one of a 'true reconciliation of nations' that was accompanied by German accountability for Nazi crimes.[14] Countering the notion that there was something fundamentally wrong with the German people, one author of a fellowship newsletter claimed, as Bishop Bell had done, that the Germans had been a misguided nation and needed to be encouraged back on to the right track. He went on to tackle the revenge-minded occupation policies implemented in Germany, stating that 'such an attitude is incompatible with those ideal and Christian motives which the Allied nations have so often proclaimed during their struggles against Nazism.'[15]

With these lofty motives, the fellowship changed its name to International Fellowship of Reconciliation (IFOR), and set out to establish national chapters, including in Germany. In 1948, IFOR established chapters in Berlin-Zehlendorf, Kassel, and Minden. The founding of IFOR's German chapters, however, did not mean that Germans were ready to pioneer reconciliation with their wartime enemies. Many German members refused to acknowledge widespread German complicity for the crimes of the Nazi era. Siegmund-Schultze, who led the German chapters, recognized the deep apathy and cynicism that had set roots in Germany during the Nazi era and, like so many other Germans at the time, claimed helplessness against the rise of the Nazi regime.[16] Echoing Bell, Siegmund-Schultze saw a solution to the bleak spiritual condition in Germany in the assistance of international organizations, which he thought could bring the German people into positive relationships with the rest of the world. The challenging task, according to Siegmund-Schultze, was for the international Christian community to reach out to the German people: 'If even those who themselves believe in divine power ... do not come to aid [the German people], these people, who have been in despair, will indeed not be able to find God. Today, perhaps more than ever before, the question of faith is for the German people a question of fellowship.'[17]

This call for the generosity of foreigners, coupled with the German fellowship's emphasis on German hardships rather than suffering over Nazi crimes, tested relations within the international organization, particularly as some IFOR members had suffered significantly under Nazi occupation. French fellowship member Pastor André Trocmé had been incarcerated in a German prison for leading his parishioners in providing shelter to five thousand Jews in Le Chambon-sur Lignon, France, and Trocmé's countryman Henry Rosser had also suffered in a German jail.[18] Moreover, Pastor Trocmé, the international secretary of IFOR, organized a lecture tour of Germany in 1947, during which he and his cousin, Eva Landwehr, organized meetings at German universities with various student organizations in Heidelberg, Hamburg, Hanover, Göttingen, Marburg, and Erlangen. In March 1948, Trocmé met with German Protestant Pastor Iwand in Sweden at a Quaker Conference, and the two became good friends.[19] Rosser, Landwehr, and Trocmé joined other French fellowship members in foregoing the personal recognition and communal benefits of victimhood when dealing with their past in order to achieve reconciliation with the German people. In response, the German branch of IFOR revealed in its official statement that its members were devoted 'to the work of justice and peace' and that it was 'deeply conscious of the responsibility of the Christian message of reconciliation.'[20] Still, it was the generosity of foreign fellowship workers that moved reconciliatory work forward.

Convinced that the Allied governments had not adequately addressed the multitude of problems in occupied Germany, IFOR members from all over Europe considered their work to be of the utmost importance for the reconstruction of Germany and the continent. IFOR declared that it had 'not been directed by governments' and in 1949 described its central purpose as to 'reach behind the governments to the sickness of civilization in individuals and our social culture; to heal division in the human family by furthering reconciliation between individuals, classes, races and nations.'[21] IFOR's goal was to further the work begun in the immediate postwar years by continuing to use the 'radiant power of love' to 'penetrat[e] and leave[n] families, churches, businesses and cultural organizations.'[22] The success of this work depended on the receptiveness of those involved and their frequent participation in intimate prayer cells, which were to expand from 'several to a dozen persons in a neighborhood [and be] multiplied throughout communities, cities and nations.' According to IFOR teachings, this concerted prayer would result in a 'widening kinship of radiant pacifism' that would unite the world 'against fear and violence across frontiers and all barriers [as the world] prepares itself for the true Kingdom of Peace's inheritance of the earth.'[23]

Although IFOR members from numerous countries maintained an exclusively religious approach in their attempts to forge new relationships between wartime enemies, their work broadened the scope of reconciliation in occupied Germany beyond strictly economic and political concerns, and extended contact to those not normally considered in state diplomacy. However, in the late 1940s, when some IFOR members attempted more overtly to fuse religious interests with social and political action, they exposed the limits of their reconciliatory efforts.

For instance, in October 1948, when German fellowship member Lydia Flügge decried the ongoing antisemitism in Germany and the pitiful living conditions in Jewish DP camps, she added that 'one could understand the reasons for antisemitism' and offered a paltry antidote of 'not being passive' and not missing an opportunity to 'pass a good word on to a Jew.'[24] Flügge asserted that 'foreigners should take over the [Jewish DP] problem' and expressed some interest in joining what foreigners, like Carl Zietlow, were doing in the realm of Christian-Jewish dialogue in occupied Germany. Thus, she acknowledged the lack of IFOR initiative in this regard.[25] Indeed, while IFOR enjoyed success in connecting Christian pacifists into an international network by 1948, it did not gain the widespread attention of larger organizations that were less committed to pacifism and more engaged with the politics of the day.[26]

World Council of Churches (WCC)

The ecumenical movement also emerged from the devastation of the First World War, but it only came to hold political significance after formal establishment of the World Council of Churches in 1948. According to ecumenists in the immediate period following the Second World War, the ecumenical movement was re-emerging for two distinct purposes: to address postwar church problems in Europe and to work for the 'spiritual reconstruction of Germany.'[27] To these ends, most prominent ecumenists, like Bishop Bell of Chichester, opposed the Allies' occupation policies, which they deemed too heavy-handed, even to the point of jeopardizing German democratization.

Bell, who had earlier cooperated with German pastor Dietrich Bonhoeffer, shared the view of most IFOR members, and laboured to incorporate Germans into a postwar Europe that would be deeply rooted in Christian values. His ecumenical experiences, and particularly his close relationship with Bonhoeffer, led Bishop Bell to frame the recent European bloodbath as a war between Christianity and unbelief. In his view, Germans could be rehabilitated, and kind and fair treatment from the outside world would reawaken the good elements in the German people.[28] In a sermon on 27 July 1945, Bell proclaimed, 'For Germany redemption and resurrection [is possible] if God pleases to lead the nation through men animated by [Bonhoeffer's] spirit.'[29] Perhaps foreign ecumenists gave the German people too much credit. As Eberhard Bethge, Bonhoeffer's biographer and close friend pointed out, most Germans were a 'long way from [Bell's] attitude' towards considering Bonhoeffer as a heroic model German, particularly because Germans continued to differentiate 'between Christian martyrdom and political resistance.'[30]

Still, many Germans in the Protestant Church welcomed the likes of Bishop Bell because he shared their view of the Nazi past and their vision for German integration in Europe. German Protestants participated eagerly in the WCC's planning meeting in Switzerland in 1946, and in preparation for its inaugural gathering at Amsterdam in 1948. In April 1948, Pastor Martin Niemöller instructed German Protestant leaders at Echzell as to how they should address the Nazi past at Amsterdam. According to Niemöller, Germans should acknowledge their troubled past, but that acknowledgment should not 'rob [Germans] of the freedom to make our own personal decisions in each situation.'[31] In order to secure the right to make these personal decisions in the future in freedom and security, Niemöller encouraged pastors to draw attention to the 1934 Barmen Declaration, which most Christians from abroad would recognize as a solid anti-Nazi document stemming from the German Protestant Confessing Church.

At the 1948 WCC conference in Amsterdam, German delegates, including Protestant Relief Work leader Eugen Gerstenmaier, employed Niemöller's approach. At the same time, they revealed their desire for political change in Germany. In his speech, Gerstenmaier first focused on the positive things that God had brought to Germany after the end of the war. Germans, he claimed, could 'not speak about Germany here without praising God.'[32] Gerstenmaier provided two grounds for this praise: the opportunity that the German people had been given after the defeat of Nazism to rebuild their society and the massive aid and generosity of the international community to the German people. Gerstenmaier praised the international group, saying that he had found in them the 'reconciliatory and delivering power of Jesus Christ.'[33] This recognition of international assistance and the use of common Christian language set the stage for his central agenda, which was twofold: to convince the international body of believers that Germans were worthy of being part of the ecumenical organization, and to increase their aid to the German people as Germany entered the Western alliance. For Gerstenmaier, these goals were intertwined: 'We pray for world peace and we are in accord with all of good will, for the reorganization of our social and economic relations. We do not want to be enslaved, neither to the dogma of Marxism nor to the views that some in Germany have for a divided world [ideologically]. We only want to fulfil the commandment of the New Testament... to fulfil the law of Christ. With this solidarity of poverty and love, we all bear together the same burden.'³⁴ While attempting to deepen spiritual and temporal bonds, Gerstenmaier advanced his specific concerns, including currency reform in Germany and German reconstruction.³⁵

Like Gerstenmaier, Bishop Horning of Silesia also took the opportunity of the gathering to pursue political goals. Horning met with Polish Bishop Szerunda in order to lobby for improved treatment of German Protestants living in Silesia after the population transfers of 1945–1946. Seemingly oblivious to the Nazi past, Horning wanted the Polish bishop to do a number of things on behalf of the Germans, including compile a list of German children who continued to reside east of the Oder-Neisse Line in Silesia and obtain a guarantee that German Protestant prisoners of war in Poland would receive improved treatment. Bishop Szerunda agreed to do these things and even went so far as to agree that former German parishes should not fall under Polish administration, thus playing into Horning's goal of maintaining a German presence in Silesia.³⁶ In this case, as in many others, it was the generosity of a foreigner who had endured years of mistreatment under German occupation that fostered reconciliation with the German people.

The German delegation to Amsterdam succeeded in gaining the sympathies of the international audience, most of whom recognized the potential adverse effects of not assisting German refugees and expellees and the costs of ignoring the specific points that Gerstenmaier had raised concerning the threat of political extremism.³⁷ Still, for the Germans, acceptance came with the price of acknowledging the evils inherent in Nazism, albeit in vague terms. The Germans were welcomed into an organization that called all Christians to counter the very things that Nazi Germany had espoused, seen in the WCC's collective statement issued at the close of the conference: 'We have to learn to resist terror, cruelty, racism... and sowing seeds of war.'³⁸ In this way, the WCC made clear that it would not tolerate the racist nationalism and aggression endemic in Nazi Germany.

This church-based diplomacy among Protestants continued after the Amsterdam meeting. Germans used the foundation established at the WCC conference to expand their relationship with French Protestants. Pastor Hans Iwand, Eugen Gerstenmaier, and others participated in the French-German Protestant gathering at Speyer, in September 1948, just weeks after the close of the Amsterdam meeting. Iwand reported on the Speyer meeting and stated that that it was clear 'from the utterances of [German] Professor Boegner that there was not the faintest doubt that his intention was to engender a political discussion.'[39] When corresponding with WCC members, Gerstenmaier admitted openly the political motives of German Protestants in their involvement in the council. To Elfan Rees of the WCC's Department of Reconstruction and Inter-Church Aid, in 1949, Gerstenmaier wrote that Germans were 'eager ... to seize the opportunity to establish international relations through the World Council.' Gerstenmaier was not writing to thank Rees for the council's aid to Germany, which was enormous,[40] but to have Rees and the WCC recognize that Germans were more than 'DPs who have become solely objects of foreign relief' and that they wanted international political and diplomatic support.[41]

Like the International Fellowship of Reconciliation, the World Council of Churches remained, by and large, a parochial organization and did not extend its work in the late 1940s beyond the familiar parameters of Christian ecumenism. Reconciliation with Jews remained outside of the council's priorities, and, in general, the WCC did not extend its activities to the political realm as much as people like Gerstenmaier would have liked.

Catholics in Germany: The Pax Christi Movement

Catholics in Germany were inspired by the legacy of committed peace activists of the interwar era, and thousands of Catholics in Western Germany became involved in international peace pilgrimages during 1947–1949. Members of the pacifist Catholic organization, the Society of Christ the King, had been executed during the Nazi era for refusing to join the Wehrmacht and for preaching pacifism after being forbidden to do so.[42] After the Second World War, Pax Christi carried on this tradition of spiritually fuelled engagement and furthered Franco-German reconciliation in a number of ways, including the release of German prisoners of war, obtaining travel passes for Germans to participate in pilgrimages to France, and international cooperative efforts to stave off the advance of Communism.

In the late 1940s, in the border areas between France and Germany, reconciliation was anything but a high priority for the majority of either nation. The horrors of German occupation were still fresh in the memories of the French. Bitterness worked its way into French occupation policies, and France proved insistent on extracting reparations from its zone. Moreover, Catholic teaching and practice in postwar

Europe prioritized construction of a Christian Europe, based on shared Western values (the *Abendland*), over preoccupation with the wartime past. Whereas this concept encouraged peaceful coexistence, it worked against the deepening of reconciliation efforts between the two countries as it ignored the horrors and destruction of the recent past, sidelined Protestants, and omitted outright the inclusion of Jews.

Some Catholics in France and Germany managed to engage critically with the Nazi past, and some even sought reconciliation with their wartime enemies. French Bishop Pierre-Marie Théas of Montauban set the foundation for Pax Christi while in a Nazi prison in 1944, but the roots of his work had already been evident earlier during the war. His stance against Nazism was public and bold as seen in the 1942 statement he had read throughout his diocese: 'I give voice to the outraged protest of Christian conscience, and I proclaim ... that all men, whatever their race or religion, have the right to be respected by individuals and by states.'[43] This statement reflected the bishop's opposition to Nazism, which led him to protest the deportation of Jews from France. That act led to his arrest in 1944 and his incarceration at Compiègne.

While in prison, Bishop Théas met Catholic prisoners who wanted him to lead them in prayer. He did so, but chose to pray for their enemies: the jailers and the German people in general. Upon his release a few weeks later, Bishop Théas returned to his diocese with the intent of focusing on reconciliation with France's enemies. This work found accord with a teacher in southern France, Marthe Dortel-Claudot. During the Christmas season, in 1944, after receiving the full support of Bishop Théas and the blessing of the Archbishop of Toulouse, Dortel-Claudot began a prayer campaign for the spiritual and moral healing of Germany. In March 1945, that prayer campaign became known as Pax Christi.[44]

Together Théas and Dortel-Claudot engendered enthusiasm for this budding group of prayerful Catholics, who laboured to make contact with like-minded German clergy. They found German priests who had also been involved in peace work before and during the Second World War. For example, Father Manfred Hörhammer had his first encounter with French Catholic youths who were promoting peace with German Catholics in the Saar in 1932. Father Hörhammer became involved in Pax Christi shortly after his release from a French POW camp in November 1945. Hörhammer questioned the possibility of postwar Franco-German reconciliation, citing heinous German wartime misdeeds like the 1944 massacre at Oradour.[45] During a stopover in the Saar while en route from the POW camp to his home in Munich, Hörhammer found that French Catholics were, once again, attempting to rekindle prewar peaceful relations across the Franco-German border. Hörhammer received a pamphlet at the train station, signed by forty French bishops, which invited German Catholics to forge new relationships of peace and trust and called for mutual forgiveness.[46] Astonished, Hörhammer moved to act on this invitation. In a few months, by 1946, the French Pax Christi members succeeded in spreading the movement to the Saar and Baden, an endeavour supported by the Bishop of Münster, Clemens August Graf von Galen. In August 1947, the Pax Christi group received Allied permission for forty-two Germans to travel to Lourdes for the international Pax Christi meeting; seventeen Germans made the trip.[47]

After meeting at Lourdes, the French-led campaign to warm French-German relations spread to Germany. From 1 to 4 April 1948, 750 German and French Pax Christi members met for the first time on German soil, at Kevelaer, in the British zone. These meetings brought together twenty thousand Catholic peace activists from France, Germany, and the Low Countries. They had a few common roots from which to draw: a common faith tradition, mutually recognized pilgrimage locations, and the desire to prevent future conflicts in Europe.[48] Bishop Théas began the meeting by offering the German people the *Friedenskuß* (kiss of peace) from the French nation.[49] Théas expressed his heartfelt desire to reconcile the two nations and explained the gesture: 'The brotherly kiss of Christian France [is] a kiss that both pardons and asks for pardon; [it is] the kiss of reconciliation. For a number of years, France suffered many things under Germany. I don't want to arouse sad memories. Rather, I want to say to you that the truly Christian part of France, for which I serve as interpreter, wants to offer Germany forgiveness and love today.'[50]

Pax Christi leaders focused on establishing common ground in the hope of securing long-term peace in Europe on the basis of Christian principles. The question during the volatile period of the late 1940s was how far Pax Christi leaders were willing to go to realize that goal, particularly regarding German responsibility for crimes of the Nazi era. At Kevelaer, discussions focused on shared values and traditions and ignored the details of the Holocaust, part of the 'sad memories' Bishop Théas tried to avoid. In his opening remarks, Théas stressed the common Catholic bonds of God, Marian devotion, and faith: 'We look to God ... [and] ... our beloved Lady of Lourdes [who] also wished that all nations express a spirit of praise towards God, and a spirit of brotherhood towards people. Who doubts that world peace would be guaranteed after all nations embraced the spirit of brotherhood and praise towards God? Modern wars are essentially atheistic in practice. God does not belong to this practice.'[51] Rather than attacking the German people for embracing Nazism, the bishop situated that regime in the broader context of modern evil: 'As Christians we are to reject each dictator, seen today in Communism, just as seen yesterday in Nazism, which was forced on people. God does not want, and does not want for us, to eliminate human personality through the control of a party or a state... Christ came into the world to produce the community of people that spans over all borders and over all differences and objects of conflict between people.'[52] With this approach, Théas worked towards the goal of drawing the German people into new relationships of trust. At the same time, he encouraged German bishops to sidestep responsibility for Nazi crimes and fight together the new evil of Communism.

The spiritual common ground accentuated by Théas – and the German whitewashing of the past – was evident in the timely gathering on Pentecost, the day when Catholics celebrate the descent of the Holy Spirit and the remission of sin for Christians. Cardinal Frings of Cologne took the podium to address the crowd, which included bishops from Germany, France, the Netherlands, the United States, and Luxembourg.[53] He emphasized that Pax Christi offered European Catholics the opportunity to reinvigorate their common faith. Only with the renewal of faith and regular prayer campaigns could peace be maintained, as 'the strength of unshakable faith [would] overcome the world.'[54] Bishop Keller of Münster emphasized the wrongheadedness of the notion of collective guilt and focused, instead, on the Christian teaching of individual responsibility before God. In his speech, American Bishop Aloisius Muench supported the German bishops' avoidance of the past, pointed to the threat of a new war in the worsening East-West tensions, and claimed that the only solution to the hatred between nations and nationalist dictatorships was to be found in Christian faith.[55] These conventional Catholic approaches towards the recent past, all couched in generic religious language, were intended to buttress the more ambitious aims of German nationalist Catholics.[56] Among them was Bishop Franz Bornewasser of Trier, who utilized the Pax Christi meeting at Trier, in June 1948, to further his efforts to stave off French annexation of the Saar.[57]

The German priest Manfred Hörhammer stressed a deeper relational reconciliation between Germans and their wartime enemies in his speech, which included admission of German wrongdoing. Hörhammer, like the others, located the foundation of Pax Christi's approach in the basic tenets of Catholicism: the liturgy, Christ, Mary, and the Gospel of peace. Hörhammer went on to admit that the German people had followed the 'false doctrine' of nationalism. He called on all participants in the meeting to practise the only antidote to this doctrine by 'keeping alive the Spirit of God,' the same Spirit that resided in German and French Christians.[58]

An indication of Pax Christi's effectiveness is evident in its successful campaign to have German prisoners of war released in time for the 1948 Pentecost celebrations. Indeed, one of the issues that preoccupied Pax Christi members was the ongoing incarceration of thousands of German POWs in France. Here again, it was the efforts of French Bishop Théas and the good will of the French government that resulted in the release of a number of German POWs in time for them to attend their child's – or godchild's – first communion. In all, 266 German children received their first communion at Kevelaer from Bishop Théas, who took the opportunity to make a pitch for political reconciliation: 'God would want this wonderful action to serve as a beautiful prelude to the release of all German POWs on French soil in the near future. Would that not be a powerful tool that would work towards the unity between both of our nations and the building of peace?'[59]

This practical and symbolic gesture led German Pax Christi delegate Josef Probst to laud the success of Kevelaer and deem it an 'historical turning point' in German history. 'For the first time,' he announced, 'German church leaders led and demonstrated on German soil their leadership of the laity in ... public determination to pray and fight for Christian peace.'[60] Bishop Théas also recognized the triumph of Pax Christi's work at the 1948 meeting: 'These days at Kevelaer revealed a successful encounter, because when we are united in God, we are also united with one another ... we belong to different nations, who were enemies just yesterday, and are now one: the same Christ lives in us. Christians in Germany and France have the same godly life in us.'[61] The conference yielded the founding of a German branch of Pax Christi, headquartered in Aachen, with Bishop John Joseph van der Velden, serving as its first president.

The popularity and momentum of the movement grew during the summer of 1948, when ten thousand people from twenty-six countries gathered for a Pax Christi meeting at Lourdes in July, revealing again the role that Pax Christi played in bringing Germans into international dialogue.[62] Foreign bishops did not interfere with the positive ramifications of these meetings by highlighting German misdeeds. To that end, Bishop Théas and French Cardinal Jules-Géraud Saliège continued to focus on personal responsibility in matters of sin and on the work of reconstruction.[63] Germans, like Cardinal Frings, were quick to show gratitude for the efforts that non-German Catholics had made to engender peaceful relations with Germans. Frings expressed his astonishment at how the French people had welcomed him consistently 'with amazing politeness.'[64]

Pax Christi delegates combined their reconciliatory actions with personal pilgrimages, seeking physical, spiritual, relational, historical, and international healing at Lourdes. Here, the sick from all over Europe would seek healing from the same source.[65] Pilgrims took communion at the same altar, commemorating Jesus, who had suffered to achieve world peace; this 'King of Nations' was to serve as the leader of all Catholics, from all nations.[66] This common 'King,' however, was not to replace nations or national affiliation. Instead, Bishop Théas explained in 1948, that Pax Christi members had an enormous responsibility in their respective countries: 'People want to participate in international action... but the Christian should be aware that he, through his country, has the obligation to work towards the unity of humanity and the collective good is the central design of international peace.'[67]

By 1949, the ambitions of Pax Christi members to establish lasting peace in the world had gained the attention and endorsement of Pope Pius XII and the Allies.[68] Pax Christi, they recognized, had something to contribute to the stabilization of Europe and the democratization of Germany.[69] In particular, the French Military Government expressed its encouragement of Pax Christi's work. According to Mr Boumard, a French artist, the French Military Government 'wants [Pax Christi's] presence to be as organized as possible, and to always have the appearance that [the French] had invited the Germans.' French authorities, he said, wanted German visitors, including artists who attended cultural exhibitions in France, to 'have a good time in France.'[70] Common ground was achieved in October 1948, when French and German authors met at an abbey in Royaumont, a setting that encouraged dialogue among the international participants on the 'German problem' and the related 'Rhenish question.'

Not all Germans took the French generosity as a way of dealing with the horrors of Nazism. At Lourdes, a German man, Dr Herder-Dornreich, stated that he had 'deplored the injustice done in the name of Germany... that affected our Christian brothers beyond our borders with injustice.' Herder-Dietrich then turned to convey his appreciation for the fact that the French had 'stretched out [their] brotherly hand from the other side.' He expressed amazement that 'Christians from other countries helped us [and they] will always remain in our hearts.'[71] After the 1948 Lourdes meeting, Manfred Hörhammer also declared that positive things had occurred between the French and the German people, but not at the expense of German critical reflection:

> We left Lourdes with the promises that we had secured friendships with our French friends and that we wanted to fight side by side with them in the spirit of prayer and towards a better future... we want to extend our personal thanks to Mr Colonel Dortel-Claudot and his wife. For us they were in Kevelaer the first revelation of Catholic France and they both won our hearts. Here at Lourdes they accepted us and we felt the inseparable tie of friendship. Particularly, [we experienced] Bishop Théas' selflessness. He is a friend of Germany who considered our concerns and needs.[72]

On this foundation of friendship and security, the work of Pax Christi shifted its focus towards the connected goals of deepening personal piety and fostering international solidarity.[73] Meeting at Oropa, Italy, in 1949, Pax Christi members agreed on the need to rebuild Europe in a concerted, international effort.[74] They revealed the more political aspects of the group that were beginning to emerge, seen in work to promote 'practical education of peace in the schools and the reorientation of teachers and history books.'[75] In 1949, Hörhammer recognized the deep significance of Pax Christi's work for the Germans, who remained pariahs in the international community. 'The German delegation,' he proclaimed, '[had] not forgotten for a moment the rubble and tears of our country and our people.' How wonderful it was, he marvelled, for Germans to represent their country, because it was 'not possible at this point to speak openly and sincerely at international conferences.'[76] After presenting the concerns of the German people, Hörhammer concluded, 'Our French friends have listened well... now I would like to be able to tell our German people about Oropa,' where Italians welcomed Germans warmly.[77]

By 1949, Bishop Théas' – and Pax Christi's – goals were ambitious, but still limited. The avoidance of the Nazi past left unattended a central component of reconciliation in Pax Christi work until the 1950s, and the organization was not focused on the laity or on ecumenical efforts. Instead, in 1948 at Lourdes, Archbishop Feltin of Bordeaux made it clear that Protestantism was one of the 'great errors of the modern world.'[78] Pax Christi work became more politically oriented as the Cold War developed, but its scope was limited. More lofty goals of global democratization and peace were left to other organizations, such as the most progressive and far-reaching international NGO in Europe in the late 1940s, Moral Re-Armament.

Moral Re-Armament (MRA)

As in the case of the International Fellowship of Reconciliation and Pax Christi, it was the victims of German aggression who took the initiative to engender reconciliation with the German people through the work of Moral Re-Armament. The group was founded formally in 1937, growing out of student gatherings of numerous universities – Princeton, Yale, Hartford Theological Seminary, and Oxford – which had organized from the mid-1920s to the early 1930s to promote a Christian-based, international moral awakening and to counter the spread of Communism.[79] For MRA founder Frank Buchman and his colleagues, creating a better world would not come via persuasion through words; instead, the stories of life-change based on the four pillars of MRA: honesty, unselfishness, purity, and love, would become contagious. Mixing these pillars with evangelical enthusiasm and popular rallies – including celebrity endorsement – proved rather successful.[80]

In 1945, MRA member John Roots encouraged Buchman to have an MRA team visit Germany in order to counter the rise of support for Communism in certain regions.[81] In 1946, Buchman invited sixteen Germans to Caux, insisting that it would be '[impossible to] rebuild Europe without the Germans.'[82] Even though this radical, inclusive approach to the German people angered many in MRA's ranks, it was consistent with, indeed foundational to, Buchman's philosophy of reconciliation, which centred on individual peacemaking that included forgiveness, allowing each individual the chance to change, ongoing communication between former enemies, and the belief that the more one had suffered, the more one could contribute to the reconciliatory process.[83] Buchman's work paid off: Germans who attended the first Caux meeting drafted a manifesto, in which they started to talk openly about the roots of Germany's problems, called on Germans to follow MRA's four absolutes, and claimed that 'men must be governed by God or they will be ruled by tyrants.'[84]

Buchman and MRA leaders were concerned equally with religious and political matters, because they considered them inseparable. For this reason, the appeal of MRA was much broader than that of IFOR and Pax Christi. MRA encouraged people of all political and religious persuasions to enter into reconciliatory dialogue, and it had a clear agenda and set of criteria for reconciliation. Moreover, unlike the latter two groups, Moral Re-Armament did not endorse pacifism. In fact, Buchman believed that 'armies with [MRA values] will give new standards of moral training to their nations' and claimed, in June 1945, that MRA was 'battling for [political] control [against] fascism and Communism.' Buchman pointed to 'that great other ideology which is the center of Christian Democracy – Moral Re-Armament' as the best solution for postwar Europe.[85]

For MRA to be effective in this battle and in the peaceful integration of Germany into Western Europe, numerous factors required alignment. By the late 1940s, the crucial components were in place. International MRA members had organized and financed international meetings, Germans were eager to participate in reconciliation at MRA conferences, and the Allies allowed, even encouraged, Germans to travel abroad to attend the meetings.[86] The Allies' encouragement of MRA work – which began in 1946, but strengthened considerably in 1947 – coincided with a shift in U.S. foreign policy towards open confrontation with the Soviet Union and containing Communism. That year, U.S. Secretary of State George Marshall moved to a more vigorous international engagement by assisting in the stabilization of Europe and staving off Communist advancement. According to MRA member Pierre Spoerri – who was active in MRA work in Caux during the late 1940s – Marshall instructed Clay to support organizations like MRA, which Clay did by brokering meetings between MRA members and German minister-presidents in the British and American zones and granting Germans travel permits to attend MRA meetings at Caux during 1946–1949. Clay told the Germans who wanted to attend the meetings, 'I ... have a directive from Washington lying on my desk, saying "What is your programme for filling the ideological vacuum?" ... it seems to me that you have come at the right time with the right answer.'[87] Clay not only granted the travel passes, he, along with the British zone's commander, General Brian Robertson, lauded MRA's anti-Communism and encouraged MRA pamphlets and productions to circulate throughout occupied Germany. Clay and Robertson even sent liaisons to represent them at the Caux conferences.[88]

This alignment of German, Allied, and MRA interests brought thousands of people together at the international meetings at Caux to realize their respective agendas. In 1947, by the invitation of foreign nationals and with the encouragement and permission of the Allies, more than 150 Germans attended the Caux conference. A year later, 414 Germans made the trip, including high-ranking political figures such as Konrad Adenauer, several minister-presidents, thirty-two cabinet members and their spouses, and labour representatives.[89] Altogether, five thousand delegates from fifty-two nations attended the 1948 meetings, including the prime minister of Denmark, the president of the Swiss Confederation, and the vice president of the Austrian parliament.[90] George Shuster, the high commissioner of Bavaria in 1950–1951, recalled Adenauer's recognition of the political significance of MRA. According to Shuster, Adenauer wanted Germans to attend 'as soon after the close of World War II as was feasible.' Further, he claimed, '[MRA conferences] were the first international meetings to cross the barriers of war [where] Germans like Dr Adenauer could state candidly [that] they wished to make retribution for the wrongs done, but that their objective was still the reconciliation of men and nations: something they had always sought after, but for a long time had been powerless to effect.'[91]

Germans who wanted to take on the evils of the Nazi era and reconcile with their wartime enemies in MRA found themselves overwhelmed with the task before them. Georg Eastman, who reported on the 1948 meeting, recalled, 'I saw the look of hopelessness on their [Germans'] faces, many of them wondering whether they would be received as friends, and with a great fear in their hearts of the French, Norwegians, Danes, Dutch and English.'[92] Frank Buchman recognized this problem in his speech at the conference, and tried to level the differences between Germans and their wartime enemies. In doing so, Buchman addressed the shortcomings of standard state diplomacy, which he felt focused exclusively on material reconstruction. For Buchman, material concerns were only part of the equation, and the Allies' policies were failing to address the heart of the problem. '[They] tr[ied] desperately to combat moral apathy with economic plans,' he claimed, but 'the problem is not just an Iron Curtain which separates nation from nation, but steely selfishness which separates man from man and all men from the governance of God.'[93]

Buchman's approach appealed to visitors at Caux, because all were uncertain regarding the future peace and stability of Europe. For

Buchman, MRA had something to offer: 'At a time when statesmen realize the lateness of the hour...[Moral Re-Armament is] a force in the war of ideas, with the training and experience which, under God, can equip the statesmen and the ordinary man with an ideology adequate to remake the nations – now...at Caux the answer has been found.'[94]

Buchman's optimism relied on the delegates' support, particularly regarding their willingness to welcome Germans into their work. In 1947, Irene Laure had exemplified the relinquishment of hatred when she answered Buchman's challenge to incorporate Germany into a unified Europe with positive action. Laure's cynicism regarding statist diplomacy was rooted in the conviction that 'men stayed what they were' and resisted personal change. But only through personal change, Laure believed, was 'there a chance to build [relationships] soundly.'[95] Laure practised this approach personally by devoting her life to MRA work. She began with a two-month tour of Western Germany for the cause of reconciliation between French and German people. Like Buchman, she recognized the central role of victims in the reconciliatory process. The importance of her focus was evident in the positive effects of her work among the German people. Laure explained, 'True, I cannot forget the devastation in France or in the other countries occupied by the Germans, but what I can do is look my own hatred in the face and ask forgiveness for it. The change which occurred in me produced a change in a great many Germans.'[96] Laure was not the only French delegate to take this posture. Eastman reported that the French delegation at Caux in 1948, which numbered around five hundred, revealed that 'every vestige of hatred and bitterness disappeared...[as French and German people sat] down together [to] plan a program whereby France and Germany could together build a new Europe.'[97]

This kind of dialogue also had a significant impact on the way that Germans viewed their own situation. Although the majority of German delegates were interested in some form of reconciliation, and they had been selected as the best candidates by political and church leaders for that work,[98] they revealed the common postwar German propensity towards defensiveness. Foreigners recognized these attitudinal obstacles to change and challenged Germans to abandon them. Buchman confronted Germans at Caux, describing MRA's goal for Germany: 'What we want is to help Germany look forward – especially young Germans – and in the process they will find the way to deal with the past, and they will have to put things right.'[99]

At its meetings, Moral Re-Armament enacted Buchman's gentleness towards the Germans. This approach had a significant impact both at Caux and within Germany. MRA's morality plays, such as *The Good Road* and *The Forgotten Factor*, were staged at Caux to emphasize the shared moral traditions of the participants. They had a powerful impact on the German delegation. After the 1948 meetings, Konrad Adenauer, Minister-Presidents Karl Arnold of North Rhein-Westphalia, Reinhold Maier of Württemberg-Baden, and Hans Ehard of Bavaria – with the encouragement of all three Western Allied powers – invited MRA's theatre group to tour Germany, and it was allowed into Germany in fall 1948. When it crossed the German border, it was 'the largest non-military operation in Germany since the war.'[100]

The MRA tour brought people from thirty countries into Germany, and the Allies and the German Land governments welcomed them officially.[101] The tour group focused its efforts on the Ruhr, a stronghold of Communism, where it staged *The Good Road* and the industrial drama, *The Forgotten Factor*, to large crowds in Essen. Tens of thousands of miners saw the plays and, according to Swiss MRA member Philippe Mottu, 'the moral transformation which took place at the time in the mines, the trade unions and even the cells of the Communist party as well as the boards of directors became a significant factor in the recovery of postwar Germany.'[102] The group's Germany tour also had political significance. Mr Knepper, who managed a mine in Germany, described that seeing *The Good Road* was 'the greatest experience of his life [because] it meant that we [Germans] were accepted again by the international community.'[103]

All Germans who were involved in Moral Re-Armament expressed the chief goal of German rehabilitation on the world stage. Commitment to this cause led them to engage actively in reconciliation. Decades later, Spoerri can recall 'hundreds' of instances in which MRA activities facilitated reconciliation between Germans and their wartime enemies. It was 'a very widespread experience,' he said.[104] One case involved the actions of Hans Lukaschek, co-founder of the Christian Democratic Union (CDU) and minister of refugees in the Federal Republic of Germany from 1949 to 1953. Angered by the lack of Allied support for the development of civil rights legislation in postwar Germany, Lukaschek lauded MRA's grassroots efforts towards reconciliation. In his words, 'the way for Germany will be the way of penance and seeing ourselves clearly ... it will be for us the way of the cross [that will bring about] Germany['s] inclu[sion] in the family of nations.'[105]

A wide variety of influential Germans embraced the work of Moral Re-Armament, as the broad campaign of moral rehabilitation served their political, and for some, personal, goals. Hans Peters, professor and CDU city council member in West Berlin, and Erwin Stein, the Hessian minister of education, reached their own conclusions at the conference. Peters, who admitted Germany's 'enormous guilt,' concluded that the '[ideas and] spirit of Caux will break the ice off the hearts' of millions of hopeless Germans.[106] Stein, who was responsible for 700,000 students, stated the deep significance of religion in state building. In his view, the message of Moral Re-Armament was crucial for German students, who ought to 'succeed in building an inspired, living democracy under the government of God.' For Stein, this goal was not only important domestically; it was 'a precondition of any success for treaties or conferences... between France and Germany [and] other nations.'[107] Baron Hans Herwarth von Bittenfeld, who was a diplomat during the Nazi era, reported that 'at Caux we found democracy at work... and we faced ourselves and our nation [in] personal and national repentance... we learned at Caux we were responsible... through the lack of a positive ideology... for the rise of Hitler.'[108]

The Germans' praise of Moral Re-Armament, and the critical reflections on their own past, influenced political figures in concrete ways, particularly in Franco-German relations. In the late 1940s, most West German politicians supported MRA,[109] and after the 1948 meetings, Adenauer claimed he had been convinced of MRA's significance for Germany and Europe and was eager to continue participation. He described his conversion this way: 'I must tell you frankly that when I arrived at Caux I looked at things with a certain scepticism... [by] the second day... I was convinced of the greatness of the work being done at Caux.'[110] Adenauer was won over after witnessing MRA's morality plays and the general meetings. He returned to Germany to champion the MRA tours and promote circulation of the MRA pamphlet, *Everything Must Change.*

On the French side, Foreign Minister Robert Schuman did not attend the Caux assemblies until the summer of 1953, but many of his close colleagues and friends did. Among them was Lille industrialist Louis Boucquey. Schuman met Boucquey in 1948, and Boucquey, who had embraced the teachings of MRA, convinced Schuman of the need to engender more cooperation between management and labour in northern France's industrial region. With support from Boucquey and others, including the secretary of the French Employers' Federation,

Robert Tilge, who had been at Caux 1947, Schuman took the first steps towards implementing these new ideas into Franco-German relations. In 1948, Boucquey arranged a meeting between Schuman and Buchman.[111]

After being convinced of MRA's approach, Schuman began to speak publicly about his plan for cooperation – and reconciliation – between France and Germany.[112] On 11 January 1949, Schuman moved towards improving Franco-German relations, first by opposing the majority French view on the Ruhr Statute, which gave France jurisdiction over the Ruhr's industrial resources and output. According to Schuman, 'each delivery of coal and iron to foreign countries [should] be paid for in full to the [German] companies. No Allied [country] should get a special advantage out of the Ruhr.'[113] These initial moves towards Franco-German cooperation in industry, which eventually developed into the Schuman Plan, came during a volatile period, when French policy towards Germany was based on fear and retribution.[114]

The significance of Franco-German reconciliation became evident to many influential figures in Allied countries. The American Military Government was also convinced of Schuman's position, which sparked hope among the German people and, in turn, guided the German approach to their Allied occupiers. On 4 April 1949, the same day that NATO's North Atlantic Pact was signed, the German Office for Peace Questions drafted a document stating how the latest developments affected Germans.[115] Now the office reported a shift in British policy, which aimed eventually to include Germany in the pact. The Americans, the statement explained, considered 'German-French reconciliation [to be] the most important factor, a powerful pillar in the stabilization of Europe.'[116] The office celebrated U.S. Secretary of State Dean Acheson's pronouncement that America's Germany policy promoted 'develop[ing] Germany into a peaceful and constructive member of the European community [and] hav[ing] Germany take responsibility for its own business development.'[117]

By the time of Acheson's speech, in April 1949, Moral Re-Armament had been working towards the same goals in the Ruhr for over a year. In its hope of having industrialists and workers embrace its moral agenda, MRA concentrated on improving working and living conditions for miners and management in the Ruhr. By the time of the founding of the Federal Republic of Germany, in May 1949, MRA had brought Germans into meaningful dialogue with more foreign nationals outside of Germany than any other association during the occupation period.

MRA gatherings had played a pivotal role in setting the stage for Franco-German reconciliation and peace in Western Europe.

Moral Re-Armament members were frustrated by the fact that they could not operate in Communist countries. Indeed, Moscow was wary of MRA, and had embarked on a propaganda campaign to malign Frank Buchman and the MRA movement, seeing it as a threat in the establishment of Cold War allies.[118] MRA members did, however, maintain contact with people in the Soviet zone and, subsequently, the German Democratic Republic. Continuing these contacts depended on individuals from Eastern Germany making it to the meetings in Berlin, which was not always easy. MRA's 'penetration' of the German East, as Spoerri called it, essentially came to an end in 1961 with the building of the Berlin Wall.[119] The SED was aware of MRA's work in the late 1940s, and following Moscow's lead, embarked on a a propaganda campaign to discredit Buchman as 'a personal friend of Hitler and Himmler.'[120] By the time of MRA's triumphs in the West, the ideological divide had been set.

International Organizations and Reconciliation Efforts in the Soviet Zone

In the late 1940s, foreign NGO workers and churchmen utilized common religious beliefs and traditions to forge bonds with the German people in the Western zones. In the Soviet zone, by contrast, the work of Communist-directed organizations focused primarily on establishing an international Socialist coalition between Germans and 'anti-fascists' throughout Europe. Both approaches played on the immense suffering and injustice experienced during the war. In the Western zones, a general progression was evident in the relationships that developed between Germans and international groups, from the initial focus on the establishment of common values and goals to the more difficult work of confronting the crimes of the Nazi era at the personal, communal, and international levels. In the Soviet zone, a different progression is discernible, one without the focus on personal change and responsibility. This difference was rooted in the dominant interpretation of recent events among Germans in the Soviet zone and their Soviet occupiers. According to this view, Nazism was a Western, capitalist phenomenon wholly foreign to those living in Soviet-dominated Central and Eastern Europe.

Differing from NGOs in the West, organizations in the Soviet zone took the initiative in addressing the Nazi past head-on. They also initiated contact with foreign organizations, in the attempt to absolve themselves of association with Nazism and gain support from like-minded anti-fascist groups. With all Communist countries and international socialist groups being officially 'anti-fascist,' and with state control and close supervision of all organizations in the Soviet zone, the Association of Victims of Nazism (VVN), the Office for International Cooperation (Büro für Internationale Zusammenarbeit), and the Society for German-Soviet Friendship (Gesellschaft für Deutsch-Sowjetische Freundschaft) were never entirely 'non-government' organizations. The fact that Western NGO workers were limited in their contact and work with Germans living in the Soviet zone, and that formation of organizations within the zone was restricted along ideological lines, left little room to manoeuvre.[121]

Association of Victims of Nazism (VVN)

In the Soviet zone, the cornerstones of the most successful NGO work in the Western zones – anti-Communism; political, military, and economic integration; and a return to traditional religiosity – were viewed as cancerous agents. The Association of Victims of Nazism, the most active and successful organization in the Soviet zone and the least aligned with the government, promoted a peace plan opposite to those offered by groups like Moral Re-Armament. Composed of a majority of Communists, the VVN was opposed to the integration of Germany with the Western world and ignored religion, except when it suited the organization's political goals.[122]

Although both the VVN and its predecessor, Victims of Fascism, focused on domestic issues during the first few years after the war, 1947 witnessed a shift in the association's work towards holding conferences with Western German and international participants. This new direction was intended to unite like-minded Germans from all four zones who agreed with one, some, or all aspects of the VVN's peaceful, socialist, anti-fascist message. The official goal was to form a united, anti-fascist, non-aggressive Germany that was led neither by Soviet Communism nor by Western capitalism and militarism, and to work in concert with foreigners who resisted Nazism.[123] The initial attempt to establish a viable, all-German, cross-zonal organization was staged at the VVN's meeting at Frankfurt am Main from 15 to 17 March 1947. Fifty-eight delegates from the Western zones and Berlin gathered with ten delegates from the Soviet zone. The eclectic gathering, which included Frankfurt publisher Eugen Kogon, Bavarian Minister of Reparations Philipp Auerbach, and Karl Raddatz – the VVN's co-founder in the Soviet zone – revealed the basic concerns of the group. Raddatz outlined the central objectives in his speech: a peace treaty between Germany and the Allies; reparations for the victims of Nazism; and freedom to join forces with international groups that had resisted Nazism during the Second World War in order to build a new Europe free of fascism.[124]

A few weeks after the Frankfurt gathering, VVN leaders in the Soviet zone met at Berlin with the hope of moving towards realization of the group's goals, which were not being met by their Soviet occupiers. The VVN's leader in the Soviet zone, Franz Dahlem, reflected on the Frankfurt meeting, and reported that he saw the 'great significance that the VVN can have for the political development of all of Germany.'[125] Even though Dahlem's, and the VVN's, goal of uniting Germany politically remained elusive, the organization did continue to labour towards more achievable ends. It became the central organization for politically motivated people, including pastors and Jewish community leaders, who wanted to further German interests in a way that was not being achieved under Soviet occupation. For example, Protestant Pastor Gabriel, who joined the Berlin meeting, espoused the 'anti-fascism' of the group and attempted, with some difficulty, to fuse the Confessing Church's theologically driven resistance to Nazi church policies with the Communist resistance movement in the Nazi era.[126]

VVN members wanted to distance themselves from any connection with Nazi Germany, and they recognized the need to have their work align with Soviet ideology. The most elaborate effort that addressed both concerns was the VVN's exhibit, 'The Other Germany,' which toured the Soviet zone during 1948–1949. In this travelling exhibition, the VVN provided massive, indisputable evidence of Nazi crimes and highlighted the regime's 'anti-fascist' resisters. In March 1947, during the final preparation stage, the VVN's General Secretary Karl Raddatz delineated the ambitions for the exhibition: 'If each city and each locale contributes to the success of this exhibit, it will gain international significance.'[127] Raddatz's efforts gained a huge audience. Between September 1948 and November 1949, over 150,000 people visited the exhibit in six cities.[128]

Through its Office of International Contacts, the VVN eventually connected with the first group to welcome the VVN into dialogue: the International Federation of Former Political Prisoners of Fascism.

Comparable to cases in the Western zones, it was foreigneers who initiated contact with the Germans, in this case the French and Spanish leaders of the federation. They arranged a meeting with VVN leaders in Berlin in 1948, where the federation revealed its desire to increase international solidarity.[129] Thereafter, VVN members, who were limited in their ability to travel outside of the Soviet zone, continued to correspond with federation members, even if they could not attend the international 'anti-fascist' meetings, like the one held in Warsaw in May 1948.[130]

The international meetings of the International Federation of Former Political Prisoners of Fascism drew the attention and participation of a wide variety of other anti-fascist and victims groups throughout Europe. These groups highlighted German crimes of the Nazi era and demanded atonement. At the federation's international meeting at Warsaw, in January 1949, Edward Kowalski, the director and general secretary of the federation, expressed the organization's goal of securing political freedom, peace, and legal security. He then went on to demand the 'denazification and democratization of Germany and the payment of reparations.'[131] Just three days earlier, the National Council of the French Federation of Former Deported and Interned Prisoners had drafted its manifesto, which exposed the fact that Germans were not paying reparations, vowed never to forget the concentration camps and the massacre at Oradour, and demanded specific amounts of money for its members' suffering at the hands of the Germans.[132] These accusations, like the ones levelled at a massive VVN-led rally in Berlin in May 1949, were directed against Germans who were involved in the remilitarization of Western Germany.[133] However sincere members of these organizations may have been about getting recognition for their suffering under Nazi rule, their efforts were instrumentalized by Communist authorities in political attacks on the West.

Office for International Cooperation

The topic of injustice was prevalent in all reconstruction work in the Soviet zone in the late 1940s. It also garnered significant attention from the Socialist Unity Party. Like the VVN, the SED sought contact with international organizations in order to further German involvement in international cooperation in postwar European development, an endeavour that hinged on recognition of past injustices. To that end, the SED's Central Committee for International Contacts laboured, in a variety of ways, through its Office for International Cooperation, headed by Max Keilson. In 1948, the office became involved in international exchange programs that included academics, journalists, labourers, and unions. That year, it authorized Germans to travel to conferences in Poland and Hungary, and invited foreigners to meetings in Saxony.[134]

In its contact and relations with Poland, the Office for International Cooperation was forthright in admitting the destruction Germany had wrought on Poland during the Second World War. It made sure, however, to stress that those evils had come by way of 'fascist German troops,' who were part of 'Hitler's Germany.'[135] In a September 1949 letter to the Polish Foreign Ministry, the office included the approximate cost to the Poles of the German occupation of Poland and offered suggestions for what each Pole should receive in compensation, complete with an admission of guilt on behalf of the German people.[136] The author of the letter lamented the ongoing anti-Polish attitudes in Germany. 'The agitators,' the letter insisted, 'are backed by the Americans and British ... the banks and industry kings of Wall Street and London city, who are planning a war against the Soviet Union.'[137] The office declared that Germans and Poles shared the same interests; it was the 'imperialistic enemy' that threatened the peaceful rebuilding of Poland and Germany, and harmed relations between the two.[138]

These comments sought to affirm solidarity between Poles and Germans, and win support for the SED's goal of creating a united socialist Germany. The SED considered the 'stance of ... Poland towards the German problem [to be] ... vital for the German people.'[139] With its letter, the Office for International Cooperation hoped to gain support from the Poles at a time when Warsaw was about to host a conference between leaders of the Soviet Union and the foreign ministers of the European socialist states. The letter urged the Polish Foreign Ministry to convince delegates at the meeting to work towards establishing an 'independent Germany ... [which would] enter into a normal peaceful relationship with ... the Polish government,' including a guarantee of Polish leadership in the 'economic development of the Soviet zone.'[140] The appeal concluded with a subtle threat: if the Polish government did not follow this path, Poles would not only sacrifice the economic benefits involved in reconstruction projects in Germany, they would again be threatened by an embittered German nation.

Society for German-Soviet Friendship

While the Office for International Cooperation was working to secure Polish support for the emerging East German state, the Society for German-Soviet Friendship was active in deepening relations between

Germans and the Soviet Union. At first glance, these groups appear to have some characteristics of Western NGOs. However, the groups served essentially as Communist front organizations in furthering the political goals of the SED and the Soviet Administration. The Society for German-Soviet Friendship was formed in 1948 by order of the Soviet Administration's propaganda minister, Major General Sergei Tiulpanov, who personally monitored the SED and the society.[141] The society's main objective was 'the task of spreading the truth about the Soviet Union, of fighting every kind of slander and opposition [to the USSR] and through this to secure and deepen the friendship of the German people with the people of the Soviet Union.'[142] It focused on establishing relations with cultural foundations and institutions in the Soviet Union and engaging in discussions, educational exchange, cultural events, and creation of Russian language centres in Germany.[143]

Like the Office for International Cooperation, the society stressed the past animosities between the two nations in the hopes of validating the suffering of the victims of Nazism, and establishing friendly relations for the future. The eagerness for improving relations between Germany and the Soviet Union was dampened by the stark reality of the postwar political and economic situation between the two nations. Although the Soviets were interested in furthering the work of the society and developing relations with the German people, they would not forgive the destruction brought by the German Army and occupation.

The restoration of positive relations between Germans and Soviet citizens would come at a high price, evident in a society pamphlet, printed after the establishment of the German Democratic Republic, in October 1949. In the pamphlet, titled 'That Is True Friendship: Through the Reduction of Reparations, the Soviet Union Gifts Each Citizen of the GDR–450 DM,' Soviet members of the society spelled out the enormous cost that the German occupation had levied on the Soviet Union and reminded the German people of the number of Soviet war dead. But, because Stalin's view was that 'Hitlers come and go, but the German people and the German state remains,' the Soviets pledged to improve relations between the two nations, beginning with a 'gift' of lowering the reparations payments that Germany was to make to the Soviet Union. The pamphlet proclaimed, 'The socialist country knows no revenge and retaliation towards the defeated.'[144]

This propaganda pamphlet included a comparative study between the Soviet zone and the Western zones, concluding that the Western Allies were damaging Germany economically through reparations.

Meanwhile, of course, the Soviets were busy with a wholesale dismantling of the industrial infrastructure in Eastern Germany.[145] Ignoring these facts, the Soviets claimed to differ from the Western Allies' 'colonial' approach. They wished to 'recognize the peaceful politics of the German Democratic Republic,' the pamphlet insisted, and support 'the democratic development of the German people.'[146] Recognizing that this new arrangement was the best that could be hoped for under the current circumstances, GDR Prime Minister Otto Grotewohl offered an immediate response of gratitude to Stalin, filled with praise for the dictator and words welcoming the onset of improved Soviet-German relations.[147] Little more than fronts for Communist power, organizations like the VVN and the Society for German-Soviet Friendship might seem to have contributed nothing to postwar processes of reconciliation. Through their detailed presentation of Nazi 'fascist' crimes and their attacks on Western 'imperialist' agitators, however, they did serve to draw attention to German wartime aggression and to some of its victims. If the blatant propagandistic nature of their efforts made it easy to discredit them, it also served to disseminate their views on both sides of the East-West divide.

Schizophrenic Reconciliation

From 1947 to 1949, the most successful organizations that operated in occupied Germany were those that aligned their goals and work with the priorities of the respective zonal occupiers. The rhetoric of peace was popular throughout all of occupied Germany. However, pacifist groups in the Western zones were not as successful as those that espoused the integration of Germany into the budding Western alliance, including militarily. Directly related to the integration of Western military might was the concern over the spread of Communism. In Eastern Germany, anxiety about Western military power drew the attention of Germans and was also used as a rallying tool for support of Communist ideology. Organizations in the Soviet zone, although bound to the Soviet Administration and the SED, supported international peace initiatives within Soviet-dominated Eastern Europe and demanded that German 'fascists' pay for the suffering of at least some of the victims of Nazism.

The initiatives of foreign individuals and groups to contact Germans in the immediate postwar period led to the first diplomatic exchanges between Germans and foreign nationals after the Second World War. Supported by the Allies, who encouraged their work in a variety of ways, Germans advanced reconciliatory work while, at the same time, they furthered their own goals. In order to do so, they were forced to meet certain criteria at Catholic pilgrimage sites, at Protestant gatherings, or at socialist rallies. Those encounters, in turn, moved Germans beyond the material and political spheres of nation building to personal reflection. Some Germans were more sincere in their religious and political beliefs than others, and some were more altruistic in their statements of reconciliation than others, but all who participated in international gatherings were pushed towards self-reflection and were exposed to personal accounts of suffering from their wartime enemies.

Reconciliatory efforts in the late 1940s mirrored the ideological contexts of political and military alliances, however, and as a result were limited and incomplete. Indeed, the largest group of victims from the Nazi era, the Jews, was ignored in the work of all of the organizations examined above, as were individual victims and minority groups, including Roma, Sinti, homosexuals, and victims of sterilization and medical experimentation. The failure to recognize all victims during the occupation period led to ongoing problems in both Germanies after 1949. Still, the contacts and reconciliatory activities of NGOs during the late 1940s were significant both for Germany and the international community, because they marked progress in addressing Nazi crimes, victimhood, and responsibility. The next chapter focuses on the long-term effects of the new relationships that emerged between Germans and their wartime enemies during the Allied occupation of Germany.

Chapter Five

The Politics of Reconciliation in the Two Germanies, 1949–1954

In May 1952, at the height of negotiations between the Federal Republic of Germany and representatives from Israel and the Jewish Claims Conference, Germany's chief negotiators, Franz Böhm and Otto Küster, resigned. Böhm and Küster could not do their job because of the resistance they experienced from fellow Germans over their efforts to finalize a compensation package for Jewish victims of Nazism. Both Böhm and Küster were actively involved in German Societies for Christian-Jewish Cooperation. As negotiators they had pursued German-Jewish reconciliation with deep personal conviction, which involved garnering substantial compensation for Jewish victims. Germans from all walks of life opposed their efforts, led by the Federal Republic's Finance Minister Fritz Schäffer, who claimed that their proposed sum would cripple Germany's economy.[1]

Schäffer's plan to reduce the compensation package from 4.35 billion DM, the agreed basis for negotiations, to 3.0 billion DM outraged Küster and Böhm and brought Schäffer and the negotiators into direct confrontation.[2] His belief in justice compromised, Küster aired his grievances in a public radio address: 'I speak with anger, but I hope to God that it [is] a just anger ... I came to the conclusion that the German people must know in which spirit the decision in Bonn was made, that the injustice of the Hitler era remains intact and that [it will] remain with our sons and grandchildren.'[3] Küster blamed the finance minister for the injustice inherent in the proposed deal, calling it 'politically intolerable.' He appealed to the German people, 'especially the young, innocent heirs of Hitler [to] cry out' in protest of the fact that 'our national honour is no longer maintained.'[4] Küster saw no option but to resign, and he did so on 7 May 1952. Three weeks later, Böhm followed Küster's lead and resigned, leaving Schäffer with regrets over hiring the pair.[5]

The Jewish newspaper *Allgemeine Wochenzeitung der Juden in Deutschland*, which monitored the level of antisemitism in Germany, lauded the two men's efforts and noted the benefits of their actions. The paper observed how Küster's resignation 'appeared to have a positive effect in a very short period of time,' because Schäffer reinstated Böhm, and the German negotiating team brought a much larger compensation offer to the bargaining table.[6] Küster never regained his position in the Finance Ministry, but his actions, and those of Böhm, facilitated the Luxembourg Agreement, in September 1952, in which the Federal Republic of Germany agreed to pay Israel 3.0 billion DM and the Jewish Claims Conference 450 million DM.[7]

This chapter examines the processes of retribution and reconciliation between Germans and their wartime victims and enemies in the years following formation of the two German states in 1949. Both Germans and foreigners operated under tense conditions and sought benefits for themselves, yet positive developments did emerge. The account of Küster and Böhm reveals the convergence of forces that affected everyone who dealt with the Nazi past: the Western Allies, who demanded democratization of the German justice system, including compensation for victims; the victims, who demanded recognition and compensation; defensive Germans, who opposed taking responsibility for Nazi crimes; and other Germans, who promoted appropriate action vis-à-vis the Nazi past and its victims. In the Soviet zone/GDR, it was much the same, although things proceeded along Stalinist lines. For personnel representing all four Allied nations, continued distrust of the German people mixed with the desire to incorporate Germany into their respective geopolitical camps. On the German side, unwillingness to tackle the evils of Nazism struggled with the necessity to do so, as Germans continued to strive for international acceptance.

In this context, traditional diplomacy in both Germanies gradually superseded the grassroots diplomacy of the occupation era. Nevertheless, the political significance and influence of NGOs and other grassroots groups remained high. Indeed, the recognition of victims of Nazism engendered largely by NGOs during the preceding years – evident in Böhm's and Küster's participation in the Societies for Christian-Jewish Cooperation – made possible the ongoing discussion of victimhood and victim compensation in semi-sovereign West Germany.

Tensions

Observations of the lack of German contrition after state formation found wide support among foreign journalists. During the summer of 1949, British journalists lamented the lack of change seen in the German people, deplored the absence of gratitude among the German people for Allied support since the end of the war, and were astounded by the lack of contrition that Germans felt.[8] For instance, Brian Colonnell wrote in the *Continental Daily Mail* about how the Germans had 'not [uttered] a word of thanks for the assistance of the American and British taxpayers, who brought them back on their legs, or a word about a feeling of debt or shame for their past misdeeds.'[9] One French journalist lamented that 'the Germany that arises today is not a new Germany, but it is under a rejuvenated mask of the Germany from yesterday,'[10] and a British writer claimed, 'Germany wants to re-establish the political and economic scene of the past [which is] a dire warning for the world, that Germany is still a strong source of evil.'[11] In Eastern Germany, the Soviet Administration had discouraged recognition of Jewish victims throughout the occupation era and, together with German Communists, had purged the SED of Jews, and of gentiles who were sympathetic to Jewish suffering.[12] Clearly, the transformation of Germany was incomplete at the end of formal occupation in 1949.

It was in this context that the Western Allies created their High Commissions and the Soviets their Control Commission, in order to maintain control over the newly established semi-sovereign German states. The commissions balanced control with the attempt to work in concert with the German people towards common goals in international politics. After 1949, the Allies continued to assume that the price of Germany's integration into Europe would require appropriate penitence – and action – in relation to the Nazi past. One British journalist wrote, 'Forgiveness is a Christian virtue, but forgetting can be an act of madness, particularly when it is extended to the Germans ... We may not deal with the Germans gently. We want them to be in the European Community, but not at the price of forgetting what they did.'[13] Indeed, the aim of the Western Allies was to have the Germans enter the family of nations, and the Allies were prepared to contribute to the difficult task of that incorporation. As one French journalist put it, only after the Allies had done the work and 'avoid[ed] disaster' in reshaping Europe would it be possible for 'Germany [to] find its place in a reconciled continent.'[14] Soviet policy in Germany continued to prioritize the unity of anti-fascist forces over critical reflection on the past, while gradually handing over control of zonal governance to appropriate Soviet-aligned 'German helpmates.'[15] Like their Western counterparts, they lacked belief that a widespread change of mind had occurred in Germany, but seemed less concerned about these matters so long as the Germans served Soviet goals.

Validating the anger and distrust that foreigners held towards the German people were the attitudes and actions of German church leaders, whom the Allies had counted on to take the lead in the type of forgiveness and reconciliation that foreign journalists broached in their articles. Even though the Western Allies voiced this connection more blatantly than the Soviets, German church leaders and their affiliated relief organizations viewed state formation as an opportunity to further their institutional and nationalistic goals. Tensions rose when church leaders from Western Germany sidelined reconciliation as they laboured towards German unification, which included efforts to frustrate the East German campaign towards political legitimacy and recognition.[16] Leading the Protestant charge was Berlin Bishop Otto Dibelius, who found much support from Protestant clergy, such as Bishop Mitzenheim of Thüringia and Reinold von Thadden-Trieglaff, who was chairman of the Protestant Church Congress, an office established in 1949 to organize all-German gatherings for Protestants.[17] At the Protestant gatherings, prominent clergy openly promoted the notion that Protestant religion bound all Germans together, even while denying that they had a political agenda.[18]

In 1949, the churches' affiliated organizations – Church's Aid Society and Protestant Relief Work – promoted the nationalist agenda of their respective churches and continued in their struggle to claim victimhood status for the expellees and for the German people in general. On the eve of the formation of West German statehood in spring 1949, Church's Aid Society published numerous articles in its periodical, *Christ Unterwegs*, monitoring the details of the Catholic expellee population and extolling their communal innocence.[19] Moreover, the Aid Society continued to work towards maintaining a German presence in former German-held territories in Eastern Europe and northern Italy,[20] and used its periodical to chastise the Allies for their inhumane treatment of the German people and to provide guidance morally – and politically – to German Catholic expellees.[21]

Protestant Relief Work also served nationalist goals after 1949, now with its president, Eugen Gerstenmaier, also serving as President of the Foreign Committee of the Federal Parliament (1949–1953). Gerstenmaier promoted the unification of Germany, telling the audience at the Protestant Church Congress in Essen, in 1950, that because Germans could not 'assume that the world powers will agree to leave Germany and to afford Germany self-determination,' German Protestants should approach the Nazi past in a 'forgive and forget' manner.[22] He called for an end to denazification, claiming that it hindered German reconstruction and 'achiev[ing] genuine solidarity in Germany, [which could] only be achieved through reconciliation.'[23] Gerstenmaier's focus on diffusing the Cold War through 'reconciliation' fit in with his broader goal of bringing an end to the political polarization in Germany, which would occur through the unification of Germany. He claimed, 'We must reunite Germany [because] Europe is for us not Europe without the territory and people over the Elbe and Oder.'[24]

Reparations in the Federal Republic of Germany: The Politics of Compensation

During the first few years of the Federal Republic's existence, German government officials prioritized two inter-related, but often incongruent, goals of national unity, and Germany's integration with the West. Consequently, tensions that arose between foreigners and Germans revolved around how the German people dealt with the victims of Nazism. In the general democratization scheme, the Allies believed that the German people required both supervision and assistance in their gradual reinstatement into the family of nations and regulated German affairs to that end. For example, the Occupation Statute promised Germans the 'maximum possible degree' of self-government, even while the Charter of the Allied High Commission for Germany stated clearly that Germans were required to take over the 'deliver[y of] reparations and restitutable property; care and administration of displaced persons; [and] disposition of war criminals.'[25] As for the victims of Nazism, the Allies monitored closely German government affairs regarding reparations and in some cases applied considerable pressure to the German government to compensate victim groups. In general, victim recognition and compensation – including reparations, restitution, and indemnity payments – were entangled in the bid for full German sovereignty, and alignment with the West.[26] At stake in these proceedings was justice for victims personally, and also the future of victim recognition and compensation in the Federal Republic of Germany.

After state formation, it became apparent to some Germans that their fears of the German government abandoning the path to fair compensation were well founded. Indeed, if justice was to be realized, the lax and at times defiant approach that most German politicians held towards reparations, particularly in the Ministries of Finance and Justice, would require external pressure if it were to change for the better. West Germany's Justice Minister during 1949–1953, Thomas Dehler – whose wife was of Jewish descent – was opposed to reparations, mostly due to the burden that they levied on the German people, and he used the West German reparations laws to restrict compensation wherever possible. In a November 1950 speech to the Bundestag, Dehler placed the blame for the ongoing problems with reparations on the Allies and expressed his displeasure at the fact that the Allied High Commissions would continue to control reparations procedures.[27] Dehler's concern for those Germans who had purchased the property of persecutees outweighed his concern for the just treatment of the victims. Instead of seeking justice for the victims, most of whom were Jews, Dehler claimed that the purchasers of the property had 'no responsibility' for the injustice done to the victims and that most cases were unsolvable logistically and morally, because 'it [is not] possible to make right nonmaterial damages.'[28] Rather than attempting to address the enormous injustice, Dehler insisted on gaining from the Allies more control of German affairs in these matters which, if achieved, would result in less generous treatment for the victims.

Dehler and other like-minded government officials continued to oppose reparations in a battle that came to the fore in 1950. While Dehler was haggling over the details of the law, the injustice towards the victims increased, because many victims – including sterilization victims, victims of medical experiments, homosexuals, and Jews – were recognized inadequately, or not at all, in the West German reparations laws. The 1933 Law for the Prevention of Hereditarily Diseased Offspring, which legalized the sterilization of people whom the Nazis deemed mentally and physically handicapped, resulted in the sterilization of 300,000 to 400,000 people against their will.[29] However, many of the victims of forced sterilization were not sterilized according to the parameters of this law, but on racial grounds – such as Afro-Germans, Jews, and Roma and Sinti people – although the exact number of these illegal operations is unknown. In 1951, the Ministry of Justice stated that it would recognize and compensate victims of forced sterilization only in such cases of 'illegal sterilization,' thus excluding those who were sterilized 'legally' under the Nazi law.[30] Meanwhile, all victims of sterilization struggled for recognition and compensation.[31]

Before promulgation of the 1953 Additional Federal Compensation Act, the ad hoc treatment of sterilization victims worked well for Dehler and the government, because cases could be dismissed rather easily without appealing to an all-encompassing federal law.[32] In October 1950, Karl Stürke of Oldenburg wrote to Dehler with the hopes of getting compensation not only for himself but for his friend Mr Hirschmöller, who had also applied. Stürke insisted that Dehler 'did not understand [their] situation [which included the fact that he was] sterilized in 1935 ... for reasons of mental deficiency.'[33] Dehler underlined these words with his own pen, proving to himself that Stürke was sterilized 'legally' in 1935 and thus was not eligible for compensation.[34] Thousands of other applicants received the same response. News of the denial of their claims arrived via a generic letter, drafted by Dr Schultheiss of the Ministry of the Interior, which emphasized that the applicant's sterilization had been done legally.[35]

The position of the Federal Government led some people, encouraged by the progressive compensation laws that had been enacted in the American zone, to support the notion that the Länder should develop their own reparations laws. This occurred in Schleswig-Holstein. In January 1951, the Land government there drafted progressive legislation that acknowledged the victimhood of those who had been forcibly sterilized and considered such individuals eligible for compensation.[36] Meanwhile, in 1951, the High Commissioners remained true to their mandate and insisted that reparations procedures move forward.[37] Dehler, however, continued to fight the Allies' position of collective restitution, wanting instead a case-by-case examination of each individual's claim to victimhood. He referred to Allied tactics as being like 'the experiences of the National Socialist era,' and insisted that the Allies reconsider their demands.[38]

Meanwhile, even the victims of 'illegal' sterilization found it difficult to gain recognition and compensation. The Ministry of Justice felt obligated, reluctantly, to compensate Roma and Sinti victims of sterilization, because in 1947 a Hamburg judge had convicted physicians for performing those sterilizations. The legal precedent, and the media coverage of it, forced the ministry to acknowledge the right of Roma and Sinti victims of forced sterilization to receive compensation.[39] But the ministry stated that it 'was not obligated to compensate' those who had suffered 'legal' sterilization, which left those victims to fend for themselves.[40]

Opposition to compensation within the government led the victims of forced sterilization, in December 1950, to form the Central Association of Sterilized and Physically Harmed People, which represented approximately eight hundred victims. In August 1951, the association held a massive rally in support of forcibly sterilized and medically maltreated individuals. The event was advertised widely in a circular drafted by the association's leader, Kurt Königer, who realized that the victims' only hope for justice was to gain public awareness of and support for their cause.[41] The federal government responded to this initiative by attempting to discredit Königer and undermine the association's work. In a letter of September 1951, the Federal Chancellor's Office informed the Central Association of Sterilized and Physically Harmed People that their leader was a fraud, who had been sterilized 'legally' in 1935 for mental deficiency. Further, government officials claimed, Königer had slandered the Wehrmacht, which resulted in his incarceration at Buchenwald in 1944, where he had supposedly suffered brain damage. This version of events implied that Königer's actions thereafter were not conducted by someone of sound mind. For good measure, the government's letter added that Königer had been convicted of theft and other sordid petty crimes since the end of the war.[42]

The collective effort of the FRG's government ministries to avert compensation of individual victims was part of a broader campaign that included all victims of Nazism in Germany and abroad.[43] While the West German government continued to hesitate and falter in reparations proceedings in Germany, foreigners were pressuring Germans to move forward and, in some cases, enacted their own justice.[44] For the West Germans, a significant, large-scale reparations deal – one that would affect victims in Germany and, more importantly, victims abroad – became a central project in the bid for Germany's normalization of international standing. Ernst Féaux de la Croix, whom the Ministry of Finance appointed to address these problems, attributed the change to Jewish influence: 'The Federal Ministry of Finance began to realize from the beginning of 1952 that it was not possible to continue the attitude prevailing thus far of Federal Government inactivity in the area of reparations ... the pressure of world public opinion, inspired and at the same time directed by the large, mainly Jewish organizations of persecutees, became greater and greater.'[45] Indeed, it was foreign demands for justice that commanded the attention of most Germans in government, and it was those demands that guided decisions regarding who was recognized. In most cases, the victims who were recognized and compensated were those with the most support domestically, and internationally.

German-Jewish Relations, 1949–1952: Restitution and ... Reconciliation?

The need for increased foreign intervention in German-Jewish reconciliation became evident in the early 1950s, particularly after the American High Commission's 1951 surveys revealed that the majority of West Germans did not feel responsible to address Jewish victimhood and that the majority also held firm in their antisemitism.[46] Antisemitic articles appeared in abundance in the German popular press and were reprinted and discussed in the Jewish *Wochenzeitung*.[47] Such articles led the *Wochenzeitung*'s editors to publish a front-page story in April 1950, titled 'Enough Already: A Comment on Antisemitism in Germany.' The cover image, a cartoon captioned 'Children at Play,' depicted German youths desecrating a Jewish cemetery. *Wochenzeitung* journalist H. Ritzel offered a scathing rendition of democracy in Germany in 1950 and encouraged Jews to engage proactively in the development of a more tolerant Germany.[48] Whereas the eighteen thousand Jews who remained in Western Germany in 1949 strove to gain recognition in the Federal Republic through the Central Council of Jews in Germany (established in 1950), it would take more powerful, international organizations to secure from the FRG a massive compensation package for Jews.

Akin to other cases of postwar reconciliation in Germany, it was the victims – or their representatives, in this case, the state of Israel and the Jewish Claims Conference – that initiated the reconciliatory process. After the formation of the state of Israel in 1948, the Israeli government demanded reparations from Germany. The fledgling East German government ignored the demand, whereas Chancellor Adenauer offered the Israeli state goods totalling 10 million DM. Israeli officials rejected the offer and, in conjunction with World Jewish Congress members – who established in 1951 the Conference on Material Claims against Germany, or the Claims Conference – continued to demand substantial compensation for Jewish victims. In September 1951, Adenauer stated in a Bundestag session that the Federal Republic of Germany had a 'duty of moral and material reparations.'[49] By this time, West German government representatives were working towards realizing this duty, while facing demands of 4.2 billion DM from the state of Israel for 'reconstruction assistance,' and 500 million DM from the Claims Conference to compensate for stolen Jewish property.[50]

Not all FRG government officials agreed with meeting these demands, despite Adenauer's stated intentions to pay reparations to Israel and Jewish victims and organizations. Franz Böhm's and Otto Küster's standoff with Finance Minister Fritz Schäffer over Jewish reparations in 1952 was rooted in the broader opposition to compensation outlined above, and in foreign demands that Germany make a significant reconciliatory gesture towards world Jewry as a prerequisite to German sovereignty. Beginning in 1951, leading German politicians, including Social Democrat Carlo Schmid and the Christian Democratic Chancellor, Konrad Adenauer, promoted a reparations deal with Israel and world Jewry. Schmid recognized in his first meeting with Adenauer that 'reconciliation with the Jewish people was an important factor in [Adenauer's] general political outlook,'[51] which was chiefly concerned with Western integration that involved, unavoidably, U.S. interests in Europe and the Middle East.[52] Indeed, it was political pragmatism that led the likes of Schäffer and Dehler to go along with the negotiations, even while Schäffer tried to stall negotiations and reduce the compensation sum.

Böhm and Küster rose to the occasion and pushed forward the negotiations on the sum of 4.35 billion DM, the figure all parties agreed on as the basis for negotiations.[53] When the Israelis proposed a larger sum of 6.3 billion DM, Böhm revealed his true feelings, stating that 'compared to the size of the damages caused, it is without a doubt completely appropriate.'[54] Moreover, after the negotiators agreed that West Germany would pay Israel a sum of 3.0 billion DM, Böhm publicly expressed his embarrassment at the reduced figure and was outraged at the slow pace of the negotiations stemming from the German side. He told a reporter, 'Elderly victims cannot wait 50–60 years for compensation!'[55] For Böhm and Küster, the moral concerns expressed in the compensation proceedings were part of their respective, and similar, worldviews, which found expression in their participation in the Societies for Christian-Jewish Cooperation.

Christians and Jews

Although the most far-reaching progress in German-Jewish reconciliation occurred via foreign pressure and international agreements, there were some significant home-grown German initiatives as well. The few

Germans who proceeded altruistically in the recognition and compensation of Jewish victims of Nazism were emboldened by their personal convictions and by the organization and support of the Societies for Christian-Jewish Cooperation. In nearly all cases, individuals who joined the societies and championed the recognition of Jewish victims had a track record of similar activity outside the organization. Küster had been an active member in Gertrud Luckner's *Freiburger Rundbrief* circle and was committed to seeing Baden-Württemberg's Restitution Office and the federal Ministry of Finance adopt a thoroughgoing restitution law for all victims of Nazism.[56] Küster joined the Freiburg society, and Franz Böhm joined Frankfurt's chapter. Böhm also served as the chairman of the societies' central coordinating committee and, in 1950, he encouraged Germans publicly to tackle antisemitism from the ground up in 'collective resistance.'[57]

Although it is impossible to know exactly what Christians and Jews felt towards each other during the first few years after West German state formation, the extant records of Christian-Jewish dialogue indicate hesitancy on both sides. In 1949, the periodical *Christ und Sozialist* surveyed 150 people, Christian and Jewish, asking them to respond to four questions: Were Germans guilty towards the Jews? What was the person's opinion on antisemitism? Did the person believe in Christian-Jewish understanding? What did that person have to say about general aspects of Jewish culture?[58]

Jewish responses demanded recognition for suffering under Nazi rule, but Jews were also generous towards the German people. One respondent stated that 'Germany has a great responsibility towards the Jews' and reminded readers that 'each of us [Jews] has had either parents, siblings, uncles, cousins, or other relatives murdered by the Nazis.' At the same time, the respondent stressed that Christian-Jewish reconciliation remained a possibility 'through understanding each other.'[59] A Jewish woman said she had experienced kindness from Germans during the Nazi era. She was optimistic that 'understanding between people of good will on both the Christian and Jewish side' could achieve positive things, particularly through education.[60] On the Christian side, a Protestant pastor acknowledged German responsibility towards Jewish suffering and expressed optimism regarding Christian-Jewish reconciliation.[61]

However, the majority of Protestants who entered into dialogue with Jews refused to abandon Christian supercessionism, the main obstacle to Christian-Jewish reconciliation. After the disheartening inaugural 'Church and Judaism' meeting in 1948 at Düsseldorf, the German Protestant Committee for Service towards Israel held its second meeting, at Kassel, from 27 February to 3 March 1950. That event brought together Erlangen's Jewish Professor Hans-Joachim Schoeps with Protestants Otto Dibelius, Heinrich Oepke, Karl Rengstorf, Heinrich Grüber, and Adolf Freudenberg. Dibelius provided the foundation for the meeting, which looked rather promising: 'the people here ... seek to understand the Jewish Question in repentant reflection ... German Christianity ... [has] a heavy responsibility towards the Jews ... [and we] have still not sufficiently identified and acknowledged it. The meetings are a hopeful attempt to use biblical grounds to bring to order a destroyed relationship and to continue conversation into which the Church cannot enter without taking on the responsibility for the damage done.'[62]

Although the Council of the Protestant Church agreed with Dibelius about the need to address antisemitism in Germany, it revealed the limits of its self-directed analysis. It was not able to shed the Nazi terminology of the *Judenfrage,* nor was it able to engage with Jews as equals. Instead, the council's efforts were self-serving, and the most vocal participants at the meeting, Oepke and Rengstorf, held to Christian supercessionism. No Jews were on the speakers' list, and there was only one interconfessional roundtable discussion 'on the Jewish-Christian problem.' Hans-Joachim Schoeps was its only Jewish participant.[63]

The mixed group of Christians and Jews did make some progress in altering Protestant teaching about Jews. One participant at the conference, Pastor Adolf Freudenberg, presented a draft of his proposal for a new Protestant approach to the 'Jewish Question.' In April 1950, the Protestant Church adopted Freudenberg's text in its official Berlin-Weissensee Statement.[64] The statement admitted some Protestant responsibility for the murderous attack on Jews – particularly regarding the Church's silence – during the Nazi era and called on Christians to regard 'Jews and Jewish-Christians' as God's people:

> We confess the Church, which is joined together in one body of Jewish Christians and gentile Christians and whose peace is Jesus Christ. We believe God's promise to be valid for his Chosen People even after the crucifixion of Jesus Christ. We state that by omission and silence we became implicated before the God of mercy in the outrage that has been perpetrated against the Jews by people of our nation ... We ask all Christians to dissociate themselves from all antisemitism and earnestly to resist it,

whenever it stirs again, and to encounter Jews and Jewish Christians in a brotherly spirit.⁶⁵

However, the statement did not present the two religions as equal. It concluded with a proclamation of supercessionism: 'We pray ... that [God] may bring about the Day of Fulfillment when we will be praising the triumph of Jesus Christ together with the saved Israel.'⁶⁶ In the end, this Protestant Church statement aimed at outward and practical changes, paying lip-service to acceptance of the Jewish religion and guaranteeing Protestant protection of Jewish cemeteries.⁶⁷ At the same time, it underscored the fundamental differences between Christians and Jews.

Future meetings of the Protestant Committee for Service towards Israel, at Düsseldorf in 1951 and in Ansbach in 1952, proceeded in the same theological vein but did evoke some positive response from Jews.⁶⁸ A *Wochenzeitung* journalist reported how, at Düsseldorf, 'we [Jews] heard so many pleasant words about the understanding between Christians and Jews, and about the love that the Christians held towards Israel.' The journalist questioned the allegations that Christians disregarded Jews in Germany, pointing to the utterances of Christians at the conference and to the Berlin-Weissensee Statement.⁶⁹ In the early 1950s, it seems Jews in Germany welcomed any positive gesture from Christians, even while they continued to focus on their own gatherings.⁷⁰ A new approach was needed to bridge the gaps that separated the two groups.

The thirteen Societies for Christian-Jewish Cooperation established in Western Germany during 1948–1953 employed such a novel approach. The societies laboured towards gentile acceptance of Jews on their own terms and towards the elimination of antisemitism in Germany. The societies spearheaded the kind of gentile-Jewish dialogue that Jews at the 1949 Heidelberg Conference had deemed necessary for Jewish survival in Germany, first with Allied support in institutional organization, structure, and finances, and then, by the early 1950s, autonomously.⁷¹ In addition to gathering thousands of Catholics, Protestants, and Jews in open dialogue just a few years after the Holocaust, society members tackled racist teaching in school curricula and academic practice and established the annual German-wide meetings, 'Weeks of Brotherhood.'

An example of the societies' success in combatting antisemitism is in the Frankfurt chapter's 1950 campaign to expunge antisemitic content from textbooks and school curricula in Northrhine-Westfalia.⁷² When a delegation of Jews and Christians found numerous short stories and poems that were clearly antisemitic in nature, the society embarked on a letter-writing campaign to the Minister of Culture of Northrhine-Westfalia, Christine Teusch. Together, Catholics, Protestants, and Jews informed Teusch on 11 June 1950: 'When a German child in school encounters a Jewish person in the schoolbooks, the Jew must be presented in an honourable way. We must take on the pedagogical duty, at the very least, to ensure that ... children must ponder the significance of the injustice done to the Jews.'[73] Moreover, society members suggested a fundamental shift in thinking: Jews did not need to convert to Christianity in order to be accepted in German society: 'We do not accept the publisher's ... attempt to present to us that baptism can change the life of the eternal Jew ... the psychological harm done to unbaptized Jews is not made right by explaining it away in ten pages.'[74] The next day, Teusch began to look into the matter, and by 13 June she had moved to ban the books in question.[75] By 14 June, Teusch informed the society: 'On my demand ... production and distribution and selling of the volumes will stop immediately and the books will ... not be used in the schools [moreover] the Cultural Ministers from other provinces will meet with me personally tomorrow morning in Unkel at the Cultural Ministers Conference, and I will pass along the information.'[76] In a span of just six days, the Societies for Christian-Jewish Cooperation succeeded in convincing Teusch of their position, and in having her remove the texts and ban their further publication.[77]

On 15 June 1950, the president of the Frankfurt society, Hugo Stenzel, sent a letter to Teusch, in which he lauded her work and the success of the society. 'For the first time since 1945,' Stenzel announced, 'a private organization, together with the authorities and offices concerned, has implemented a form of self-cleansing.' Stenzel pointed to the need to eradicate the deeper problem in Christian teaching: 'Henceforth we call on all church authorities to think through again their theological foundations of the Christian stance towards the Jews, and be awakened to the subtle and dormant aspects therein.'[78]

Professional academics also used society gatherings to challenge the traditional Christian view towards the Jews. At a society meeting in March 1950, a Catholic member of the Berlin society, anthropologist Professor Hermann Muckermann, director of the Kaiser Wilhelm Institute for Applied Anthropology in Berlin, gave an address titled 'Fundamental Problems of Solidarity between Jews and Christians.' In his address, Muckermann, who had been forced into retirement during the Nazi era because of his opposition to the sterilization program, claimed that 'the new anthropology is not limited to the physicality of people.' He stressed that the 'biological unity of humanity' meant there were no 'real differences' between Jews and Christians or anyone else.[79] For Muckermann, after the anthropological differences had been stripped away, the divide between Christians and Jews became entirely a religious issue, which he claimed was 'not a hindrance for the development of real solidarity.'[80] The solution for Muckermann was to be found in theological common ground, evident in a shared deity, shared morality, and common eschatology.[81]

Muckermann's focus on seeking common theological ground, while dissolving superficial differences between Christians and Jews, was typical of the agenda of the Societies for Christian-Jewish Cooperation, and evident in the development of the annual Weeks of Brotherhood.[82] Beginning in 1951, the week-long, inter-faith sessions became a hallmark of the societies.[83] Although foreign influence and organization – including the work of Everett Clinchy and the World Brotherhood organization – assisted the development of the Brotherhood Weeks, the impetus for stepping up the work of the societies in general came from domestic sources, both Jewish and Christian. The *Wochenzeitung* ran numerous articles in 1950 on the widespread activities of the Societies for Christian-Jewish Cooperation, and the societies in Berlin and Frankfurt appealed to the newspaper's readers to join in their work. The invitation attempted to convince Jews that the societies' work was genuine and 'not political, but a moral prerequisite' for the new Germany.[84]

The first Week of Brotherhood was held throughout Germany from 17 to 25 February 1951. In keeping with the precedent set by President Heuss at the founding of the Wiesbaden society in 1949, high-profile political figures participated in the meetings. Munich's Mayor Dr Karl Scharnagl, Bavarian Minister-President Hans Ehard, and the American High Commissioner for Bavaria George Shuster all attended the Munich gatherings. The *Wochenzeitung* endorsed the meetings and printed Benno Ostertag's confirmation that the Societies for Christian-Jewish Cooperation had dismissed the charge of deicide vis-à-vis the Jews.[85]

Christians also offered positive grounds for the gatherings, evident in Joseph Brandlmeier's opening address at Munich. Brandlmeier, the president of the Munich society, stated that the society was 'making efforts to help prepare for a better ordering of our social life [through] deepening...understanding and brotherly cooperation [while] refus[ing] proselytization, and...indifferentism.'[86] Participants took in plays, films, lectures, and gatherings where students learned approaches to reconciliation through the use of shared religious values. Sessions were broadcast throughout Germany by radio.[87]

Jewish responses to these initiatives ranged widely, but all revealed less enthusiasm than did their Christian interlocutors. All Jewish participants had lost family members in the Holocaust and had little faith in the German people's willingness to abandon antisemitism. At the Brotherhood Week meetings in Munich in 1951, Senator Dr Nürnberger, a Jewish resident of Nuremberg, highlighted numerous contributions that Nuremberg's Jews – numbering ten thousand in 1933 – had made to the city, and to Germany, for generations. Nürnberger lauded Karl Thieme's emphasis on racial, religious, and international tolerance but pointed out that the mere 150 Jews who remained in Nuremberg in 1951 comprised a socially ostracized minority. 'Jews today are really on the receiving end of things,' he said, 'contributing little ... and [they] are insignificant and do not have a great deal of influence.'[88] He concluded with a call to remember the destruction unleashed by Nazism: 'The Week of Brotherhood should remind us to never forget the extent of misfortune that came upon humanity through prejudice and hatred, and how much good will and brotherly love needs to be employed to bridge the gap between countries, people and confessions. If we can do that, then the Weeks of Brotherhood will prove effective.'[89]

Jewish participation in the Societies for Christian-Jewish Cooperation was discouraged further when some Christian society members revealed questionable attitudes towards Jews, which became particularly problematic when charges of antisemitism against society administrators came to light.[90] These disappointments included Munich Mayor Scharnagl, who upheld anti-Jewish prejudices in the economic realm, and the president of the Munich society, Joseph Brandlmeier, who had distinguished himself in 1951 with his opposition to proselytization of Jews. Two years prior in 1949, however, he had revealed a proclivity to blame the victim with his claim that the continuation of 'godless and inhuman antisemitism must not surprise anybody.'[91] Heated exchanges followed Brandlmeier's remarks, resulting in Philipp Auerbach's resignation from the society in Munich. By 1951, only nine of fifty-one members of the Munich society were Jews, and according to Anthony Kauders, they were the 'more acculturated Jews in the postwar community [and] less inclined ... to challenge the hegemony of certain views within the [societies].'[92]

The few Jews who remained active in the Societies for Christian-Jewish Cooperation championed inner change as a solution to present problems. Julius Spanier, president of the Jewish community in Munich, and Erlangen Professor Hans-Joachim Schoeps both highlighted personal responsibility and, like their Christian counterparts, viewed common religious ground as a constructive tool for engagement. At the 1951 conference, Spanier claimed, 'We people are children of a father and a God who created us, we must learn again mutual respect and love, so that we again can know the dignified word: peace, inner peace and outer peace as well ... *in this spirit* I welcome the purpose of the Week of Brotherhood ... and hope for [its] success.'[93]

Hans-Joachim Schoeps refused to shy away from the enormous obstacles to Christian-Jewish reconciliation. As he had done in his 1949 speech, Schoeps again drew attention to the problems of attempting to have Jews and Christians enter into cooperative relationships after the Holocaust. In his address to the Brotherhood Week gathering at Munich in 1951, he reminded the audience of the compelling reasons for Jewish scepticism: 'Jews have the most grounds for doubt regarding brotherly convictions and are sceptical to affirm them ... People of good-will have gathered here – but this is a ridiculous minority in the broader world. The majority remains of ill will ... we Jews are generally realistic people ... our question is: will the good-will of brotherly conviction stand firm when put to the test?'[94]

Schoeps challenged the audience using the biblical story of Cain and Abel, which appears in both Jewish and Christian Scriptures. Cain, who killed his brother Abel, avoided answering for his actions, asking God: 'Am I my brother's keeper?' 'The way Cain thought,' Schoeps explained, 'is the way we all think ... we abandon the responsibility, the solidarity with our neighbour [and avoid] making things right.'[95] For Schoeps, the solution was obvious: 'if you want to take on yourself the commandments of God, you will need to take up the responsibility of being brotherly.'[96] Schoeps concluded by pointing to the crossroads before which German gentiles stood: whether to 'maintain their confidence in the lies, in violence and murder, or to turn again to God, whose commandments are clear and simple.'[97]

Others echoed Schoeps' challenge to gentile Germans to take responsibility for Christian-Jewish reconciliation and expressed negative feelings about the progress of that work thus far. Elliot Cohen stressed that 'the dialogue can, in no way, begin with the Jews,'[98] and Holocaust survivor Nathan Levinson expressed outrage at Christian ignorance towards the significance of initiating brotherly exchange. Eventually, Levinson, and many other Jews, saw the Societies for Christian-Jewish Cooperation as the only option available to express the depth of their personal and communal suffering and to combat antisemitism in Germany.[99] To that end, most who participated in the societies tried to find connections between Christianity and Judaism, even while many Catholics proceeded with reservations in light of the Vatican's prohibition of such activities on the grounds that they led to indifferentism, and many Protestants shared that view. Rabbi Freier of Berlin, for example, stressed the concept of 'brotherhood' in Jewish and Christian traditions, and the Jewishness of Jesus which, he concluded, would 'make easier' the process of reconciliation.[100] Together, the efforts of Nürnberger, Baeck, Schoeps, Levinson, Freier, and others, challenged Christians to accept Jews on their own terms and to prove they were sincere about engaging in meaningful dialogue.

The reality was that Jews, and the Christians who supported them, continued to face enormous challenges in their struggle for recognition and equality in the Federal Republic of Germany. Auschwitz survivor Philipp Auerbach continued to labour towards recognition of Jewish suffering and Christian-Jewish reconciliation in Germany, serving as Bavarian State Commissioner for Reparations and on the board of the Central Committee of Jews in Germany, established after the Heidelberg Conference in 1949.[101] Auerbach secured compensation for Jews from all over Europe. His reward was a ruthless attack from Joseph Müller, Bavaria's justice minister. Müller framed Auerbach in an embezzlement scandal involving false claims that Auerbach had garnered money for people who were not victims, including himself. On 15 August 1952, in despair, his reputation ruined, Auerbach committed suicide in prison.[102]

The West German government's stand on reparations also affected Jews and gentiles in the general public. In August 1952, Katherina Grumbach, a widow living in Mannheim, wrote to President Heuss appealing for financial assistance. Grumbach, eighty-two years old at the time, was the gentile widow of a Jewish man who had died in 1936. After her husband's death, Grumbach received a pension from the Association of Jews in Germany, until it was dissolved in 1943. Baden-Württemberg's Finance Ministry resumed pension payments to Mrs Grumbach until August 1951. Thereafter, Grumbach became ineligible for a German pension due to her involvement in the Jewish community, even though she had not converted to Judaism and was not eligible for support from Jewish organizations.[103]

The reason for this apparent discrimination was tied to the FRG's 450 million DM agreement with the Jewish Claims Conference in 1952. Jewish organizations, such as the Jewish Restitution Successor Organization (JRSO), were to handle Jewish claims and pensions. German Jews found, however, that the money was not easy to access, because international Jewish organizations did not support the re-establishment of Jewish communities in Germany.[104] The JRSO in Mannheim refused to pay Grumbach's pension, as did the Mannheim Jewish Community, which claimed no responsibility for assuming state pensions. The Office of the President waited three months to reply to Grumbach, and when it did, it stated bluntly that it was the responsibility of Jewish organizations to pay the pension.[105]

This decision outraged a family friend, Erwin Vossler, who wrote numerous letters on Grumbach's behalf to the Ministry of the Interior. Throughout 1953, Vossler lambasted the ministry, pointing out that the Nazi regime, 'which was no friend of the Jews,' had allowed this woman to receive a pension, whereas this new government allowed an old widow to go hungry.[106] The dismissive reply from the ministry's Dr Fiegel[107] prompted Vossler to counter-attack: 'It appears to me that you have learned nothing from the past!' In a subsequent letter he asked, 'Are we, after the democratic election of 1949, still under the authority of the thousand-year Reich?'[108] Ultimately, Vossler's efforts were in vain, except for the fact that they raised public awareness of the plight of victims in the FRG and the government's disinterest in such matters.[109]

Moreover, in West Germany, the cost of accepting Jews as equals, recognizing their suffering, and offering compensation was often high and meant political and social isolation. After Otto Küster was relieved of his duties in the federal Ministry of Finance in 1952 for opposing Schäffer's restrictive policies on reparations, he continued to publicize the FRG government's inadequate reparations plan, especially after the creation of the 1953 Federal Act. In a speech to the Frankfurt society in 1953, Küster expressed his disgust towards the actions of some government officials: 'One senses that the legislature is only really satisfied when it arrives at the immense section on hardship compensation [in the Federal Act], in which everything which it had previously cut, dismembered, and forgotten is mildly cleansed with philanthropic gestures ... all the parties behave as though this is an act of generosity ... in the countless distribution of benefit laws [which were] oriented towards a comparison [of suffering].'[110] In 1954, Küster was fired from his position as Baden-Württemberg's reparations commissioner on account of his fervour for reparations and, as Böhm commented afterward, due to the fact that most people in the ministry felt that Küster was 'not a convenient man to have around.'[111]

International Relations: Renewed Animosities or Reconciliation?

Although a new reconciliatory approach was required to set all relations between Germans and other Europeans on a new diplomatic footing, Franco-German and Danish-German relations required immediate attention during the first decade after the Second World War. For France, the concern was the Ruhr, because French citizens feared the Germans would use their industry there to replenish their destroyed military as they had after the First World War. In northern Germany, long-standing animosities between Germans and Danes came to the fore after the FRG restricted voting rights and political representation for Danes in Germany. In both cases, Moral Re-Armament offered new solutions to old problems.

After West German state formation, the underlying animosities between France and Germany continued, as did the struggle for full German sovereignty. The connection between these two issues was evident in July 1949, when a number of influential German political and social figures met with French General Marie Pierre König, commander of the French zone, to discuss transition to the Occupation Statute and the High Commission. Among the Germans present were Württemberg's SPD Chairman Carlo Schmid and Gustav von Schmoller. Schmid and Schmoller had co-founded the Institute for Occupation Issues and had been directly involved in drafting the Basic Law of the Federal Republic of Germany. Their main goal, along with other parliamentary officials and academics, was to encourage König to soften France's Germany policy and to garner more direct control of German affairs.

The German participants attempted to draw König's attention to what they saw as the wrong-headed restrictions of the Occupation Statute and to further Franco-German rapprochement. Karl Gengler, president of Baden-Württemberg's State Parliament thanked the French for their liberation of Germany and expressed Germany's willingness to develop democratically and enter into peaceful international relations.[112] Meanwhile, Professor Erbe, rector of Tübingen University, offered telling insights into how German attitudes had hindered the realization of German goals after the war. According to Erbe, 'the doubt of others regarding our sincerity resulted in our retreat again into isolation scarcely after the new-found victory of having gained our spiritual freedom.'[113] For Erbe, the solution to this problem was for Germans to focus on a different approach, as 'our subjectivity, party politics, our ideological mythologizing about the past ... had become weary.'[114] In other words, the stubbornness of the German people towards their past was getting them nowhere in the present.

General König's response began with an acknowledgment of the new boldness Germans were displaying, which he attributed to the contemporary political context. 'It would be from my side naïve to believe,' König pointed out, 'that you all would not have spoken so critically had this not been a meeting to mark our parting of ways.'[115] König took the opportunity to remind the Germans that, '[during] the last war so many French families [underwent] misfortune and grief.'[116] He then expressed astonishment at how many Germans had written to him, claiming that the French wanted to ruin Europe. For König, it was clear: a 'democratic and peaceful' Germany – and Europe – would 'be achieved only under the protection of a longer occupation.'[117]

German words and actions substantiated König's concerns regarding the condition of German democratization, even though German statesmen dismissed those attitudes. In November 1949, newly elected West German Chancellor Konrad Adenauer, at the time engaged in peacebuilding with his French friends, acknowledged French fears of a future attack from Germany, but disregarded them as purely 'psychological.' Nevertheless, Adenauer did not dispute the relevance of the fears: 'We must, first of all, neither flatly deny nor trivialize the security question. It is irrelevant whether we actually are dangerous; what matters is whether France considers us harmless. Psychology always lags behind the actual historical development ... [and it becomes] a political reality.'[118]

The situation in November 1949 proved that the political reality lagged behind Adenauer's confidence. A major point of contention was control and administration of the Saar. In November, public disputes over the Saar erupted, often around Trier's Catholic Bishop Franz Rudolph Bornewasser. Immediately after the war, Bornewasser had initiated a campaign to stave off French plans to incorporate part of the diocese of the Saar into France, an issue that re-emerged after West

German state formation. Throughout 1949, the German Office for Peace Questions monitored the situation at a time when Bishop Bornewasser was called 'a thorn in the side of the French Military Government,' because his German nationalism and resistance of the Allies' goals had caused 'increased tension.'[119]

The views of Bornewasser and like-minded German nationalists raised concern beyond the French Military Government, seen in French journalist Geneviève Tabouis' article titled 'The Saar Is Content with Its Economic Affiliation with France,' which appeared in the Parisian paper, *L'Information*. In this 1950 publication, Tabouis expressed outrage at the founding of the Democratic Party of the Saar, which sought to unify the Saar with the Federal Republic of Germany, and lambasted Bishop Bornewasser, to whom she referred as a '100% Nazi.'[120] Her observations, based on a trip to Saarbrücken, led her to conclude that the French had a serious security problem in the Saar.[121]

The response to Tabouis' article confirmed her fears of German aggression, and revealed ongoing hostility between the French and German people. The Office for Peace Questions defended the character of Bornewasser and claimed, in writing, that one 'required a microscope' to find the few Nazis who lived in the Saar. It was not the Germans, the office's statement claimed, but the current French-led regime in the Saar that showed 'similarities to the methods used by Himmler and Hitler.'[122] The likelihood of an organic solution to tensions around control of the Saar was small, unless someone, on one side or the other, made significant concessions. The French were the first to give, but they required assistance. It came from an international network of people who laboured towards interpersonal, national, and international reconciliation under the auspices of Moral Re-Armament.[123]

On 25 October 1949, just a few weeks after the Caux World Assembly, Louis Boucquey took the initiative to invite Robert Schuman to his home for dinner, along with MRA leader Frank Buchman. At the dinner, Schuman expressed his frustration to the two other men over the dismal state of Franco-German relations, which were mired in disputes over control of the Saar and the Ruhr.[124] Chancellor Adenauer had written to Schuman, stating that 'the Saar seems to develop to my great regret into a decisive and, I am afraid, a fatal political factor.'[125] Schuman lamented to his dinner companions, 'One of my difficulties is that I don't know whom I can trust among the German politicians. For example, I've only met Adenauer once.'[126] Buchman promised to introduce Schuman to the 'wonderful German visitors' who attended MRA meetings, including Ministers Karl Arnold and Hans von Herwarth and Chancellor Adenauer. Schuman agreed.[127]

Schuman was dedicated to finding a new approach to relations between Germany and France. In December 1949, two months after meeting Buchman, Schuman addressed the Catholic Congress in Brussels: 'In the past, the impulse for revenge was too alive ... [now] it is time to seize the initiative, to secure our final reconciliation with Germany.'[128] Shortly thereafter, in December, Frank Buchman visited Adenauer and West German President Theodore Heuss in Bonn in order to arrange a meeting between Schuman and the chancellor. Adenauer told Buchman he was 'extremely interested [in Buchman's] conversation with Schuman about the relations which ought to exist between France and Germany.'[129] One month later, Schuman made good on his promise to Boucquey and Buchman, meeting with Adenauer in Bonn for the first time on 13 January 1950. The conversation included an open exchange on Franco-German relations, particularly concerning the Saar.[130]

During the first few months of 1950, Schuman and Adenauer cemented the foundation of one of the most important relationships in postwar Europe, a relationship brokered by Frank Buchman and his colleagues in Moral Re-Armament. Both statesmen continued to uphold MRA principles throughout the early 1950s, a crucial period for Franco-German relations, and throughout the remainder of their political careers. Days prior to the Foreign Ministers Conference that would decide the position of West Germany vis-à-vis the North Atlantic Treaty, Schuman declared in a personal note to Adenauer that 'Europe ... will be built by means of a series of concrete achievements that will create a real solidarity [which] requires the elimination of the age-old opposition between France and Germany.'[131] The far-reaching impact of the reconciliation engendered by Schuman and Adenauer was seen in the ratification of the Schuman Plan on 5 September 1950.[132] As for the Saar, the two countries decided to share administration of the region until it was incorporated into the Federal Republic of Germany by plebiscite, in 1957. According to Pierre Spoerri, this success can be attributed 'partly to the relationship of trust that had been established between the German and French leaders' and particularly to Schuman's successful program of Franco-German cooperation in the Ruhr.[133]

Moral Re-Armament played a significant role in promoting Franco-German reconciliation by bringing powerful political players to the bargaining table. Influential politicians, businessmen, and laymen met at Caux, where new relationships of trust began.[134] At Caux, Danish and German politicians also made contact. Together they resolved the disputes that had erupted in both countries over the rights of the Danish minority in Schleswig-Holstein and the German minority residing north of the border.

On the Danish side, Paul Brodersen, Valdemar Hvidt, Christian Harhoff, and many other political, labour, and military men began to attend meetings at Caux in 1946. The first acts of rapprochement between the two countries took place at Caux in 1947, when two hundred Danes and 150 Germans attended the meetings.[135] This time, the Germans took the lead in the form of an initiative by businessman Werner von Tippelskirch. During a plenary session at Caux, he asked the Danes to forgive Germans for what they had suffered under German occupation. Tippelskirch had been a colonel in the Wehrmacht General Staff and was part of the team that had planned the invasion of Denmark. 'I do not ask you to forget what we Germans have done to you,' he said, 'but to forgive.'[136] The Danish delegation responded favourably.

The new trust that was built between Germans and Danes at Caux in the late 1940s formed the groundwork for negotiations a few years later. Although the West German government had assured members of the Danish minority of their rights in the 1949 Kiel Declaration, the new Kiel government elected in 1950 discriminated against the Danish minority, barring them from representation in government. Eventually, Danish and German friends at Caux brokered the Bonn-Copenhagen Declarations of 1955, which secured equal rights for Germans and Danes living on both sides of the border.[137]

German Democratic Republic: Temporary Solutions to Ongoing Injustices

A comparison between the Federal Republic of Germany and the German Democratic Republic with regard to victim recognition, compensation, and reconciliation with Germany's wartime enemies reveals similarities and differences. Both governments opposed reparations – at least unofficially – and when reparations were deemed necessary, both paid as little as possible. In both countries, thousands of victims fell through the bureaucratic cracks in legal codes. Still, the overall situation in the GDR was worse than in the FRG. Whereas some influential

West Germans laboured against the majority in championing atonement for past misdeeds, fewer such individuals were to be found in East Germany, due mostly to overwhelming pressure to conform to the regime and to the threats such people faced to the well-being of themselves and their families. Still, men like Helmut Lehmann, Leo Zuckermann, Paul Merker, Heinrich Grüber, and Julius Meyer fought against hopeless odds and a repressive regime to garner recognition and compensation for victims of Nazism, only to have their work snuffed out by the government in the early 1950s.

With regard to victim recognition and compensation, in 1949, the situation in the GDR was similar to that in the FRG. Although reparations laws were more limited in the GDR, some people, notably victims of forced sterilization, were recognized in the East before their counterparts in the West, thanks to the labours of the Victims of Fascism group.[138] Jews, however, did not experience comparable support within the Victims group, nor from the GDR government. In fact, members of the Victims group continued to perpetuate stereotypes of Jews and downplay the significance of the Jews as victims of Nazism.[139]

Without support from the organization in the GDR that was most sympathetic to Jewish suffering, Jews were left to deal with the GDR's Restitution Law. That law did not allow them to attain property that had been stolen from them during the Nazi era. This injustice led Jews to lobby for their rights through appeals to Jewish community leaders, but to no avail.[140] Jews were robbed of their homes and then again denied the right to live in them, even after – as Julius Meyer put it in an appeal to the SED – 'the thousand-year Reich no longer stands.'[141] In this regard, Jews in the same situation in the FRG were treated better, although appeals for justice – like those from victims of sterilization, and people such as Mrs Grumbach – sometimes also went unheard.[142]

Unlike Jews in West Germany, who – after passing of the Additional Federal Compensation Act in 1953 – were able to claim their former property, Jews in the East faced restrictions on compensation from the Soviet Military Administration and the GDR government. The 1952 change in the Restitution Law and its arbitrary enactment gave way to even more restrictive restitution laws that were set in stone in by Wolfgang Vogel, the GDR's chief reparations officer in the Ministry of Finance.[143] Vogel's antisemitism was widespread in the GDR and throughout the Soviet bloc. The bloc-wide antisemitic attack that began in 1948 targeted 'American-Israeli imperialists,' including Rudolf

Slansky in Czechoslovakia, Raszlo Rajk in Hungary, and numerous people in the GDR. Those who championed Jewish restitution – Lehmann, Merker, Zuckerman, and Meyer, all of whom held influential positions – were perceived as a threat by the Communist government of the GDR. Harassed by governments agents, these men were eventually imprisoned or forced to flee abroad.[144]

By 1952, the attempt to muzzle the Jewish community in the GDR – particularly in the realm of reparations – had succeeded, as was evident in the defensive and cautious posture of Jews in the GDR at that time. For instance, when Leon Löwenkopf – a prominent leader of the Jewish community in Dresden – answered an American journalist's request for information on the situation of Jews in the GDR in 1952, Löwenkopf provided a glowing report that highlighted the differences between the Jewish communities in East and West Germany. Rather than pointing out the favourable reparations laws in the Western Länder, and the Additional Federal Compensation Act developed at the time, Löwenkopf pointed to the widespread antisemitism in West Germany, the new injustices that Jews faced there, and plans for West German rearmament. He lauded the VVN for securing compensation for Jews in the GDR, but failed to describe the ad hoc nature of that compensation or to mention the Jews' status as second-class victims within that organization. Instead, he presented the GDR as a great place to live and praised its government for punishing racists.[145] In fact, by early 1953, in the GDR and throughout the Soviet bloc, purges of so-called Western imperialists targeted Jews and those sympathetic to the Jewish cause. Many Jews and supposed fellow-travellers were deported and others, like Merker and many like-minded men, particularly in Berlin, were imprisoned as enemies of the state.[146]

The attack on the Jewish community in the GDR was part of a campaign to consolidate the East German dictatorship under Stalinist ideology. In this setting, all religious groups, including the mainline churches, held a precarious position. Like the Jews, the churches in the GDR enjoyed the legal right to practise their religion under the protection of the Constitution, but they too faced the stark reality of Stalinist repression, albeit for different reasons. In early 1950, the government started to clamp down on religious freedoms which, in turn, engendered a tense relationship between the churches and the GDR government that would extend throughout the 1950s. The regime responded harshly to the efforts of the churches to undermine its legitimacy in 1950 by seizing control of religious education in the GDR and, starting in 1952, by forbidding East German churchmen from travelling to the Federal Republic of Germany. GDR authorities also attempted to defame the character and reputation of clergy, including Otto Dibelius, who promoted a Western agenda.[147] As challenging as these attacks were for the churches, their consequences were not as dire as those of the anti-Zionist campaign.

In April 1950, GDR government representatives met with church leaders from all the Eastern Länder in order to reach an agreement regarding the role of the church in the GDR. A joint document released on 28 April, stated that 'the churches were prepared to cooperate in the reconstruction of national life. The Government declared its willingness to give the church freedom to work ... according to the Constitution.'[148] This agreement, however, was followed by what Bishop Horning of Görlitz termed the government's 'very heavy attacks' on the churches, complete with press support.[149] The *Tägliche Rundschau* publicized the SED's position in an article titled 'The Role of the Church in the German Democratic Republic.' It first attacked church leaders for not falling into line with the government – for acting aggressively even after gaining 'constitutional liberties' – and then attempted to coerce churchmen to align themselves with Stalinism: 'Certain church leaders undertook one reactionary attack after the other against the movement of those who are fighting for peace and against the democratic regime in the German Democratic Republic. They are the same outstanding church leaders who always fought for the regime of monopolists and "Junkers," who approved of Nazi terror and blessed the arms for Hitler's predatory war. At present these church leaders have again taken the stand at the front of the war-mongers and reactionaries carrying out the orders of the Anglo-American imperialists and their German collaborators.'[150] The SED claimed to be acting in defence of the state, not in opposition to the churches. Much as the Nazis had done, the SED criticized the churches for not falling in line ideologically, and exaggerated the number (i.e., 'hundreds') of 'aligned' churchmen in its bid for political support.[151]

In June 1950, the World Council of Churches' representative, Pastor Bengt Hoffmann, assessed the situation in Eastern Germany, and discovered that Protestant pastors diverged in their approaches to the Nazi past and the Communist regime. Some Protestants, including Bishop Horning, were repentant and longed to reconcile with their wartime enemies. In June 1950, Horning stated that Germans had 'worshipped the Golden Calf' during the Nazi era, which resulted in God 'withdrawing his presence from them.'[152] This worship of a false god, according to Horning, included the fact that Christians had 'tolerated in silence that atrocious injustice and sin against the Jews.'[153] Perhaps the pressures of persecution in the GDR had alerted some Protestant clergy to what was at stake in the continuation of their inflexible approach not only to the past but to their current situation.

Not all agreed with Horning, however, and many pastors, if not the 'hundreds' of which the SED boasted, lined up with the regime.[154] The lines between Christian service and political aims were blurred, as the pastors in the GDR, regardless of their political views, sought the material support of Hoffmann and the WCC's Department for Inter-Church Aid and Service to Refugees. The department, however, wanted to see East German pastors resist Communism. The mixture of interests became evident in correspondence between the two groups. One East German pastor, in his attempt to receive the same kind of sympathy he said was accorded to Jews from the outside world, told Hoffmann that 'the Oder-Neisse border is an injustice, fundamentally the same kind of gross injustice we, the Germans, did to the Jews.'[155] Such remarks did fall on fertile ground, although not precisely as many Germans had hoped. The WCC's refugee branch recognized the significance of maintaining correspondence with churchmen in the GDR, but maintained its focus on spiritual matters.[156] It was left to more politically aligned organizations to tackle broader social concerns in the GDR.

Grassroots Initiatives and Cold War Politics

Although all work in the GDR necessarily aligned with Stalinism, numerous organizations continued to play a significant role in reconstruction, and reconciliation. One organization that consistently thrived in the GDR was People's Solidarity, which included grassroots people and political figures, such as Helmut Lehmann, the association's president. From 1948 to 1952, all other organizations in the GDR – NGOs and church-affiliated groups – were either limited in the scope of their work or forced to close down operations. After 1949, People's Solidarity continued the ideologically driven work it had begun in 1945, and maintained its ties to the Protestant Relief Work only as long as that group served Solidarity's purposes. Thus, it became the task of Relief Work leader Christian Berg to convince People's Solidarity – and the GDR government – of the usefulness of his organization, which he attempted to do on many occasions.[157] At a People's Solidarity meeting in Weimar, Berg stressed that the Protestant Relief

Work's assistance was 'not based on class, race, or confession or political affiliation' and pledged to continue to fight to help all people in need.[158]

People's Solidarity was not convinced and, after the September Congress at Weimar, Helmut Lehmann pressed Protestant Relief Work personnel to clarify their political orientation. Protestant Relief Work members explained that they could not forbid others to join the Communist Party or the National Front but they themselves would not do so.[159] Because of this refusal, Lehmann concluded that 'it would no longer be possible for there to be continuing work between the People's Solidarity and Relief Work.' Even though church and relief organizations were no longer tolerated in the country, the much-needed aid that came through the Relief Work office continued to flow unabated into the GDR.[160]

By the early 1950s, the ideological positions of East and West Germany, and the position and work of the NGOs and other organizations that operated within each country, were firmly entrenched. During these years, the organizations developed and furthered their social and political work and increased their significance. For Pax Christi, the early 1950s marked the onset of a trend that fused its spiritual revivalism with a political agenda. Symptomatic of this shift was its move to join the ranks of NGOs that combatted Communism. Throughout the early 1950s, Pax Christi members in Germany continued to labour with a 'missionary purpose' towards 'the return of Europe' to Christianity,[161] and kept the annual pilgrimages from Cologne to Lourdes.[162] However, from 1952 on, Pax Christi began to incorporate a more politicized agenda, evident in its work in Franco-German reconciliation, and in its anti-Communism. With Pope Pius XII supporting its anti-Communist work,[163] Pax Christi members sought to infiltrate the Eastern bloc and address proactively the 'East-West question' in occupied Germany and Austria.[164] After 1950, Pax Christi branched out from Germany, France, and Italy to work in England, and the Netherlands,[165] and endeavoured to 'end the war in Indochina and Vietnam [and begin] a mission to Catholics in Poland.'[166] This anti-Communism went unnoticed for the most part by Communist governments, who preferred to extol the peaceful work of Pax Christi. In August 1955, Pax Christi was even permitted to hold an international congress in Warsaw.[167]

Other developments reveal the combination of personal reconciliation and political action in Pax Christi's work, seen both within Germany and in the FRG's foreign relations. By 1953, some Pax Christi members began to confront racism of the past, and present. 'People of different blood can learn to understand one another as comrades,' one Pax Christi member claimed, underscoring equality as a Pax Christi tenet.[168]

In the realm of Franco-German reconciliation, German Pax Christi members addressed contritely the slaughter of French citizens at Oradour in 1944. In 1948, The Office for Peace Questions had made overtures on this issue, but it tried to force reconciliation without considering the feelings of the French people.[169] Pax Christi had a different approach. In 1955, German Pax Christi members offered the Oradour parish a chalice made of melted jewelry from a German family. It was accepted by the parish through Bishop Théas. Similar gestures were made in Lille, Mauthausen, Salzburg, and Speyer.[170]

In the early 1950s, not all Germans and international NGOs shared Pax Christi's anti-war stance. Most Germans were interested in improving Germany's place in the international order and in establishing security for themselves. Although some NGO workers championed the pacifist principles of Pax Christi, among them Siegmund-Schultze, the International Fellowship of Reconciliation, and the International Opposition to Military Service organization, few others shared their views.[171] Indeed, MRA supported the mainstream political agenda of the Western powers, which included arming Western Europe morally and militarily in defence against Communist expansion. Just two months after the 1951 creation of the European Coal and Steel Community, Adenauer stated, 'The nations of the world will only have stable relations with one another when they have been inwardly prepared. In this respect, MRA has rendered great and fruitful services. During these last few months we have witnessed the success of difficult negotiations and the signing of important international agreements. MRA has played an unseen but effective role in reducing the differences of opinion between the negotiating parties and has guided them towards a peaceful agreement by helping them to seek the common good.'[172] By the end of the 1950s, Adenauer was convinced of MRA's central role in staving off Communist expansion. He addressed other European political leaders at Caux in 1959 with these words: 'You know what great significance I attach to the ideological fight which MRA is waging in the whole world against Communism. We need the unity of all these spiritual forces which are mobilized against materialism and communism if we are to master the present critical situation in the world.'[173]

The ideological battle of the Cold War both fostered and hindered reconciliatory work throughout postwar Germany. The opposing positions on Western European integration posed challenges to reconciliation on both sides. In the realm of gentile-Jewish reconciliation, the labours of Gertrud Luckner were among the most noteworthy in occupied Germany in terms of sincerity, courage, and positive results. However, due to her cooperation with the Western branches of the VVN, Luckner's activities came under the scrutiny of Carl Zietlow and his assistant. Luckner was forced to defend herself against the attacks of foreigners who had come to Germany to introduce gentile-Jewish reconciliation at a time when she was already devoting herself to that work in Freiburg. Although Luckner conceded that the VVN was comprised mostly of Communists, she assured her accusers that it was a diverse group, and stated that she was not certain of the number of attendees in her Christian-Jewish circle of cooperation who were affiliated with the VVN. After formation of the Federal Republic of Germany, its Interior Ministry also took an interest in Luckner's work, fearing the inroads that Communists had made into Freiburg. Fanning the flames was Baden's VVN leader, Harry Dobberkau, who proclaimed that 'the war-minded policy of the West German Government' was 'hereby actively assisted by the Occupation Powers' and accused it of 'splitting all forces striving for peace.'[174]

The battle between the VVN, which had representation in both Germanies, and both German and Allied governing bodies overflowed into the public sphere. The West German press denounced the VVN as a Communist affiliate, warned citizens of the FRG against the evils of the organization, and called on them to boycott its meetings.[175] When the VVN planned a massive peace rally for 14–15 April 1951 in Gelsenkirchen, local anti-Communists mounted posters depicting Communists as evil beasts bent on enslaving humanity.[176] For many in the VVN, like non-Communist member Arthur Katterer, the association's good intentions were being thwarted by Cold War politics: 'If the fight for peace is actually a concern of the Communists, one can only congratulate them on their decision. As a matter of fact, we are of the opinion that we must advance together with Communists fighting for peace. For this reason it is our task also to influence all non-Communists so that they too commit themselves to fight for peace.'[177]

Declarations of shared objectives notwithstanding, Western Allied personnel refused to cooperate with any Communist organization. Zietlow's assistant Karl-Heinz Fehsenfeld dismissed Katterer's words and concluded that Luckner's actions and assertions were an obvious cover-up of Communist activity. In his view, Luckner's activities compromised not only herself but the Society for Christian-Jewish

Cooperation and its American overseers. Because of the 'important political issues' at stake, Zietlow's assistant recommended tough measures: 'There are only two alternatives left as far as I can see it, 1. Miss Luckner has to decide either to stay away from all work connected with the Freiburg or Baden-Baden VVN activities completely, or 2. Miss Luckner has to give up her leading position with the society, if not all her related work.'[178] Although Zietlow did not follow through on these recommendations, they reveal that some Allied personnel prioritized anti-Communism over gentile-Jewish reconciliation. This priority limited reconciliatory work because organizations like the VVN included many victims who had nothing to do with Communism. In their quest for political stabilization, the Western Allies interfered with the work of a handful of altruistic Germans who sought to reconcile with their wartime victims.[179]

Fear of Communism also influenced Moral Re-Armament, but in this case, results were more positive. Beginning in 1950, by invitation of the Bundesrat president and Northrhine-Westfalia's Minister-President Karl Arnold, MRA held regular meetings in the Ruhr at Gelsenkirchen, Essen, and Düsseldorf. MRA viewed the Ruhr 'as an area of special significance,' due to its idustrial base.[180] With Adenauer's support, Arnold lauded MRA's work and wanted to incorporate it into his agenda of blocking Communist influence in the Ruhr.[181] With this backing MRA held weekly meetings at Gelsenkirchen that fostered positive relations between labour and management, while helping to stave off Communist expansion in the Ruhr, Germany, and Europe.

Meanwhile, refusal to align itself along strict ideological lines led the VVN into difficulties on both sides of the East-West divide. In February 1953, the SED dissolved the organization in the GDR. The reasons for this remain unclear, but evidence indicates that the SED did not view VVN members as politically loyal, particularly because many members were Jews. In the highly charged political context of the early 1950s, the people in power paid much more attention to combatting perceived political threats than they did to victim recognition or gentile-Jewish reconciliation.[182]

Foundations for the Future

After the two Germanies gained semi-sovereign status in 1949, both sought to align themselves in the optimum manner with their ideological backers. This task proved complicated, but the rewards were enormous. In pursuit of those rewards, West Germans had to fall in line with Western liberal values, which included some measure of justice for the victims of Nazism. In East Germany, aligning that country with the Soviet Union was paramount, and Stalinist ideology paid little heed to reparations, unless they could be used for propaganda purposes. As a result, after its founding in 1949, the government of the German Democratic Republic refused to take responsibility for Nazi atrocities. Its intransigence brought an end to diplomatic exchanges between the GDR and Israel after 1956. Together, the lack of recognition of Jewish suffering under Nazism and the failure to compensate the Jews of East Germany contributed to a festering of the wounds of the Third Reich, which continues today.

Grassroots initiatives, including those of NGOs and other organizations, filled some of the gaps left by government bureaucracies and general indifference to the situation of former victims. On many levels, processes of reconciliation in both Germanies depended on the labours of a variety of organizations. To be sure, these organizations could only do so much, and their work required recognition and support from government bodies if success was to be achieved. In the end, the work of these organizations, and their relations with the German governments exposed the pervasive indifference of many Germans to the suffering of their wartime enemies and victims. At the same time, NGOs, particularly in the Western zones and the FRG, provided a forum for those who genuinely wanted to develop new relationships of trust with Jews, Poles, French people, and others. This work was especially significant in overcoming the deep distrust in Franco-German relations. The transformative potential of such new relations was manifest in the Bonn-Paris Agreements of 1954 that incorporated West Germany into the European Alliance.[183] Although successes were few, they were significant because they laid a foundation for future cooperation between Germans and the victims of Nazism.

The long-term effects of Nazism, and the implications of how Nazi atrocities were handled in the immediate postwar era, are enormous. The approach in the three Western zones and, after 1949, in the Federal Republic of Germany, produced an open-ended dialogue around past suffering, compensation, and reconciliation. In contrast, the approach in the Soviet zone and the GDR of ignoring the depth of Jewish suffering under Nazism, and their urgent needs thereafter, formed a toxic foundation for future relations between Jews and Christians in Germany.

The repercussions of these divergent paths are evident in events since German unification in 1990. In the ongoing quest for justice, Jews of the former GDR and the Jewish Claims Conference have levelled material claims against the Federal Republic of Germany. Meanwhile, Jewish cemeteries and buildings, and sometimes Jews themselves, remain targets of attack from members of the far right, and antisemitism and anti-Zionism provide a language of resentment that, although publicly discredited, can on occasion be heard from individuals across the political spectrum.

Conclusion

Examination of the new relationships that emerged during the first decade after the Second World War between Germans and their wartime victims and enemies yields significant insights into the political and social development of postwar Germany. As Hans Asmussen stated to the Allies in 1946, the world, indeed, did not allow Germans to leave the Nazi past behind, and simply 'forget it all.' The encounters highlighted in this book are immersed in this tense environment. They show that people who, in principle, opposed reconciliation and those who participated altruistically in it – even with their contradictory aims and inconsistent approaches – contributed to the larger goal of reconciliation. At base, reconciliation required development of new relations of mutual trust. Building trust involved recognition of past injustices, acknowledgment of the ongoing suffering of Nazism's victims, and some form of atonement. But most Germans were resistant to reconciliation, avoiding contact with victims of German racism and aggression. Lauding their morality and their history, they opposed change. Yet many of these same people longed to be accepted by the outside world and to re-establish Germany's international standing. Germans wanted to rebuild their country – and their state – on their own terms and rid themselves of foreign occupiers. A much smaller group of Germans laboured towards reconciliation as an end in itself.

Whereas the methods of pragmatic and idealistic reconciliation were both effective, it was the combination of these two approaches that yielded the most significant results in occupied Germany. The two impulses led the German people to acknowledge the evils of the Nazi past in a variety of ways. The idealists proceeded against public opinion in Germany and against forces that opposed them and their work. The pragmatists usually couched their admissions of guilt in references to international conflict and the horror and barbarism of warfare. That way, all nations would be implicated in the human tragedy of the Second World War. German politicians, churchmen, relief workers, and philanthropists of all kinds admitted that they had become caught up in the fervour of Nazism, but held the leaders responsible. Those leaders, they assumed, were all dead, in prison, or somehow elsewhere.

In the early postwar stage, during the Nuremberg trials and initial denazification efforts, the German people in all four occupied zones showed an attitude of defiance, reluctant recognition of the past, and grudging reconciliation with their wartime enemies only insofar as the outside world required. German organizations monitored the actions and attitudes of the Allies during occupation, attempting to ascertain the bare minimum that Germans would have to pay, financially and morally, for the crimes of the Nazis before Germany would be granted full sovereignty. Political activities were buttressed by the work of the mainline German churches, to which the Allies granted a central role in German democratization, on account of their presumed anti-Nazi record. Proving to be more recalcitrant than the Allies had initially thought, German churchmen infused their co-religionists, and their churches' affiliated relief organizations, with an interpretation of Nazism that absolved them of collective and institutional responsibility and focused, instead, on the cultivation of personal piety as the best 'cure' for the ills of the day. With a few notable exceptions, most German religious bodies ignored the crimes of the Nazi era, claimed innocence towards them when forced to address the past, and contributed to the discourse on German suffering that, they claimed, the Allies had wrought on Germany.

Akin to Daniel Bishop's sketch, the German people required assistance in the difficult ascent to international integration, but – unlike Bishop's image – the German people were very involved in that process. To be sure, beginning as early as 1944, the impulse for reconciliation came mostly from victims of German aggression who lived abroad, starting with material aid. By 1946, grassroots initiatives extended beyond correspondence and material aid to personal encounters between Germans and foreigners outside Germany. This impulse aligned with Frank Buchman's belief of the central role that victims play in initiating, steering, and achieving reconciliation after conflicts. However, the advent of this work coincided with the ambitions and policies of the Allied powers as Cold War tensions intensified, evident in economic divisions – particularly after Stalin refused Marshall Aid in 1947 – and in the Soviets' permanent departure from the Allied Control Council in 1948. The Allies' interest in consolidating power within their respective spheres of influence guided their support of initiatives that served their purposes of democratization in the West, and Stalinization in the East. To that end, Moral Re-Armament brought high-profile Germans into contact with a wide variety of prominent international figures, who helped bring peace and stability to postwar Europe.[1] Also in 1947, the emerging International Council of Christians and Jews welcomed Germans to its meetings and worked in concert with Allied occupation personnel to establish Societies for Christian-Jewish Cooperation, beginning later that year. Franz Böhm, a sincere proponent of mending relations between Jews and Germans, utilized his positions on the executive committee of Frankfurt's Society for Christian-Jewish Cooperation and in West Germany's Finance Ministry to secure significant compensation for Jews in 1952.

Other efforts by the World Council of Churches, Pax Christi, and the International Fellowship of Reconciliation also contributed to reconciliatory discussion but had less impact, due to their narrow approach and, for Pax Christ and IFOR, their pacifist beliefs. By the mid-1950s, IFOR founder Friedrich Siegmund-Schultze acknowledged the woefully inadequate attempts of the group to further gentile-Jewish reconciliation in Germany and lauded the efforts of individual Protestants who had taken up the cause.[2] In doing so, Siegmund-Schultze exposed the fact that the institution he had founded lacked the vision to address with any consequence German antisemitism. To be sure, the German branch of Pax Christi became more politically active in the decades to come, which was evident in its encouragement of Willi Brandt's Ostpolitik during the early 1970s and its efforts to have the West German government compensate Polish victims of German occupation.[3]

In the Soviet zone, the Association of Victims of Nazism had the broadest impact, at least until it was shut down in 1953. It won compensation for victims, even some Jews, in a political context that was hostile to Jews and where politicians opposed the compensation of individuals as a violation of their doctrines against private property. After some early overtures, gentile-Jewish reconciliation failed outright in the zone, because Stalinist ideology dictated that Jews were not a distinct nation and therefore could not have been persecuted as such during the Third Reich. Moreover, Stalinist conventions insisted that the perpetrators of Nazi crimes resided in Western Germany, a position that freed Germans in the East to acknowledge Nazi crimes because they were not implicated in them. Other organizations that were more directly aligned with the SED and the Soviet Administration, such as the People's Solidarity Association and the Society for German-Soviet Friendship, also contributed to international dialogue in the Soviet bloc, although without recognition of Jewish victimhood or encouragement of Germans in the GDR to take responsibility for the Nazi past. In all four zones, it became politically acceptable – even required – to express disgust for the Nazis and the horrors that they had wrought, but the motivations and rewards for doing so differed across the East-West zonal boundaries.

A great deal was achieved despite the often problematic and self-serving reconciliatory efforts in occupied Germany. As the Federal Republic of Germany and the German Democratic Republic moved through the four decades of the Cold War, politicians – and the German people – proceeded to treat the victims of Nazism in much the same way that they had during the late 1940s. The criteria for recognition and reparations established during occupation continued to be followed and, as Franz Böhm recognized in 1952, the Allies had a great deal to do with the establishment of those criteria.[4] The battle for compensation was real, and the stakes were high. After 1949, discussion of the recognition and compensation of Jewish victims continued in Western Germany, whereas it was silenced in the GDR. The absence of Christian-Jewish dialogue in East Germany meant little progress towards gentile-Jewish reconciliation occurred there. The negative ramifications of Stalinist ideology were enormous for Jews, as seen in the widespread antisemitic purges in 1952, the same year that the Luxembourg Agreement paid billions of dollars to Jews internationally, including Jews in West Germany.

This study has revealed that reconciliation in postwar Germany was most often fostered through performance, and did not require that participants undergo a genuine change of mind. Instead, it was a combination of outside resources that provided the necessary support to empower internal action at all levels of society. Together, Germans and international figures played a significant role in the early stages of European cooperation. Further research is needed to better understand the role of grassroots initiatives, NGOs, and religious organizations in the stabilization of Germany after the Nazi catastrophe, and how a similar wide range of actors may factor into post-conflict reconciliation in other contexts.

The victory over Nazism and the successful embedding of democracy in all parts of Germany was due to the valiant efforts of the few who saw the need, and seized the opportunity, to promote the cause of reconciliation, despite discouragements, public rejection, or bitter resentments. Their success has been little acknowledged or praised. This book is a tribute to their efforts and eventual, if long delayed, success, which deserves to be better known as a striking contribution to the history of modern Germany.

Notes

Preface

1 Daniel Bishop, 'Der lange schwere Weg zurück in die Familie der Nationen,' *Die Neue Zeitung*, 25 Oct. 1945, 1. The caption under the sketch states: '[This] is an optimistic perspective,' because it presents the 'possibility that a changed Germany will once again be received into the family of nations.'

Introduction

1 Victor Gollancz, *In Darkest Germany* (London: Victor Gollancz, 1947), 18.
2 Heinrich August Winker, trans. Alexander J. Sager, *Germany: The Long Road West*, vol. 2, *1933–1990* (Oxford: Oxford University Press, 2007 [German ed. 2000]), 116.
3 Ronald Granieri, *The Ambivalent Alliance: Konrad Adenauer, the CDU/CSU, and the West, 1949–1966* (New York: Berghahn Books, 2003); Philip H. Gordon, *France, Germany, and the Western Alliance* (Boulder, CO: Westview, 1995); Norbert Frei, *Adenauer's Germany and the Nazi Past: The Politics of Amnesty and Integration* (New York: Columbia University Press, 2002); and Daniel E. Rogers, *Politics after Hitler: The Western Allies and the German Party System* (London: Macmillan, 1995).
4 Norman Naimark, *The Russians in Germany: A History of the Soviet Zone of Occupation, 1945–1949* (Cambridge, MA: Harvard University Press, 1995); Richard Merritt, *Democracy Imposed: U.S. Occupation Policy and the German Public, 1945–1950* (New Haven, CT: Yale University Press, 1995); and Jeffrey Herf, *Divided Memory: The Nazi Past in the Two Germanys* (Cambridge, MA: Harvard University Press, 1997).
5 Ralf Kessler and Hartmut Rüdiger, *Wiedergutmachung im Osten Deutschlands 1945–1953: Grundsätzliche Diskussionen und die Praxis in*

Sachsen-Anhalt (Berlin: Peter Lang, 1996); Angelika Timm, *Jewish Claims against East Germany: Moral Obligations and Pragmatic Policy* (Budapest: Central European University Press, 1997); and Christian Pross, *Paying for the Past: The Struggle over Reparations for Surviving Victims of the Nazi Terror* (Baltimore, MD: Johns Hopkins University Press, 1998).

6 Garth Lean, *On the Tail of a Comet: The Life of Frank Buchman* (Colorado Spings, CO: Helmers and Howard, 1988); Pax Christi, *Pax Christi: Veröffentlichungen der Deutschen Pax-Christi Sektion* (Idstein: Komzi, 1995); and Elke Reuter and Detlef Hansel, *Das kurze Leben der VVN von 1947 bis 1953: Die Geschichte der Vereinigung der Verfolgten des Naziregimes in der sowjetischen Besatzungszone und in der DDR* (Berlin: Edition Ost, 1997). A more widely distributed work on MRA is Daniel Sack, *Moral Re-Armament: The Reinventions of an American Religious Movement* (New York: Palgrave Macmillan, 2009).

7 Matthew Hockenos, *A Church Divided: German Protestants Confront the Nazi Past* (Bloomington, IN: Indiana University Press, 2004); Michael Phayer, *The Catholic Church and the Holocaust, 1930–1965* (Bloomington, IN: Indiana University Press, 2000); Gerhard Besier, *Der SED-Staat und die Kirche: Der Weg in die Anpassung* (Munich: Bertelsmann, 1993); and Björn Krondörfer, Katherina von Kellenbach, and Norbert Peck, *Mit Blick auf die Täter: Fragen an die deutsche Theologie nach 1945* (Gütersloh: Gütersloh Verlagshaus, 2006).

8 See Konrad Jarausch, *After Hitler: Recivilizing Germans, 1945–1995* (New York: Oxford University Press, 2006), and Hermann-Josef Rupieper, 'Der Bund für Bürgerrechte: Transnational Relations and the Problem of Democratization in West Germany, 1949–1954,' in David Wetzel, ed., *International Politics and German History: The Past Informs the Present* (Westport, CT: Greenwood, 1997), 87–102.

9 Margaret Myers Feinstein, *Holocaust Survivors in Postwar Germany, 1945–1957* (Cambridge: Cambridge University Press, 2010); Atina Grossmann, *Jews, Germans, and Allies: Close Encounters in Occupied Germany* (Princeton, NJ: Princeton University Press, 2007); Jay Geller, *Jews in Post-Holocaust Germany* (Cambridge: Cambridge University Press, 2005); and Irena Ostmeyer, *Zwischen Schuld und Sühne: Evangelische Kirche und Juden in der SBZ und DDR 1945–1990* (Berlin: Institut Kirche und Judentum, 2002).

10 See Josef Foschepoth, *Im Schatten der Vergangenheit: Die Anfänge der Gesellschaften für Christlich-Jüdische Zusammenarbeit* (Göttingen: Vandenhoek and Ruprecht, 1993); Anthony Kauders, *Democratization and the Jews: Munich, 1945–1965* (Lincoln, NB: University of Nebraska Press, 2004).

11 Lothar Mertens, *Davidstern unter Hammer und Zirkel: Die jüdischen Gemeinden in der SBZ/DDR und ihre Beziehung durch Partei und Staat 1945–1990* (Hildeshiem: Olms, 1997); Ulrike Offenberg, *Seid Vorsichtig gegen die Machthaber: Die jüdischen Gemeinden in der SBZ und der DDR 1945 bis 1990* (Berlin: Aufbau Verlag,1998); and Angelika Timm, *Hammer, Zirkel, Davidstern: Das gestörte Verhältnis der DDR zu Zionismus und Staat Israel* (Bonn: Bouvier, 1997).
12 Jörg Friedrich, *Der Brand: Deutschland im Bombenkrieg, 1940–1945* (Munich: Propyläen, 2002); Robert G. Moeller, *War Stories: The Search for a Usable Past in the Federal Republic of Germany* (Berkeley, CA: University of California Press, 2001); and, Bill Niven, ed., *Germans as Victims: Remembering the Past in Contemporary Germany* (New York: Palgrave, 2006).
13 Laurel Cohen-Pfister and Dagmar Wienröder-Skinner (eds.), *Victims and Perpetrators: (Re)presenting the Past in Post-Unification Culture* (New York: De Gruyter, 2006); and Devin Pendas, *The Frankfurt Auschwitz Trial, 1963–1965: Genocide, History, and the Limits of the Law* (Cambridge: Cambridge University Press, 2006).
14 Douglas Johnston and Cynthia Sampson, eds., *Religion: The Missing Dimension of Statecraft* (New York: Oxford University Press, 1994); Amy Benson Brown and Karen M. Poremski, eds., *Roads to Reconciliation: Conflict and Dialogue in the Twenty-First Century* (Armonk, NY: M.E. Sharpe, 2005). Lily Gardner Feldman, 'The Principle and Practice of "Reconciliation" in German Foreign Policy: Relations with France, Israel, Poland and the Czech Republic,' *International Affairs* 75/2 (1999): 333–56; John Paul Lederach, *Building Peace: Sustainable Reconciliation in Divided Societies* (Washington, DC: U.S. Institute of Peace Press, 1997); and Stephen Rock, *Why Peace Breaks Out: Great Power Rapprochement in Historical Perspective* (Chapel Hill, NC: University of North Carolina Press, 1989).
15 Yinan He, *The Search for Reconciliation: Sino-Japanese and German-Polish Relations since World War II* (Cambridge: Cambridge University Press, 2009); Muna Ndulo, ed., *Security, Reconstruction, and Reconciliation: When the Wars End* (London: University College London Press, 2007); and Kai Ambos et al., eds., *Building a Future on Peace and Justice: The Nuremberg Declaration on Peace and Justice* (Berlin: Springer, 2009).
16 Daniel Philpott, *Just and Unjust Peace: An Ethic of Political Reconciliation* (New York: Oxford University Press, 2012); Lily Gardner Feldman, 'Reconciliation and Legitimacy,' in Thomas Banchoff and Mitchell P. Smith, eds., *Legitimacy and the European Union: A Contested Polity* (New York: Routledge, 1999), 1–9; David Crocker, 'Reckoning with Past Wrongs: A Normative Framework,' in Carol A.L. Prager and Trudy Govier, eds., *Dilemmas of Reconciliation: Cases and Concepts* (Waterloo: Wilfrid Laurier University Press, 2003), 39–63; Paul Komesaroff, 'Pathways to

Reconciliation: Bringing Diverse Voices into Conversation,' in Fleming Rothfield and Paul Komesaroff, eds., *Pathways to Reconciliation: Between Theory and Practice* (Burlington, VT: Ashgate, 2008), 1–12; Andrew Schaap, *Political Reconciliation* (London: Routledge, 2005); and Mark Gibney and Rhoda E. Howard-Hassmann, 'Introduction: Apologies and the West,' in Mark Gibney et al., eds., *The Age of Apology: Facing Up to the Past* (Philadelphia, PA: University of Pennsylvania Press, 2008), 1–9.
17 He, *Search for Reconciliation*, 19.
18 Feldman, 'Reconciliation and Legitimacy,' 2.

1. The German People and Allied Demands: Pressures and Initiatives towards Reconciliation

1 Marshall Knappen, *And Call It Peace* (Chicago, IL: University of Chicago Press, 1947), 185.
2 Ibid., 75.
3 'Coordinating Committee [CORC]: Control Council Responsibilities' (19 Aug. 1945), in *Report of the Tripartite Conference at Potsdam*, Objective IV, Bundesarchiv Koblenz (hereafter BAK), Z 46/17 CORC/P(45)2, Appendix A, 2.
4 'Declaration on Atrocities Issued after the Moscow Conference of the Foreign Ministers of the United Kingdom, the United States, and the Soviet Union,' 30 Oct. 1943, in *Documents on Germany under Occupation, 1945–1954*, ed. by Beate Ruhm von Oppen (New York: Oxford University Press, 1955), 2.
5 *Report of the Tripartite Conference at Potsdam*, Objective IV, Appendix A, 2.
6 Joseph Grew, U.S. Undersecretary of State, noted in August 1945, 'The ultimate success of the entire policy of the Government toward Germany will depend upon the extent to which the Germans are brought to change their ideals and ways.' Letter from Grew to George Shuster, 1 Aug. 1945, George Nauman Shuster Papers (hereafter SHU), Box 5, Archives of the University of Notre Dame (hereafter UNDA).
7 The Christian Democratic Union (CDU) was established in Cologne on 18 May 1945. By the end of 1945, five other political parties had been established, and five more by 1947. See Rogers, *Politics after Hitler*, 20–48.
8 Winkler, *Germany: The Long Road West*, 114–15.
9 See Wolfgang Leonhard, *Child of the Revolution* (London: Regnery, 1958), 359.
10 Bert Schloss, 'The American Occupation of Germany, 1945–1952: An Appraisal,' Chicago, IL: University of Chicago, 1955, 165.

11 See Uta G. Poiger, *Jazz, Rock, and Rebels: Cold War Politics and American Culture in Divided Germany* (Berkeley, CA: University of California Press, 2000); and Bishop Berning's notice that warned Catholics against viewing decadent foreign films, 'Für den Filmbesuch Ausländische und neue deutsche Filme in den drei Westzonen' (Aug. 1948), BAK, Z 18/2.
12 See 'Unser Schuld,' *Neues Abendland* (Oct. 1946): 3–35, and articles on German guilt, democratization of Germany, the Nuremberg Trials, the 'dark side' of Germany, and the fate of the Jews under Nazi rule, in *Gegenwart* no. 2/3 (24 Dec. 1945).
13 See *Pocket Guide to Germany*, which was given to all American serviceman upon their arrival in Europe. It stated, 'Germans have sinned against the laws of humanity and cannot come back into the civilized fold by merely sticking out their hands and saying "I'm sorry"' (4). *Stars and Stripes* magazine reprinted a poem found in the *New York Herald Tribune* that mocked the idea of being kind to the Germans; see 'Be Gentle to the Germans' (9 Feb. 1945, 2). Another article included a cartoon depicting a German man running out to greet American troops, his hand dripping with blood. The caption reads: 'No, Heinrich, it won't wash,' 'Civilians Determined to Make Friends with Conquerors' (7 March 1945, 2).
14 U.S. Department of State, 'Directive to Commander-in-Chief of United States Forces of Occupation Regarding the Military Government of Germany; April 1945 (JCS 1067),' *Foreign Relations of the United States: European Advisory Commission, Austria, Germany* 3 (1945): 484.
15 Historian Oliver Frederiksen explains how, although the policy changed, 'it was still official policy that contacts should be discouraged.' See *The American Military Occupation of Germany, 1945–1953* (OMGUS, Darmstadt: Historical Division, 1953), 131–2.
16 Naimark, *The Russians in Germany*, 69–94.
17 CORC, 'Recall of German officials and obnoxious Germans from neutral countries' (31 Aug. 1945), BAK, Z46/17 CORC/P(45)29, 1.
18 CORC, Report on the Tripartite Conference at Potsdam, Objective IV, Appendix A, 9.
19 CORC, 'Progress Report to the Coordinating Committee with regard to Section XIII of the Resolutions of the Potsdam Conference (orderly transfer of German Populations)' (10 Sept. 1945), BAK, Z46/17 CORC/P (45)72, Appendix C, 3.
20 Ibid. The total number of expellees was approximately 12.5 million. Jarausch, *After Hitler*, 240.

21 Eagle Glassheim claims that approximately two million ethnic Germans were expelled in an orderly and humane manner during Jan.–Dec. 1946, but that during the summer months of 1945, approximately 700,000 ethnic Germans were victims of wanton acts of violence leaving 30,000 dead in Czechoslovakia alone. 'National Mythologies and Ethnic Cleansing: The Expulsion of Czechoslovak Germans in 1945,' *Central European History* 33/4 (2000): 463.

22 'Das Probleme der deutschen Minderheiten: Ein Interview mit Präsident Beneš – Polen und Österreich im Mittelpunkt,' *Die Neue Zeitung*, 18 Oct. 1945.

23 Ibid.

24 The *Neue Zeitung* reported how, in early fall 1945, the British wanted the Poles to slow their pace of transferring Germans to the British Zone, as the British Military Government was having difficulty absorbing the 3,000 refugees arriving in its zone every day. Ibid.

25 For details on the difficulties surrounding the influx of refugees in the British and American zones, see 'Ergebnisse der Volkszahlung' (29 Oct. 1946), BAK, Z1/1349. Difficulties in the Soviet zone were considerable; in some cases (e.g., Pomerania and Mecklenburg), the refugees equalled or even outnumbered the residents. See 'Treysa Report' (4 May 1946), Archiv des Diakonischen Werkes der EKD (hereafter ADW), ZB 74.

26 For example, the U.S. Army forced Germans from Ludwigslust to view the graves of victims of the concentration camp at Wobbelin. See Richard Overy, *Interrogations: The Nazi Elite in Allied Hands* (New York: Penguin, 2001), 44–5. In another case, Germans living in Weimar were forced by the U.S. Third Army Military Police to view the mass graves and transport the dead to graves at Buchenwald. See Harry Truman Library, at *http://www.trumanlibrary.org/photographs/view.php?id=3862&rr=.*

27 CORC, Report on the Tripartite Conference at Potsdam, Objective IV, Appendix A, 3.

28 According to Richard Overy, the acts deemed criminal at this stage were mostly drawn from a list of crimes created in 1919 by the Allied victors of the First World War. See *Interrogations*, 46.

29 Allied Control Council (ACC) Law No. 10, 'Punishment of Persons Guilty of War Crimes, Crimes against Peace and Crimes against Humanity, 20 Dec. 1945,' in *Official Gazette of the Control Council for Germany* 3 (31 Jan. 1946).

30 Heinrich Winkler argues that denazification 'proved to be a failure,' due to the fact that once the tials were over, many Germans 'would no longer be confronted with their political biographies.' *Germany: The Long Road West*, 111.

31 The American Military Government oversaw the German administration of 900,000 cases; the British Military Government investigated 296,798 cases; and the French Military Government witnessed 195,000 cases in the courts. See Office of the Military Government of the United States (hereafter OMGUS), *Denazification in the Four Zones* (1947), OMGUS pamphlet, published 1947.

32 Provincial Advisory Council, 'Law on the Purging of Bavaria of Nazism and Militarism (draft)' (24 Oct. 1945), BAK, Z1/1337. For the Allied Law, see Directive 24 of 12 Jan. 1946, 'The Removal from Office and from Positions of Responsibility of Nazis and Persons Hostile to Allied Purposes,' *Official Gazette for the Control Council of Germany* 5 (31 March 1946).

33 Letter from Goetz to Erich Rossmann, Generalsekretär beim Länderat Stuttgart, 'Unzulänglichkeiten in diesem Gesetz: Für Kabinettsitzung,' 12 Jan. 1946, BAK, Z 1/1337.

34 Letter from Bishop Wurm to OMGUS, April 1946, BAK, Z 1/1337.

35 Winkler, *Germany: The Long Road West*, 111.

36 Herf, *Divided Memory*, 72, and Timothy Vogt, *Denazification in Soviet-Occupied Germany: Brandenburg, 1945–1948* (Cambridge, MA: Harvard University Press, 2000), 3.

37 Association of Victims of Nazism (hereafter VVN), *Zwei Jahre Hauptausschuss OdF* (Berlin: Hauptauschuss OdF, 1947), 82.

38 Ibid., 80–1.

39 Constantine Goschler, *Wiedergutmachung: Westdeutschland und die Verfolgten des Nationalsozialismus 1945–1954: Quellen und Darstellung zur Zeitgeschichte*, no. 34 (Munich: Oldenbourg, 1992), 642.

40 'Die Landesverwaltung Württemberg, Abt. Inneres Bekanntmachung betr. Einrichtung des Amts für Wiedergutmachung der Folgen des Naziterrors Stuttgart' (21 June 1945), Institut für Zeitgeschichte (hereafter IfZ) -Archiv, Bestand OMGUS. Found in Bibliothek, Bundesarchiv Berlin.

41 Direktor, das Innenministerium Württemberg-Baden an die Landräte und die Bürgermeister der kreisfreien Städte Erlass: Hilfsmaßnahmen für ehemalige politische Gefangene Stuttgart (17 Dec. 1945), IfZ-Archiv, OMGUS 12/26-2/26. Found in Bibliothek, Bundesarchiv Berlin.

42 Direktorat für Reparationen und Rückerstattung (hereafter DRDR), 'Draft Reply to the Yugoslav Mission,' BAK, Z 45f 2/128-1/7–13 DRDR/P(46)5.

43 Ibid. This procedure included everyday personal belongings and larger objects, such as automobiles.

44 Ibid.

45 See F. Roy Willis, *The French in Germany 1945–1949* (Stanford, CA: Stanford University Press, 1962), Chapter 6.
46 See Kessler and Rüdiger, *Wiedergutmachung im Osten Deutschlands*, 22–3.
47 Martin Broszat and Hermann Weber, eds., *SBZ-Handbuch: Staatliche Verwaltungen, Parteien, Gesellschaftliche Organisationen und Ihre Führungskräfte in der SBZ Deutschlands, 1945–1949* (Munich: Oldenbourg, 1990), 749.
48 For example, the Victims of Fascism fundraiser 'Rettet die Kinder' brought in over 6 million German Marks by 30 June 1946 (nearly 200,000 more Marks by 31 Dec. 1946), of which just under 5.2 million was used in support of the Victims group during 1945–6. See VVN, *Zwei Jahre Hauptausschuss OdF*, 90.
49 Geschke was joined by other founding members of Victims of Fascism: Otto Brass, Heinrich Grüber, Theodor Steltzer, Hildegard Staehle, Julius Meyer, Margarete Jung, Hermann Landwehr, Dr R. Havemann, Annedore Leber, and Dr Marion York von Wartenburg. See ibid., 8.
50 A bank account was set up for donations, which needed to have about 360,000 Marks in it in order to meet the demands for the emergency funds. See, 'Introduction,' ibid.
51 *Berliner Zeitung* article in ibid., 45. The *Berliner Zeitung* report on the rally claimed that the anti-fascist fighters and victims of Nazism were the 'only heroes we have today' and that their work was planting the 'seed of our new state.' The mixed motives of the participants in the rally were addressed towards the end of the article, with reference to the rally being a *Sühnegang* (atonement pilgrimage) for many who were present. See ibid., 42.
52 Geschke speech, quoted in *Die Toten, Den Lebenden: Gedenkschrift zur Gedächtnis-Kundgebung OdF, Berlin-Neukölln, 9.9.45* (Berlin: Stadt Berlin Magistrat, 1945), 3.
53 Geschke speech, quoted in VVN, *Zwei Jahre Hauptausschuss OdF*, 46.
54 Dahrendorf speech, quoted in *Die Toten*. Similarly, speaking on behalf of women's groups that had resisted the Nazis, Mrs Wiedmeyer put it this way: 'the acknowledgment of our collective guilt gives us the strength to rebuild and to make things right.' Quoted in VVN, *Zwei Jahre Hauptausschuss OdF*, 46.
55 In his speech, Franz Dahlem proclaimed, 'Germany needs, above all, fighters ... who in no way compromised with any aspect of Nazism ... these people have the duty to tell the Germans the naked truth of their permission and complicity in the crimes of the Nazi regime and that they have to take on the collective responsibility of reparations and making things right

with the people of other nations [so that we can forge] friendly ties and relationships with other nations.' Quoted in *Die Toten*, 5.
56 According to Michael Brenner, 6,000 Jews survived the war in Germany, most of whom had lived in Berlin. See 'Epilogue or Preface? Five Decades of Jewish Life in Postwar Germany: A Balance Sheet,' in Otto R. Romberg and Suzanne Urban-Fahr, eds., *Jews in Germany after 1945: Citizens or "Fellow" Citizens?* (Frankfurt: Tribune, 2000), 51.
57 Mertens, *Davidstern unter Hammer und Zirkel*, 30. See also Angelika Königseder and Juliane Wetzel, *Waiting for Hope: Jewish Displaced Persons in Post – World War Two Germany* (Evanston, IL: Northwestern University Press, 2001), 6.
58 Stalin asserted that Jews comprised an ethnic group in Russia, rather than a distinct nation. *Marxism and the National Question* ([1913]; transl. and published, Moscow: Marx-Engels-Lenin Institute, 1946), 12.
59 Letter from the General Secretary of the Berlin Jewish community (Gemeinde) to the Sowjetische-Russische Zentralkommandatur, titled 'Bildung der Jüdischen Gemeinde zu Berlin,' 12 Dec. 1945, and the response from the Magistrat der Stadt Berlin, Beirat für kirchliche Angelegenheiten und, Referent für die jüdischen Angelegenheiten, Siegmund Weltinger, 21 Feb. 1946, Centrum Judaicum (hereafter CJA), 5 A1:1. The central administration of the Berlin Jewish community, whose headquarters were at the burned-out synagogue on Oranienburgerstraße, was comprised of Erich Nehlans, Dr Hans Münzer, Dr Hans-Erich Fabian, Dr Leo Löwenkopf, Karl Busch, and Julius Meyer; see CJA, 5 Bl:50.
60 Letter, 12 Dec. 1945, CJA, 5 A1:1.
61 Ibid.
62 Letter from Der Vorstand der Jüdische Gemeinde zu Berlin to international Jewish groups, 15 July 1945, CJA, 5 A1:16. The letter appears here in its original form, emphasis added.
63 VVN, *Zwei Jahre Hauptausschuss OdF*, 18. For the separation of victims groups ('Fighters' and 'Victims'), see letter from SED's Sozialfürsorge office to SED, 19 July 1946, Stiftung Archiv der Parteien und Massenorganizationen der DDR im Bundesarchiv (hereafter SAPMO), DY 30/ IV 2/2027/29. The compensation criteria were complex, and practice differed in each region of the Soviet zone, as the Soviet Military Administration (SMAD) had delegated each region (Bezirksozialamt) control over reparations. Helmut Eschwege and Paul Merker both continued to defy the Stalinist non-recognition of Jewish nationhood and demanded recognition for Jewish victims on that basis. See letter from Merker and Eschwege to SED, 10 Feb. 1946, SAPMO, DY 30/ IV 2/2027/29. In

mid-1946, Victims of Fascism counted 42,287 'Victims of Nuremberg Laws' and 57,823 'Fighters'; in Berlin, both groups received the one-time payment of 450 DM, but not in Brandenburg, where it was only for 'Fighters.' In Saxony, 500 DM were available for compensation in a communal fund for 'Nuremberg' victims, but that fund was based on donations. In the end, most victims did not receive ongoing compensation. For example, in Berlin, a person receiving a salary of 75 DM a month would receive 25 DM a month from the Victims of Fascism fund, but pensions were reserved for 'Fighters' only.

64 Heinz Brand's speech at the Leipzig meeting held 27–28 Oct. 1945, SAPMO, DY 54/V 277/1/1.
65 VVN, *Zwei Jahre Hauptausschuss OdF*, 19.
66 See, e.g., speeches by Dr Havemann and Hildegard Staehles at Victims of Fascism rally, titled 'Wir Klagen An!' quoted in ibid., 66–7.
67 Ottomar Geschke's speech, ibid.
68 Other sub-groups included: Victims of Political Opportunism, Victims of Religious or Ideological Persecution, Military Offenders, Family Arrests; and Victims of Recognized Political Offence. VVN, *Zwei Jahre Hauptausschuss OdF*, 23.
69 Roma and Sinti victims were encouraged to submit individual claims for reparations if they could prove that they fit the criteria for being a 'victim.' Jehovah's Witnesses found that they were no more welcome in the GDR than in Nazi Germany, and the organization was banned in the GDR in 1950. Kessler and Rüdiger, *Wiedergutmachung im Osten*, 243.
70 The SED considered resistance fighters and their widows as victims of Nazism. See Ministerpräsident Otto Grotewohl, 'Regierungserklärung zur Stellung der Verfolgten des Naziregimes Berlin,' *Neues Deutschland*, 12 Oct. 1949.
71 Deutsche-Zentralverwaltung Sozialfürsorge (OdF Zusammenfassung), 'Bestehen Bestimmungen über die Rückgabe der seinerzeit arisierten Betriebe?' (18 June 1946), SAPMO, DY 30/IV 2/2027/29. The law applied to Thuringia only.
72 Letter from Berlin Gemeinde to JOINT, the Jewish Agency for Palestine, the American Jewish Committee, the World Jewish Congress and the American Jewish Congress, Jan. 1947, CJA, 5 A1:16.
73 Organizations authorized to assist Jews in the Soviet zone: Swedish Red Cross, Jewish Agency for Palestine, Belgian Military Mission, World Jewish Congress, American Jewish Joint Distribution Committee, Association of Jewish Refugees in Great Britain, Australian Jewish Welfare Committee, Jewish Immigrant Aid Society of Canada, Council of Jewish Communities in Bohemia and Moravia CSR, Commita

Israelitica Ufficio Ricerche (Italy), South African Jewish Board of Deputies, Canadian Jewish Congress Western Division Winnipeg, Swiss European Union, Do Zydowskiego Komiteto (Poland), Cisroco, Comite Israelita de Socorros (Chile), Comite Auxilier do Joint no (Brasil), Comite Auxiliar del Joint en Paraguay Para Socorro y Reconstrution (Paraguay), Joint Relief Committee (Cuba). CJA, 5 A1:86.

74 Victims of Fascism, planning session, titled 'Über die Bildung einer Kommission in Berlin, zur Aufdeckung der Morde an Geisteskranken und Zwangssterilisierten' (22 Feb. 1946), SAPMO, DY 54 V/277/1/19.

75 The *Berliner Zeitung* printed an article on the Nazi 'Euthanasia' Program (T4 Program), on 1 June 1945. Found in SAPMO, DY 54 V/277/1/19.

76 The screening of applicants for victim recognition and compensation was thorough, and ideologically driven. SS men who tried to obtain membership in Victims of Fascism paid for their false applications with arrest. VVN, *Zwei Jahre Hauptausschuss OdF*, 17. Of 23,897 applicants for political persecution, only 9,529 were accepted; of 25,000 applicants who sought designation as 'Victims of the Nuremberg Laws,' 10,268 were accepted. Ibid., 88.

77 *Jahrbuch von 1945 bis 31. März 1947 Arbeit und Sozialfürsorge* (Berlin: Deutsche Verwaltung für Arbeit und Sozialfürsorge SZO, 1947), 7.

78 Victims of Fascism, Interzonen-Besprechung, 'Völkerversöhnung,' SAPMO, DY 54 V/277 1/45.

79 See Herf, *Divided Memory*, 94–5.

80 The Allies did not have to look far to find many reasons to doubt the political appropriateness of the German church leadership. For example, the pro-Nazi German Christians appealed to the ACC for separate Protestant Church denominational status in 1946, but were refused (16 Sept. 1946), BAK, Z 45 f RG 260 DOACARACP(46)27.

81 See Bishop of Chichester, George Bell, *Christianity and World Order* (New York: Penguin, 1940), 105–6, quoted in Peter Raina, *Bishop George Bell: The Greatest Churchman – A Portrait in Letters* (London: Churches Together in Britain and Ireland, 2006), 229, 92.

82 Knappen, *And Call It Peace*, 48. This view was widespread. For example, OMGUS historian Harold Zink noted that 'the German church was considered by the Occupying Powers as one of the most important instruments for the reorientation of German society,' cited in Beryl McClaskey, *The History of U.S. Policy and Program in the Field of Religious Affairs under the Office of the U.S. High Commissioner for Germany* (HICOG, 1951), i.

83 Directive from Zentralsekretariat der SED, Abteilung Kultur und Erziehung, an alle Landes-, Provinzial- und Bezirksorganisationen, 'Unsere Stellung zur Kirche' (July, 1946), SAPMO, DY 30/IV 2/14/1.

84 Protestant SED Party Members to the Zentralsekretariat der SED, 'Christentum und Sozialismus sind keine Gegensätze' (30 Sept. 1946), SAPMO, DY 30/IV 2/14/1.
85 Befehl des Oberbefehlshabers der sowjetischen Besatzungstruppen in Deutschland, 'Über die Leitung der Arbeit in Kinderheimen' (26 July 1946) SAPMO, DY 30/IV 2/14/238.
86 Lucius Clay, *Decision in Germany* (Garden City, NY: Doubleday, 1950), 305.
87 In Clay's view, 'the Military Government should [not] take an active part in religious life. The purpose of our Religious Affairs Branch [is] to encourage German church leaders by helping them solve their immediate problems ... [while] guarantee[ing] full freedom of worship.' Ibid., 303.
88 See the VVN document, 'Martin Niemöller ohne Maske: Aus den Protokollen einer 1938 gegen ihn geführten Strafverhandlung, and Erklärung' (28 July 1947), SAPMO, DY 55 V 278/2/13. In contrast, The Department of Reconstruction and Inter-Church Aid: Division of Material Aid, World Council of Churches (hereafter WCC) admonished Niemöller in a report to OMGUS in a telegram in 1947, 'Martin Niemöller, Telegram no.143/2' (22 June 1947), SAPMO, DY 55 278/2/13, 3. In 1945, American Lutheran WCC member, Sylvester Michelfelder provided his rendition of Niemöller: 'You cannot be in the presence of such a great personality as Martin Niemöller without realizing that here is a man like a re-incarnated Jeremiah or John the Baptist.' Sylvester Michelfelder's Report to WCC, 'My Interview with Pastor Niemöller' (7 Nov. 1945), ADW, ZB 311.
89 OMGUS, Confidential Special Report No. 5, APO 742, 'Pastor Niemoeller: The Evolution of an Anti-Nazi' (27 Oct. 1947), John Conway Collection, John Richard Allison Library, Regent College, Vancouver, B.C. (hereafter Conway Collection), BX 8080 N48 M35 1997 File 6.
90 Knappen, *And Call It Peace*, 126–7.
91 By August 1946, 136 of 2,168 clergymen and employees were removed in greater Hesse; in Baden-Württemberg, 144 of 5,730; in Bavaria, 41 of 11,236. Ibid., 135–6. For the case in the British zone, see Gerhard Besier, *'Selbstreinigung' unter britischer Besatzungsherrschaft: Die Evangelisch-Lutherische Landeskirche Hannovers und ihr Landesbischof Marahrens, 1945–1947* (Göttingen: Vandenhoeck and Ruprecht, 1986).
92 British Member's statement to the ACC Religious Affairs Branch, 'Exchange of Informal Information on the Development of the Religious Situation in the Different Zones' (11 Oct. 1945), BAK, Z 45 f RG 260, 2.
93 French Member's statement, ibid., 3.
94 British Member's statement, ibid., 2.

95 Soviet Member's statement, 'Eighth meeting of the ACC Religious Affairs Branch' (23 Dec. 1945), BAK, Z 45 f RG 260 DIAC/ARAC/M(45), 8.
96 Joint statement, 'Ninth meeting of the ACC Religious Affairs Branch' (12 Jan. 1946), BAK, Z 45 f RG 260 DIAC/ARAC/M(46)1, 1.
97 Knappen, *And Call It Peace*, 173.
98 The U.S. members of CRALOG included: the National Catholic Welfare Conference, Church World Service, Lutheran World Relief, Mennonite Central Committee, and Unitarians. McClaskey, *History of U.S. Policy and Program*, 24.
99 Letter from the WCC's Department of Reconstruction and Inter-Church Aid to General Dwight Eisenhower and Staff, 6 Nov. 1945, ADW, ZB 331.
100 German Protestant Church, 'Preparatory Document: Amsterdam' (1946), ADW, ZB 331.
101 After opposing the appointment of a liaison, the Soviets finally agreed to allow the WCC's Dr Bachman to serve as an 'unofficial' liaison in the American zone. ACC Religious Affairs Branch, 'Appointment of Liaison Officer between the WCC and the German Churches' (3 Sept. 1947), BAK, Z 45 f 2/11-12 DIAC/ARAC/M(47), 10, 126.
102 Memorandum from Dr Herman to the WCC, 'Relations between German and Polish Church leaders in Silesia,' 15 July 1946, ADW, ZB 332, 1.
103 Ibid., 1, 5.
104 Ibid., 2.
105 *In Namen der Wahrheit: Erklärung des Rates der Evangel. Kirchen in Polen*, Methodist Pastor K. Najder and Lutheran Pastor Z. Michelis, 1–4, ADW, ZB 85.
106 Memorandum from Dr Herman, 3. Pastor Niemczyk explained that 30 German deacons were working at a Polish hospital, where a Polish doctor who had survived Ravensbrück provided them with jobs.
107 Ibid., 5–6.
108 Correspondence from Clay to Secretary of War Patterson, 13 Oct. 1945, quoted in Clay, *Decision in Germany*, 104.
109 Frederic Spotts, *The Churches and Politics in Germany* (Middletown, CT: Wesleyan University Press, 1973), 81.
110 McClaskey, *History of U.S. Policy and Program*, 24.
111 Knappen, *And Call It Peace*, 106–7.

2. German Church and Political Groups

1 Hockenos points out that Asmussen's tempered criticism of Nazi church policies and racist ideology gave way to a pro-German viewpoint in

the immediate postwar period, as he 'tried to put the best spin possible on the Church's conspicuous silence about Nazi brutality.' *A Church Divided*, 48.
2. Letter from Asmussen to ACC, 29 Jan. 1946, BAK, Z 45 f RG260 DIAC/ARAC/MEMO (46)1, Annexure 4.
3. Ibid.
4. Ibid. Asmussen reasoned: '[We] kept silent when we ought to have spoken ... we are all guilty.'
5. Stewart Herman, *The Rebirth of the German Churches* (New York: Harper, 1946), 24.
6. See Hockenos, *A Church Divided*, 15–41. The pro-Nazi German Christians appealed to the ACC for separate Protestant Church denominational status in 1946, but were refused. Letter from Deutsche Christen to ACC Religious Affairs Branch, 16 Sept. 1946, BAK, Z 45 f RG 260 DOACARACP(46)27.
7. Hans Iwand claimed at Treysa, 'God achieved the enormous work of reconciliation through Jesus Christ, and he now offers reconciliation ... to anyone who wants to reconcile with Him ... and we are those who assist God in this work.' Fritz Soehlmann, *Treysa 1945: Die Konferenz der evangelischen Kirchenführer 27–31 August, 1945* (Lüneburg: Im Heliand Verlag, 1946), 37–8.
8. Dibelius' Pentecost sermon, 'Ein Neuer Anfang' (1945, Berlin), BAK, Z 1439/6, 2–3.
9. For an example of the utilization of the motif of Christians as the Chosen People in occupied Germany, see Steven Schroeder, 'Mennonite-Nazi Collaboration and Coming to Terms with the Past: European Mennonites and the MCC, 1945–1950,' *Conrad Grebel Review* 21/2 (2003): 6–16.
10. Dibelius' sermon, 'Die Stellvertretende Minderheit' (17 June 1945, Berlin), BAK, Z 1439/6, 4.
11. The Stuttgart Declaration stated: 'We are conscious of being united to our people not only by a common bond of suffering but also of guilt ... it is with great sorrow that we say ... through us endless misery has been inflicted on many people and countries,' ACC Religious Affairs Branch, 'Report, Annexure 1' (18 Jan. 1946), BAK, Z 45 f RG 260 DIAC/ARAC/P(46), 1.
12. Ibid.
13. Ibid.
14. Letter ACC Religious Affairs Committee to Wurm, 26 Feb. 1946, BAK, Z 45 f RG 260 DIAC/ARAC/MEMO(46), 10.

15 Letter from Bishop Wurm to the Protestant Church in England, titled 'An die Christen in England,' 14 Dec. 1945, ADW, ZB 7, 1.
16 Ibid.
17 Ibid.
18 Letter from Heinrich Grüber to Bishop Bell, in *Das Hilfswerk* (7 Aug. 1945), ADW ZB 6.
19 Wurm letter, 'An die Christen in England,' 2.
20 Letter from the German Protestant Church to the ACC, Military Governments, German governmental bodies, Church administrators, 9 May1946, BAK, Z 45 f RG 260 DIAC/ARAC/P(46), Appendix 1.
21 Ibid.
22 Ibid.
23 Otto Dibelius' sermon, 'Schuld und Vergebung' (2 June 1946, Berlin), BAK, N 1439/6, 3.
24 Ibid.
25 Ibid., 4.
26 Ibid., 6, 8.
27 See Frank Buscher, '*The Great Fear: The Catholic Church and the Anticipated Radicalization of Expellees and Refugees in Post-War Germany,*' *German History* 21/2 (2003): 204–24, and Ian Connor, 'The Protestant Churches and German Refugees and Expellees in the Western Zones of Germany after 1945,' *Debatte* 15/1 (2007): 43–63. See also Catholic Church's Aid Society circulars: 'The Expellee Problem in Germany – A Social-Revolutionary Atom Bomb for Europe,' 'The Ackermann-Gemeinde,' and 'Water on Moscow's Mills,' BAK, Z 18/211.
28 Protestant Relief Work report, 'Besprechung mit Vertretern der Ökumene und Beauftragten der Landeskirchen' (23 Oct. 1945), ADW, ZB 331.
29 Otto Dibelius, Theophil Wurm, Heinrich Grüber, and Friedrich von Bodelschwingh claimed that they had anticipated in 1942 Germany's loss in the war and secretly proposed the formation of Protestant Relief Work (hereafter, PRW). This claim was intended to garner favour, and assistance, from the Allies as it was to show the Protestant Church's lack of support for the German war effort. See ADW, ZB 7.
30 Letter from Gerstenmaier to OMGUS, 1 Oct. 1945, ADW, ZB 7.
31 Eugen Gerstenmaier, 'Hilfe für Deutschland,' in Evangelisches Hilfswerk, *Eugen Gerstenmaier: Reden und Aufsätze, Zusammengestellt Anlässlich seines 50. Geburtstages am 25.8.56*, Evangelisches Hilfswerk (Stuttgart: Ev. Verlagswerk, 1956), 54.
32 Ibid., 57.
33 Ibid., 53, 69–70.

34 Gerstenmaier's speech, 'Das Hilfswerk der EKD: Bericht auf dem II. Kirchentag und der Tagung des Wiederaufbau/Auschusses der EKD Treysa' (1 May1946, Treysa), ADW, ZB 8.

35 Some rare exceptions were made to the travel prohibition for Germans (e.g., Bishops von Galen and Preysing were granted permission to travel to meet with fellow Catholics in Rome). Minutes of the meeting between PRW personnel and OMGUS (23 Jan. 1946), ADW, ZB 8.

36 Bengt Hoffmann, 'Journey in Germany's East Zone, June 1950,' ADW, ZB 338. For difficulties in the distribution of herring, see 'Transport schwedischer Liebesgaben in der russischen Zone' (April 1946), ADW, ZB 84. Also see Gerstenmaier's 4 Feb. 1946 report on the Soviet zone, in which he claims that the PRW had succeeded in distributing packages of food, clothing, medical supplies, paper, and Bibles to ethnic Germans in Eastern Germany and Eastern Europe, ADW, ZB 8.

37 The East German government published a book, titled *From SD-Agent to Parliamentary President: The Life of Eugen Gerstenmaier,* in which it accused Gerstenmaier of having utilized the 'moral credit' of the Protestant Church in his personal life, and had, 'with journalistic talent ... found asylum under the mask of Christian charity' as head of PRW. Nationalrat der Nationalen Front des DDR,*Vom SD-Agenten P38/546 zum Bundestagpräsident: Die Karriere des Eugen Gerstenmaiers* (Berlin: Staatliche Verlag, Drückerei Tribüne Berlin, 1969), 68. This attack, although clearly politically motivated, has never been refuted and corresponds to the facts of Gerstenmaier's early and enthusiastic support of the Nazi regime.

38 Letter from Siegfried Preuss to Eugen Gerstenmaier, 'Buss- und Versöhnungsaktion der Kirchen anlässlich der Moskauer Konferenz,' 10 Jan. 1947, ADW, ZB 840, 1.

39 Ibid.

40 Ibid.

41 Siegfried Preuss, 'Die Flüchtlingsnot und die Völker: Vergeltung oder Vergebung?' (10 Jan. 1947), ADW, ZB 840, 1.

42 Ibid.

43 Ibid., 2.

44 Preuss evoked the example of the crucifixion of Jesus and Jesus' response to his murderers: 'Father, forgive them, for they know not what they do.' Ibid., 1.

45 Letter from PRW to Marshal Zhukov, 1 Aug. 1945, ADW, ZB 6, 6.

46 Berg's speech at Kirchheim, 'Was will das Hilfswerk der EKD und was will es von uns?' (13 Oct. 1945), ADW, ZB 7.

47 Berg's address at Ludwigshafen, 'Was erfordert die heutige Notlage von der evangelischen Christenheit in Deutschland?' (17 July 1946), ADW, ZB 8.
48 See 'Vatican, Polen, und Ausweisung der Ostdeutschen,' *Chist Unterwegs* (July 1948), 4.
49 Letter from Pope Pius XII to German Bishops, 1 Nov. 1945, BAK, Z 18/100, 4.
50 Letter from Pope Pius XII to Bavarian Bishops, 15 Aug. 1945, BAK Z 18/100, 2.
51 Ibid.
52 Letter from Pius XII to German Bishops, 2.
53 Ibid. Pius' views find accord in Suzanne Brown-Fleming's study of Bishop Muench, who highlighted differences between 'Nazi gangsters' and the average German, who deserved mercy and forgiveness. Suzanne Brown-Fleming, *The Holocaust and Catholic Conscience: Cardinal Aloisius Muench and the Guilt Question in Germany* (Notre Dame, IN: University of Notre Dame Press, 2006), 139–57.
54 Letter from Pope Pius XII to German Bishops, 8.
55 Bishop Michael of Regensburg's sermon, 'Christus gestern, heute und in alle Ewigkeit,' Dec. 1945 (no day provided), BAK, Z 18/100, 1.
56 Ibid., 3.
57 Ibid.
58 The bishop claimed that the Germans had been 'brought down ... from their elevated position to which they had aspired beyond reproach, due to their excellent spiritual and emotional training, their deep religious consciousness, their rich and noble mind, their solid creativity in all intellectual spheres and in culture.' Ibid., 4.
59 Ibid., 5.
60 Ibid.
61 Ibid.
62 Cardinal Frings, 'Post-Defeat Pastoral Letter of the Archbishop of Cologne,' 27 May 1945 SHU Box 2, UNDA.
63 German Archbishops' Statement, 'An die Pfarr- und Pfarrvikarie-Ämter des Erzb. Paderborn,' 30 Jan. 1946, Cologne, BAK, Z 18/100.
64 Bishop Gröber's address, 'Aus dem Hirtenwort des Erzbischofs von Freiburg zum Jahresschluss 1945,' BAK, Z 18/100, 1–2.
65 Ibid.
66 Archbishop Gröber's sermon, 'Am Feste Petri Stuhlfeier' (22 Feb. 1946), BAK, Z 18/100.
67 Letter from Bishop of Ermland to diocesans, first Advent Sunday 1945, BAK, Z 18/100, 3.

68 Papal Nuncio Eugenio Pacelli – later Pope Pius XII – introduced Catholic Action into Germany in 1928. Various Catholic groups served the goal of Catholic renewal, such as the Catholic Rural Youth Movement, Catholic Workers Union, and Young Christian Workers. See Mark Edward Ruff, *The Wayward Flock: Catholic Youth in Postwar West Germany, 1945–1965* (Chapel Hill, NC: University of North Carolina Press, 2005), 26, 41.
69 Letter from Kreutz to the Verehrlichen Diozesan-Caritasverbände, commissioning a poster, titled 'Christus als Pilger,' 3 May 1946, BAK, Z 18/7.
70 Church's Aid Society, (hereafter CAS), 'Landjugendseelsorge: Zur Situation auf dem Lande (Bayern),' *Freie Vereinigung für Seelsorgehilfe* 3 (April 1946), 7. The CAS encouraged retreat into Catholic spiritualism, evoking the eleventh-century patron saint of Eastern European ethnic Germans, St Hedwig, and in supporting Angelicum Banz and the St Ralphsverein. See BAK, Z 18/7 and BAK, Z 18/132.
71 See letter from Generalvikar Buchwieser to the Ordinariate des Erzbischof München und Freising, 'An die Hochwürdigen Seelsorgestellen der Erzdiözese,' 15 March 1946, BAK, Z 18/6.
72 See letter from Professor Otto Reinhard to Kardinal Faulhaber in Munich, 'Die kirchliche Lage in der Erzdiözese Breslau am Ende des Jahres 1945,' 6 June 1946, BAK, Z 18/6.
73 See Silesian Pastor (name unknown), 'Bericht aus Schlesien: Polnische Pressberichte 1945–6' (Nov. 1945), BAK, Z 18/131, 5.
74 Caritas report, 'Aus den Schicksalen deutscher Ostflüchtlinge' (Feb. 1946), BAK, Z 18/ 11.
75 CAS, 'Und die Kirche?: Der kommissarische polnische Bischof von Breslau, Karol Milik, schreibt in seinem ersten Hirtenbrief' (1 Sept. 1945), BAK, Z 18/3.
76 Letter from Prälat Richard Popp to the Archbishop Ordinariate Bayerns, 10 May 1946, BAK, Z 18/3.
77 See CAS circulars, 'Fall Lidice und die Dana' and 'Stellungsnahmen der Kirchen zur Vertreibung der Deutschen aus den Ostgebieten ... Eingaben an den Hl.Stuhl 1945–1946,' BAK, Z 18/ 133.
78 For example, see Professor Franz Bednar's account,'Zur Sudetendeutsche Frage: Ein tschechische – evangelischer Theologe zur Ausweisung der Sudetendeutschen,' BAK, Z 18/103.
79 CAS circular, 'Hier Irrt das Tribunal' (1947), BAK, Z 18/113.
80 CAS circular, 'Die Orgie des Mordes' (1947), BAK, Z 18/ 113.
81 Paulus Sladek, 'Predigt zur Förderung der caritativen Flüchtlingshilfe,' BAK, Z 18/101.
82 Ibid.

83 Of the expellees, 5.5 million ended up in the Soviet zone; 20%–30% of them were Roman Catholic. 'Die Not der deutschen Katholiken in russischen Zone' (March 1946), BAK, Z 18/7, 1.
84 Michael Schwartz's study finds accord with this report. He states that the expellees were deemed 'resettlers' in the Soviet zone, and that they were to find their own means of sustenance. Some charitable donations from churches and the Volkssolidarität assisted these people until the Soviet authorities founded the Resettlers Association, which began relief work in summer 1946. 'Refugees and Expellees in the Soviet Zone of Germay: Political and Social Problems of their Integration, 1945–1950,' *Journal of Communist Studies and Transition Politics* 16/1&2 (2000): 148–74.
85 'Die Not der deutschen Katholiken,' 2.
86 Ibid., 3.
87 Ibid., 5–7.
88 Letters from the German Catholic Youth groups at Kersthold and Rommerskirchen to the ACC, 'Zur Ostfrage' and 'Ruf an die christliche Jugend der Welt' (March 1947), BAK, Z 18/113.
89 Letter from the German Catholic Youth addressed to German POWs, 'Gruss der DKJ an die POW' (1947), BAK, Z 18/113.
90 First Annual Report of the Ackermann-Gemeinde (1947), BAK, Z 18/110.
91 See 'Jahresbericht der Kirchliche Hilfsstelle München 1947,' BAK, Z 18/211, and 'An Unsere München Ackermann-Gemeinde Freunde!' BAK, Z 18/110.
92 A joint statement of Sudeten German politicians and scientists, 'The Sudeten German in a Federated Europe' (1950), BAK, Z 18/211.
93 'Ansprachen zur feierlichen Eröffnung der Münchner Volkshochschule' (23 June 1946), BAK, B 259/67, 6.
94 Ibid. (emphasis added).
95 Ibid., 6–7.
96 Ibid.
97 Ibid., 11–12.
98 See 'Deutsches Büro für Friedensfragen, Informationem zum Bestand,' BAK, Z 35, and 'Institut für Besatzungsfragen: Informationen zum Bestand,' and the Institute's *Handbuch des Besatzungsrechts, Tübingen 1951–1955*, BAK, B 120.
99 Gustav Harmssen, *Reparationen-Sozialprodukt-Lebensstandard: Versuch einer Wirtschaftsbilanz* (Bremen: Friedrich Truejen Verlag, 1947).
100 See 'A Minor Mein Kampf,' *Economist*, 13 March 1948.
101 See '"So sagt Harmssen" und so sagt der "Economist" zur Bremer Denkschrift,' *Bremer Roland: Mitteilungsblatt der Bremer demokratischen Volkspartei Bremen* 2/6 (1948), in BAK, Z 35/382.

102 Letter from German Office to Herausgeber der 'Gegenwart' in Freiburg i.Br., 'Entmilitärisierung/Entnazifizierung, 1947–49,' 28 July 1947, BAK, Z 35/423.
103 Expellee Association, 'Die Wahrheit über die Kriegsverbrecherprozesse in Frankreich,' BAK, B 120/348.
104 See Expellee Association circular, 'Freiheitsglocke,' 'Wiedergutmachung???' Kamerad pass auf, was Dir blüht!!' BAK, B 150/4114.
105 Victims of Fasicm cicular, 'An alle Frauen an alle Familien in Deutschland: Wo sind die Kinder von Lidice?' SAPMO, DY 54/V/277/1/13.
106 'Licht in das Dunkel von Lidice,' *Berliner Zeitung*, 8 Feb. 1946. Found in SAPMO, DY 54/V/277/1/13.
107 People's Solidarity, 'Bericht über den Zentralausschuss der Volkssolidarität in der sowjetischen Zone' (4 June 1946), ADW, ZB 84, 1.
108 'Bewerbung Tillichs zu der Stelle eines Leiters des Sekretariäts f.d. Zonen-Kuratorium der Volkssolidarität' (26 April 1946), ADW, ZBB 67.
109 People's Solidarity, 'Bericht über den Zentralausschuss,' 2.
110 Ibid.
111 Letter from Büro Pfarrer Grüber, Evangelische Hilfsstelle, Berlin, drafted by Dr Curt Radlauer, 28 Oct. 1945, ADW, ZB 192A, 1–2.
112 Central Committee, 'Arbeitsgemeinschaft christlicher Hilfsstellen für Rassenverfolgte nichtjüdischen Glaubens in Deutschland' (22 Nov. 1946), BAK, Z 1/1291. Members: President Heinrich Grüber, Schmand (American Zone), Berkowitz (British Zone), Gertrud Luckner (French Zone).
113 'Rasseverfolgte night jüdischen Glaubens,' *Caritas Werkbrief* 3 (1946), BAK, Z 18/7, 7.
114 See Offenberg, *Seid Vorsichtig gegen die Machthaber*, 48–65.
115 Autobiography given to Ms. Zewi in an interview, 27 Aug. 1946, ADW, ZB 9.
116 Letter from Mennonite Central Committee (MCC) Levi Jost to Robert Krieder (MCC Representative in Germany), 9 Dec. 1947. MCC and CRALOG were involved in getting supplies to 'First Hebrew Christian Synagogue' in Bremen in order to divert supplies to Berlin, Karlsruhe, Frankfurt, and Mannheim, wishing to assist 'Jewish Christians' in these locations. Another letter from Dr von Lukowicz (PRW, Stuttgart) to Pastor Gross, 29 Dec. 1947, requested food and clothing for 'non-Aryan Christians,' ADW, ZB 840.
117 Letter from Protestant Relief Work Berlin to the organization's Stuttgart office referring to the 'Vereinigung Nichtarischer Christen,' 15 June 1948, ADW, ZB 840.

118 Letter from Eugen Gerstenmaier to the Protestant Relief Work office in Stuttgart regarding the case of a Protestant man who was seeking aid for his Jewish wife, 11 Oct. 1947, ADW, ZB 11.

3. Steps towards Christian-Jewish Reconciliation

1. See Greenstein's opening statement: 'The conference has been planned on the premise that there are at the present time and there will continue to be, Jewish communities in Germany.' *Conference on the Future of the Jews in Germany* (Heidelberg: Office of Adviser on Jewish Affairs, 1949), 5.
2. According to United Nations Relief and Rehabilitation Administration (UNRRA) reports, 96.8% of Jewish Displaced Persons (DPs) in Germany wanted to emigrate. See Susann Heenen-Wolff, *Im Land der Täter: Gespräche mit überlebenden Juden* (Frankfurt: Fischer Taschenbuch, 1994), 5.
3. 'Remarks by John J. McCloy, High Commissioner U.S. Zone, Germany,' in HICOG, *Conference on the Future of the Jews* (Heidelberg: Office of Adviser on Jewish Affairs, 1949), 20. Of sixty participants, only five were gentiles or represented non-Jewish organizations: Eugen Kogon and his wife (*Frankfurter Hefte*); Max Braudo (International Refugee Organization); Ludwig Eisenhardt (*Frankfurter Neue Presse*); and, John McCloy. Ibid., 1.
4. Remarks by McCloy, ibid., 21.
5. Eugen Kogon, 'Jewish and Non-Jewish Relations,' ibid., 25.
6. Ibid. See also Foschepoth, *Im Schatten der Vergangenheit*, 101, 245.
7. 'Discussion,' HICOG, *Conference on the Future of the Jews*, 27.
8. Ibid.
9. Ibid., 28. In the British zone, the Jewish population was split evenly between German Jews and Eastern European Jewish DPs. The complicated mixture of people, feelings, and ideologies led to a variety of positions on emigration.
10. Wollheim and Ostertag were key figures in the Committee's establishment, which began with the formation of a *Dachkomitee* at the Heidelberg Conference. Ibid., 56–60.
11. Max Cahn, ibid., 30.
12. See Geller, *Jews in Post-Holocaust Germany*, 38, 64, and Mertens, *Davidstern unter Hammer und Zirkel*, 30.
13. For example, Jewish representatives at the 1948 World Jewish Congress at Montreaux, France, stated that 'never again [should Jews] settle on the blood-stained German soil.' Quoted in Brenner, 'Epilogue or Preface?' 48.

14 Offenberg, *Seid Vorsichtig gegen die Machthaber*, 13. For East Berlin's Jewish population, see Mertens, *Davidstern unter Hammer und Zirkel*, 29–30, 40.
15 For example, when German police raided the Jewish DP camp at Stuttgart with the hopes of breaking an illegal black market operation, Auschwitz survivor Samuel Danziger was shot and killed by a German policeman. See Abraham S. Hyman, *The Undefeated* (New York: Gefen Books, 1993), 290.
16 Kurt Nettball, 'Bericht über die Lage der jüdischen Bevölkerung,' 28 Feb. 1947, SAPMO, DY 30 IV/2/2.027/30, 2. Paul Merker read the report, and marked this section of Nettball's document with an exclamation mark.
17 Letter from Jewish Gemeinde to Berlin ACC, 15 Jan. 1947, CJA, 5A1:16. Also see letters from: Löwenkopf to Merker, 31 May 1947; Merker to Ulbricht, 4 June 1947; Rudolf Weck to Merker, Lehmann, and Nettball, 5 June 1947. SAPMO, DY 30/ IV 2/2027/30.
18 See numerous 1948 appeals in SAPMO, DY 55 278/1/1.
19 Herf, *Divided Memory*, 88–9.
20 Part of the restructuring of Soviet zone politics in 1947 included the forced dissolution of Victims of Fascism in the Soviet zone, and the creation of the VNN in March of that year. Like its institutional predecessor, the VNN's official policy separated the Jews as second-class victims after Communists. The VVN's general secretary for the Soviet zone, Helmut Lehmann, furnished a report on the first meeting of the association in Berlin, on 30 March 1947, SAPMO, DY 30 IV/2/2.027/30,
21 See Herf, *Divided Memory*, 88–9.
22 Timm, *Jewish Claims*, 26–9.
23 Leo Zuckermann, 'Restitution und Wiedergutmachung,' *Die Weltbühne: Wochenschrift für Politik-Kunst-Wirtschaft*, no. 17 (27 April 1948), 430–2, SAPMO, DY 30/IV 2/4/124, 245–7. For further discuission, see Herf, *Divided Memory*, 88–91.
24 Letter from Leo Zuckermann to Paul Merker, 30 April 1948, SAMPO, DY 30 IV/2/2.027/31. Also see letter from Paul Merker to Wilhelm Pieck, 4 May 1948, SAPMO, DY 30/IV 2/2.027/31.
25 See letter from Jewish community in Dresden to Julius Meyer on Befehl 82, 24 Oct. 1949, CJA, 5B1:50.
26 See 'Einleitung,' SAPMO, DY 30/2027.
27 Paul Merker, 'Eine Darstellung meiner Stellungnahme zur Judenfrage,' 1 June 1956, SAPMO, DY 4102/27, 1–2.
28 Ibid., 4.
29 See Walter Lacquer, *Generation Exodus: The Fate of Young Jewish Refugees from Germany* (London: I.B. Tauris, 2004), 244.

30 For example, one church in East Berlin commemorated, in 1949, the Kristallnacht pogrom of 1938, CJA, 5A1/ 6: Protokoll 1949.
31 The government made efforts to restore and protect synagogues and cemeteries, CJA, 5B1/50.
32 Goschler, *Wiedergutmachung*, 343.
33 'Die nächste Phase: Wiedergutmachung,' *Tagesspiegel* (22 April 1948). See also Ernst Heller, 'Gutmachung Nationalsozialistischen Unrechts,' *Die Neue Zeitung*, 19 March 1949.
34 Letter from office leader Professor Kaufmann to Staatssekretär Dr Fritz Eberhard, concerning his recommendations on the remuneration of racial persecutees. Note the section, 'Besonderes Statut für Juden,' 4 Oct. 1947, BAK, Z 35/166.
35 Jewish welfare organizations did not support the establishment of permanent Jewish communities in Germany, which drove German Jews like Ostertag to self-reliance. 'Discussion,' HICOG, *Conference on the Future of the Jews*, 37, 56.
36 See Karl Hauff's flyer, 'Denkschrift über die Lage der vom Naziregime politisch, rassisch und religiös Verfolgten' (5 Feb. 1947, Stuttgart). Copy found in Bibliothek, Bundesarchiv Berlin.
37 'Message of the foreign ministers of France, the United Kingdom, and the United States to the Parliamentary Council in Bonn,' BAK, Z 35/507.
38 'Agreement as to Tripartite Controls,' BAK, Z 35/507.
39 See Geller, *Jews in Post-Holocaust Germany*, 58.
40 Louis Barish, 'Preliminary Survey of Jewish Communities in Germany,' HICOG, *Conference on the Future of the Jews*, 7, 8.
41 'Discussion,' ibid., 31.
42 Ibid.
43 Ibid., 31.
44 Even the most outspoken supporters of the maintenance of Jewish communities in Germany found it difficult to sustain their vision and work. Norbert Wollheim, for example, emigrated to the United States, asserting, 'German Jewry can only live on its memories, and that is not characteristic of a living community.' See Geller, *Jews in Post-Holocaust Germany*, 76.
45 'Concluding Remarks by Harry Greenstein,' HICOG, *Conference on the Future of the Jews*, 59.
46 Ibid.
47 Isaac Klein, 'Religious and Cultural Program,' ibid., 38, 41.
48 The Gestapo shut down the last Protestant Missions group in 1941. See Christopher Clark, *The Politics of Conversion: Missionary Protestantism and the Jews in Prussia, 1728–1947* (Oxford: Clarendon Press, 1995), 303.

49 John Conway, 'Protestant Mission to the Jews, 1810–1980: Ecclesiastical Imperialism or Theologcial Aberration?' *Holocaust and Genocide Studies* 1/1 (1986): 127–46.
50 German Protestant Church, 'Wort zur Judenfrage vom 8 April 1948,' in Rolf Rendtorff and Hans Hermann Henrix, eds., *Die Kirchen und das Judentum: Dokumente von 1945–1985* (Munich: Kaiser Verlag, 1988), 540.
51 See the Württemberg Society's Statement of 9 April 1946, in Wolfgang Gerlach, trans. Victoria Barnett, *And the Witnesses Were Silent: The Confessing Church and the Persecution of the Jews* (Lincoln, NB: Nebraska University Press, 2000), 227–8.
52 The July 1946 statement from the Westphalian Synod stated, 'We did not raise our voice loudly enough against the extermination of the Jews and other ostracized peoples,' ibid., 228.
53 See 'Synode der evangelisch-lutherischen Landeskirche Sachsens: Erklärung zur Schuld am jüdischen Volk,' 17–18 April 1948, in Rendtorff and Henrix, *Die Kirchen und das Judentum*, 544–5.
54 Ibid.
55 'Wort zur Judenfrage vom 8 April 1948,' in ibid., 542.
56 Letter from Asmussen to Protesant pastors, 'Israelitische Religion,' 4 Nov. 1947, Evangelisches Zentralarchiv (hereafter EZA) Collection 4/445.
57 Ibid.
58 See John Conway's comments on Asmussen in his article, 'How Shall Nations Repent? The Stuttgart Declaration of Guilt, October 1945,' *Journal of Ecclesiastical History* 38/4 (1987), 596–622.
59 Minutes from the 21 Oct. 1947 Protestant Church Council's meeting at Assenheim, EZA, Collection 4/445.
60 Frank Stern asserts that German philosemitism and antisemitism were closely related in occupied Germany. See *The Whitewashing of the Yellow Badge: Antisemitism and Philosemitism in Postwar Germany* (New York: Pergamon, 1992).
61 Letter from Brandenburg Superintendent Harder to EKD leadership Berlin, 18 Nov. 1947, EZA, Collection 4/445.
62 The International Missionary Council was established in 1921, and its Committee on the Christian Approach to the Jews – the proselytizing arm of the Council – was established in 1930, EZA, Collection 6/7290.
63 Franz Delitzsch (1813–1890) founded the Institutum Judaicum and Mission unter Israel in Germany. By 1948, Rengstorf, Professor of Theology at Münster, had succeeded in establishing a Delitzschianum at the University of Munich and, by 1949, fifteen Protestants – and one

Catholic priest – were engaged in full-time studies at the centre. See 'Kirche und Judentum' Scotland conference report (13–18 June, 1949), EZA, Collection 6/7290.

64 Karl Rengstorf, 'Eine Kirche aus Juden und Heiden,' 1948 Deutsche Evangelische Ausschuss für Dienst an Israel, 'Kirche und Judetum' conference (11–18 Oct. 1948, Darmstadt), EZA, Collection 6/7290.

65 Leo Baeck's address, 'Kirche und Judentum' (1948 conference, Darmstadt), EZA, Collection 6/7290.

66 See speeches and summaries: 'Kirche und Judentum' conferences, 27 Feb. to 3 March 1950 in Kassel, and 26 Feb. to 2 March 1951 in Düsseldorf, EZA, Collection 4/445. In the opening address at the conference in Scotland, International Missionary Council Chairman Birger Pernow admonished Protestants to follow God's guidance 'so that the evangelization of Israel may indeed come to pass.' Karl Rengstorf's speech, 'Spiritual Basis for Jewish Evangelism,' provided an update on Hebrew Christian Alliance assistance of children who had suffered under racial persecution of 'Jewish-Christians' – particularly at the bequest of Mr Hedenquist, who claimed that these 'Hebrew Christians' needed assistance as they 'were as much victimized by the Nuremberg racial laws as any out and out Jew.' EZA, Collection 6/7290.

67 See Ostmeyer, *Zwischen Schuld und Sühne*, 242, 272.

68 When asked in the 1960s why he thought the Holocaust had occurred, Grüber implied that it was because the Jews had rejected and killed the Messiah. See Richard Rubenstein's account of a meeting with Heinrich Grüber in *After Auschwitz: Radical Theology and Contemporary Judaism* (Indianapolis, IN: Bobbs-Merrill, 1966).

69 Lothar Mertens notes that of the 1,000 Jews in Mecklenburg in 1933, only 47 survived the war and returned home. The situation in Saxony was similar. For example, only 12 of Dresden's 6,000 Jews survived the war and returned to the city in 1945. *Davidstern unter Hammer und Zirkel*, 27.

70 See Bischöfe der Kölner und Paderborner Kirchenprovinz, 'Gemeinsamer Hirtenbrief: Die Ehrfurcht vor Gott und Mensch,' 29 June 1945, and Die Deutsche Bischöfe, 'Gemeinsamer Hirtenbrief nach beendetem Krieg,' 23 Aug. 1945, in *Kirche und Judentum*, 232–9.

71 See 'Deutscher Katholikentag in Mainz: "Entschliessung zur Judenfrage vom Sept. 1948,"' in *Kirche und Judentum*, 239–40. Also see Phayer, *The Catholic Church and the Holocaust*, 145.

72 Foschepoth, *Im Schatten der Vergangenheit*, 59–60.

73 *Der Morgen* was abolished by the Nazis in 1938, BAK, B 259/9.

74 'Deutsche Institut zur Psychologie und Überwindung des Antisemitismus: Die Bisherige Arbeit und die weiteren Aufgaben,' BAK, B 259/9, 3–4.

75 See letter from Müller-Claudius to Sterling Brown, 27 Aug. 1948, BAK, B 259/9.
76 See Elsbet Hoffmann's review of *Der Antisemitismus und das Deutsche Verhängnis* (Feb. 1949), BAK, B 259/9, 1.
77 Ibid., 2.
78 See Point VII: 'From the spiritual basis of Christianity, man cannot further antisemitism. [Today, however], religious instruction of all confessions is a constant flowing source of antisemitism, with its general acceptance of Salvation History, which is learned by children. [It] is a source of early education in antisemitic hatred.' Letter from Müller-Claudius to Sterling Brown, 27 Aug. 1948.
79 Ibid.
80 Foschepoth, *Im Schatten der Vergangenheit*, 167.
81 Gertrud Luckner, 'Geleitwort,' *Freiburger Rundbrief*, no.1 (1948), 1.
82 Ibid.
83 Zietlow correspondence with the Freiburg group, BAK, B 259/186. Also see, Phayer, *The Catholic Church and the Holocaust*, 191.
84 See Sterling Brown's Report (July 1951), BAK, B 259/68. Lucius Clay ordered the creation of the Societies for Christian-Jewish Cooperation, with the belief that they would serve in the broader goal of German democratization through developing a 'spiritual movement [and a] spirit of tolerance' in Germany, which he viewed as being of 'deep significance for the future.' See Clay, *Decision in Germany*, 235, 305.
85 Letter from Müller-Claudius to Sterling Brown, 27 Aug. 1948. Other correspondense reveals the interaction between Germans and foreign actors in Christian-Jewish relations. In a letter from Müller-Claudius to Carl Zietlow of the ICCJ, Müller-Claudius stated that his meeting with Zietlow in August 1948 was one of his happiest days in years, because his work was finding widespread support. Letter, 7 Nov. 1948, BAK, B 259/9.
86 See William Simpson and Ruth Weyl, *The Story of the International Council of Christians and Jews* (found at http://www.iccj.org/redaktion/upload_pdf/201102021125090.Final%20version%20ICCJ%20-%20The%20Story.pdf), 1995, 16–29, and Christian Rutishauser, 'The 1947 Seelisberg Conference: The Foundation of the Jewish-Christian Dialogue,' *Studies in Christian Jewish Relations* 2/2 (2007): 37.
87 Jacques Maritain, 'Eine Botschaft Jacques Maritain,' *Freiburger Rundbrief* 1/1 (1948): 2.
88 ICCJ, *Reports and Recommendations of the International Conference of Christians and Jews, Seelisberg* (Geneva: Author, 1947), 3

89 Rutishauser, 'The 1947 Seelisberg Conference,' 34–53.
90 ICCJ, *Reports and Recommendations*, 3.
91 Ibid., 6.
92 Brown's Report (July 1951), 1.
93 Ibid.
94 Ibid., 4.
95 Ibid., 5. Also see 'Im Anfang: München,' *Zusammenarbeit* no. 1 (1949): 10, BAK, B 106/38.
96 Societies would be established in the French and British zones beginning in 1950. See Foschepoth, *Im Schatten der Vergangenheit*, 244–6.
97 See 'Praeambel,' *Zusammenarbeit*, no. 1 (1949), BAK, B 106/38.
98 Ibid., 20.
99 Ibid. Germans expressed desire to achieve financial self-sufficiency. One society member stated: 'We owe this obligation to ourselves and to our own country in its struggle to develop a democratic way of life.' Brown's Report, 11.
100 'Praeambel,' *Zusammenarbeit*, no. 1: 22.
101 See Foschepoth, *Im Schatten der Vergangenheit*, 207.
102 Report of the Coordinating Council at Bad Neuheim, which stated, 'One finds also in Germany, people [from all walks of life who] decided to push for and support the German drive for the societies,' i, 14, BAK, B 259/193.
103 Knuden's invitations found in BAK, B259/192. Also see HICOG Report on Munich Conference (May 1949), BAK, B 259/188.
104 See Norbert Wollheim's reply to Knudsen upon receipt of the invitation, BAK, B 259/192.
105 Dr Lichtenstein's speech, 'Antisemitismus: Eine Frage an uns' (1949), BAK, B259/67, 1–2.
106 Ibid., 3–4.
107 Ibid., 4.
108 The same reminder was expressed by Alfred Meyer of the Wiesbaden society when he stated, 'The terrible things that happened to us during and after the war shall be the basis for our present understanding and our common work,' BAK, B 259/188.
109 Hans Joachim Schoeps' speech at Munich (30 May 1949), BAK, B 259/188, 1.
110 Ibid.
111 Ibid., 2.
112 For example, at a World Brotherhood meeting in July 1951, Berlin Rabbi Freier's speech focused on the 'brotherhood of Christ,' which included both Christians and Jews, BAK, B 259/238.

113 Hans Joachim Schoeps, *The Jewish-Christian Argument: A History of Theologies in Conflict*, trans. David Green (London: Faber and Faber, 1963 [German 1st ed., 1937]), 5.
114 Schoeps' Speech, 30 May 1949, 5–6.
115 HICOG Report on Munich Conference (May 1949), BAK, B 259/129.
116 Ibid., 6–17.
117 Ibid., 4.
118 Ibid., 5.
119 Ibid.
120 German press reports on Munich 1949, see *Die Neue Zeitung*, 2 June 1949, articles, 'Für reine Luft' and 'Versuch Christlich-Jüdischer Verständigung.' The latter claimed that 'democracy begins in the schools' and that 'clean air is where men can be with each other and to understand each other and to fight the animal within and to bring peace.'
121 Heuss' address was given to hundreds of attendees, including German professors and deans of universities in Hesse; the Hessian cabinet; representatives from business and labour groups; Protestant and Catholic bishops; the laity; rabbis; and HICOG Commissioner John McCloy and representatives of OMGUS Religious Affairs Branch. Moreover, it was broadcast live on German radio and was a major story in German newspapers the following day,
122 President T. Heuss' speech, 'Mut zur Liebe,' Wiesbaden Gesellschaft für christlich-jüdische Zusammenarbeit, 7 Dec. 1949, BAK, B 259/ 67, 2.
123 Ibid., 3.
124 Ibid.
125 See HICOG, *Conference on the Future of the Jews*, 29, and Geller, *Jews in Post-Holocaust Germany*, 207, 218, 224.
126 Quoted in Michael Brenner, *After the Holocaust: Rebuilding Jewish Lives in Postwar Germany* (Princeton, NJ: Princeton University Press, 1997), 109–10.
127 Brown reported that Germans were more preoccupied with the following: the withdrawal of Russian troops from Germany, issues of German participation in European defence, a desire to participate in the international arena in politics, and otherwise, concerns over the costs of Allied occupation, and their own misfortunes. See Brown Report, BAK, B 259/68.
128 See HICOG, *Conference on the Future of the Jews*, 7–8.
129 See Geller, *Jews in Post-Holocaust Germany*, 174. Also see Leon Löwenkopf's essay, 'Die Juden in der DDR,' CJA, 5Bl:50, and the SED

Zentrale Parteikontollkommission's (ZPKK) 1948 campaign against Jews, especially Mr Katten, Julius Meyer, and Paul Merker, SAPMO, DY 30/ IV 2/4/404.

4. Broadening International Contacts and Reconciliation Work

1 Quoted in Gabriel Marcel, ed., trans. Helen Hardinge, *Fresh Hope for the World: Moral Re-Armament in Action* (London: Longmans and Green, 1960), 24.
2 Laure's 1947 speech at Caux, quoted in ibid.
3 Ibid.
4 Lean, *On the Tail of a Comet*, 353.
5 Furthermore, Schuman claimed: 'What MRA brings us is a philosophy of life applied in action ... it is not a question of a change of policy, it is a questions of changing men. Democracy and her freedoms can be saved only by the quality of the men who speak in her name.' Robert Schuman, 'Preface,' in Frank Buchman, *Remaking the World* (London: Blandford, 1961).
6 'Adenauer Calls MRA World's Hope,' *New York Journal-American*, 31 Jan. 1960, 1.
7 Dr Vogel of the Office for Peace Questions garnered information from a journalist at the *Neue Züricher Zeitung*, who had learned – via personal interviews – the current positions of top Allied personnel. Accordingly, Vogel encouraged Germans to affect change in their occupiers by mingling with them at social gatherings. See 'Wandlungen in der britischen Deutschlandpolitik widerstrebende Tendenzen im Lager der Alliierten,' 11 Nov. 1948. BAK, B 120/331, 5.
8 The lack of popularity for pacifist groups is consistent in additional examples beyond the ones mentioned here. This is evident in the case of the German League for Human Rights, established during the Weimar era. When the founders re-emerged after 1945, trumpeting the pacifism they had espoused prior to 1933, they were shunned by the newer members, who embraced a tough stance against Communism, and who found support from the Allies. See Lora Wildenthal, 'Human Rights Activism in Occupied Germany and Early West Germany: The Case of the German League for Human Rights,' *Journal of Modern History* 8 (Summer 2008): 515–16.
9 In August 1914, Protestants formed at Constance the World Alliance for Promoting International Friendship through the Churches, with its central office in Berlin. See Eberhard Bethge, *Dietrich Bonhoeffer*

(New York: Harper and Row, 1970), 146. See also John Conway, 'Resisting Militarism: The Peace Movement in the German Evangelical Church during the Weimar Republic,' Kirchliche Zeitgeschichte 4/1 (1991): 29–45.

10 Marian Parmoor was a very active peace advocate, and served as president of the British National Peace Council and president of the British Section of the Women's International League for Peace and Freedom. Her husband, Lord Charles Cripps, First Baron of Parmoor, founded and chaired the Fight the Famine Council. See Sybil Oldfield, 'England's Cassandras in World War One,' in Sybil Oldfield, ed., *This Working-Day World: Women's Lives and Cultures in Britain, 1914–1945* (Bristol, PA: Taylor and Francis, 1994), 100.

11 Marian Parmoor, 'Problems of Peacemaking,' *Fellowship Quarterly Newsletter* 44 (Nov. 1944), EZA, Collection 626/205, 1.

12 Ibid.

13 Ibid.

14 One Fellowship member wrote, 'a new policy of aggression on Germany's part can be effectively prevented [but] opportunities [must be] afforded the German people for spiritual and material recovery and for their peaceful contribution to European and world development.' Author Unknown, 'Of the Coming Peace,' *Fellowship Quarterly Newsletter* 46 (March 1945), EZA, Collection 626/205, 1.

15 'The Treatment of Germany,' *Fellowship Quarterly Newsletter* 46 (March 1945), EZA, Collection 626/205, 2.

16 Friedrich Siegmund-Schultze claimed that the Nazis had forcibly conquered the will of the German people and that efforts of 'courageous leaders during the war were sure to fail.' 'Religious Life in Germany,' *Fellowship Quarterly Newsletter* 48 (Sept. 1945), EZA, Collection 626/205.

17 Ibid.

18 In June 1945, Henry Rosser claimed that the Fellowship's ideals had acted as 'a preservative against the temptations of despair and hatred ... and a calm retreat for the heart,' for him in prison. For Rosser, the message of peace and the unified support of others in the Fellowship organization contributed to his cultivation of a peace-minded approach to conflict even in the face of injustice and suffering. See Versöhnungsbund Korrespondenz, 1946–1958, EZA, Collection 626/191.

19 According to Trocmé, the German Pastors Iwand and Niemöller were 'preoccupied with problem of non-violence [which was of the] greatest importance for the future of our ideas in Germany, and perhaps the world,'

Letter from André Trocmé to German Fellowship, Lydia Fluegge, 5 June 1948, EZA, Collection 626/191.
20 'Zweck des Vereins,' Official Fellowship Document from Untersekretariat des Versöhnungsbunds (1948), EZA 626/180.
21 Fellowship Document, 'An Order of Peacemakers,' 1949, EZA, Collection 626/180.
22 Ibid.
23 Ibid.
24 Lydia Flügge, 'Den Kasseler Freunden des Versöhnungsbundes: Zum Nachdenken und zur Anregung,' Oct. 1948, BAK, B 259/89, 1-2.
25 Letter from Lydia Flügge to the German Fellowship, 6 June 1949, BAK, B 259/89, 2. Regular Fellowship meetings took place in Germany beginning in 1947. Like Flügge in Kassel, Sigrid Klinghammer invited Carl Zietlow to join their meetings in Berlin, which he did. See letter from Klinghammer to Zietlow, 10 March 1948, and Zietlow's written response, 11 April 1949, BAK, B 259/89.
26 The Fellowship's work was recognized and supported by the World Council of Churches and the United Nations. See Christa Stache, *Das EZA in Berlin und Seine Bestände* (Berlin: Alektor, 1992), 1.
27 Letter from WCC, Department of Reconstruction and Inter-Church Aid to General Dwight Eisenhower and Staff, 6 Nov. 1945 (signed: Sylvester Michelfelder, Stewart Herman, James Hutchison Cockburn), ADW, ZB 331.
28 See Bell, *Christianity and World Order*, 105–6, quoted in Raina, *Bishop George Bell*, 229.
29 When giving the address at Bonhoeffer's memorial service at Holy Trinity Church, on 27 July 1945, Bell stated, 'His death is a death for Germany – indeed for Europe too ... for him ... there is the resurrection of the dead; for Germany redemption and resurrection, if God pleases to lead the nation through men animated by His spirit, holy and humble and brave like Him ... [there is] hope of a new life.' Eberhard Bethge, *Bonhoeffer Gedenkheft* (Berlin, unpublished paper, 1947), quoted in Eberhard Bethge, *Dietrich Bonhoeffer*, 834.
30 Ibid.
31 See Martin Niemöller's statement, Erste Vollversammlung des Ökumenischen Rates der Kirchen in Amsterdam 1948, ADW, ZBB 1460A.
32 Eugen Gerstenmaier, 'Was sagt uns Amsterdam?' *Mitteilungen aus dem Hilfswerk der Evangelischen Kirche in Deutschland* 19 (Oct. 1948): 1.
33 Ibid.
34 Ibid.
35 Ibid.

36 Report from Bishop Horning of Görlitz (in the Soviet zone), on the Amsterdam meeting, 28 Sept. 1948, ADW, ZB 85.
37 Gerstenmaier, 'Was sagt uns Amsterdam?' 2.
38 Ibid., 3.
39 See Französisch-Deutsche Kirchentagung September 1948, ADW, ZB 840.
40 The WCC's Inter-Church Aid Work Budget offered 3,634,806.61 SFr in aid to Europe, of which Germany received 1,742,515.89 SFr. WCC financial report 1949, Appendix IV, 12, ADW, ZB 338.
41 Letter from Gerstenmaier to Elfan Rees, Department of Reconstruction and Inter-Church Aid, WCC Refugee Division, Geneva, 16 May 1949, ADW, ZB 1.
42 Pax Christi – Deutsches Sekretariat, ed., *Rundbrief der Bistumsstelle Rottenburg-Stuttgart: Sonderausgabe, 50 Jahre Pax Christi Rottenburg-Stuttgart, 1948–1998* (Bad Vilbel: Pax Christi, 1998), 3.
43 Quoted in http://www.paxchristi.net/about/html/history.html.
44 Manfred Hörhammer, 'Die Idee von Pax Christi,' in *Pax Christi: Kevelaer 1948–1988: Die Anfänge der Pax-Christi-Bewegung in Deutschland* (Kevelaer: Butzon und Berger, 1988), 10. Catholic prisoners in Dachau were also part of the prayer campaign. In 1944 Germans, Poles, Italians, Czechs – priests and laypeople – prayed together and held Mass in the camp. Henri Ferrers, 'Deutsche Priester in Dachau,' *Pax Christi: Zeitschrift des Gebetskreuzzuges für die Nationen* 1/3 (1949): 30–2.
45 Hörhammer, 'Die Idee von Pax Christi,' 8.
46 Karl Grüner, 'Das Zugabteil war seine Klosterzelle,' in *Münchner Kirchenzeitung* (27 Nov. 2005): 13.
47 Manfred Hörhammer, 'Pionierarbeit in den ersten Jahren,' *Pax Christi* 10 (1973), 9.
48 Kevelaer and Lourdes were universally recognized pilgrimage sites, after papal acknowledgment of Marian apparitions at both locations. See Josef Heckens, 'Kreuz-Weg,' in *Pax Christi: Kevelaer 1948–1988*, 47.
49 Franz Bardua, 'Was ist und was will die Pax-Christi Bewegung?' Speech given to Una Sancta group in Stuttgart, 19 Sept. 1949, in Pax Christi, *Rundbrief* 9, 1949.
50 Bishop Pierre-Maria Théas, 'Der Bruderhand des christlichen Frankreichs' (Ansprache von Bishop Pierre-MarieThéas vom 4 April 1948 in Kevelaer), in *Pax Christi: Kevelaer 1948–1988*, 22.
51 Ibid., 24.
52 Ibid, 26.
53 Bishops from the British and French zone who were in attendance included: Cardinal Frings, Cologne; Bishop Keller, Münster; Bishop

van der Velden, Aachen; and a representative of the Bishop of Trier. Other bishops in attendance included Lourdes' Bishop Théas; Cardinal Aloisius Muench from the United States; Dutch Bishop Lemmons from Roermond; and a representative of the Bishop of Luxembourg. *Rheinische Post*, 7 April 1948, '1. Internationaler Pax-Christi – Kongress in Kevelaer, 1948,' in *Pax Christi: Kevelaer 1948–1988*, 16.

54 Ibid., 18.
55 Ibid.
56 The tendency of Muench, Frings, and other Catholic leaders to side-step German responsibility for Nazism while promoting German interests is well documented. See Brown-Fleming, *The Holocaust and Catholic Conscience*, and Cardinal Frings, *Post-Defeat Pastoral Letter of the Archbishop of Cologne*, SHU Box 2, UNDA. Moreover, Cardinal Frings was outspoken in his repeated condemnation of the Allied-ordered expulsion of ethnic Germans from Eastern Europe. See, e.g., 'Kardinal Frings an die Ostvertriebenen: Protest gegen das Unrecht der Vertreibung,' *Christ Unterwegs* 2/12 (1948): 3–4.
57 Joseph Probst, 'Bischof Théas in Trier,' *Pax Christi: Zeitschrift des Gebetskreuzzuges für die Nationen* 1/2 (1949): 17.
58 Hörhammer's address, Pax Christi Archives (hereafter PCA), Folder 1/6.
59 Théas, 'Der Bruderhand,' 24.
60 'Weisser Sonntag in Kevelaer,' PCA, Folder 1/6, 1,3.
61 Théas, 'Der Bruderhand,' 33.
62 *Pax Christi: Zeitschrift des Gebetskreuzzuges für die Nationen* 1/1 (1949): 1.
63 Bishop Théas maintained at Lourdes his emphasis on the fact that all of humanity – not just the German people – had sinned and that 'we all bear the blame for it, and are answerable for it.' 'Eröffnungsansprache des Hochwürdigsten Herrn Bischofs von Tarbes und Lourdes bei der internationalen Wallfahrt am 26. Juli 1948,' ibid., 12.
64 'Ansprache von Kardinal Frings in der Rosenkranzbasilika,' ibid., 44.
65 'Die Kranken als Friedensboten auf der internationalen Wallfahrt,' ibid., 3–4.
66 'Hirtenbrief des Hochwürdigsten Herrn Bischofs von Tarbes und Lordes gelegentlich der erstern internationalen Wallfahrt zu unserer lieben Frau von Lourdes,' ibid., 5, 8.
67 Ibid., 1, 9–10, 11.
68 'Gebetskreuzzug für die Nationen,' ibid., 1, 55.
69 In late 1948, the pontiff admonished Catholics to emerge out of their 'self-interest and comfortable isolation' to serve Displaced Persons and to

engage in general 'acts of strength' that would oppose 'war and imperialism' in the world. 'Die Päpste und der Friede: Die Christen Wille zum Frieden,' *Pax Christi: Zeitschrift des Gebetskreuzzuges für die Nationen* 1/3 (1949): 1,4.
70 L.A. Boumard, 'Die französisch-deutsche Begegnung von Royaumont,' ibid., 40.
71 Dr Herder-Dorneich, 'Wört an die Brüder in Aller Welt,' *Pax Christi: Zeitschrift des Gebetskreuzzuges für die Nationen* 1/2 (1949).
72 'Ansprache des P. Manfred Hörhammer,' ibid., 49.
73 Manfred Hörhammer, 'Pax Christi – Herz der Welt!' PCA, Folder Ifd. 2/15 Nachlass Pater Hörhammer, 1
74 Pierre Lorson, 'International Begegnungen und Weltfrieden,' *Pax Christi: Zeitschrift des Gebetskreuzzuges für die Nationen* 1/3 (1949): 37.
75 Manfred Hörhammer, 'Kirche und Welt,' Speech at Oropa Conference, 3 May 1949, PCA, Folder 2/15, 4.
76 Ibid., 5.
77 Ibid.
78 Archbishop Feltin von Bordeaux, 'Die Rolle des Laien in der Kirche,' *Pax Christi: Zeitschrift des Gebetskreuzzuges für die Nationen* 1/2 (1949): 46.
79 Garth Lean describes the growing rivalry over political loyalties at universities, seen in the establishment of Communist student groups, such as the October Club at Oxford in 1932, and the Oxford Group, established formally in 1930. See *On the Tail of a Comet*, 154; for a more detailed description of the establishment of the Oxford Group, see 109–62.
80 Daniel Sack, *Moral Rearmament: The Reinventions of an American Religious Movement* (London: Palgrave), 2–5.
81 Ibid., 152.
82 Lean, *On the Tail of a Comet*, 234.
83 Pierre Spoerri, interviewed by author, 24 Feb. 2005 (hereafter Spoerri interview). See also, 1998 speech given by Pierre Spoerri at the Initiatives of Change International Centre at Caux, Switzerland, 'Frank Buchman and His Philosophy of Reconciliation,' Archives Cantonales Vaudoises (hereafter ACV), PP 746/2.1/951, 5–8.
84 Sack, *Moral Rearmament*, 153.
85 Buchman, *Remaking the World*, 220, 204.
86 For information on the personal financial donations of thousands of supporters of MRA, see Robert Hahnloser, *How Caux Is Financed*, 1949, ACV, PP 746/2.1/388.

87 Gabriele Müller-List, 'Eine neue Moral für Deutschland? Bewegung für Moralische Aufrüstung und ihre Bedeutung beim Wiederaufbau, 1947–1952,' *Das Parliament*, 31 Oct. 1981, 3, ACV, PP 746/5.2.3/2. Spoerri explained how Germans required the consent of Paris, London, and Washington to attend MRA meetings, and explained how a French Army chaplain secured permits for Germans to attend meetings at Caux in 1946. Spoerri interview.
88 Georg Eastman, *Report from Europe, 1948*, ACV, PP 746/2.1/288, 28–9.
89 Lean, *On the Tail of a Comet*, 349–50. Also see Eastman, *Report from Europe*, 19.
90 Buchman, *Remaking the World*, 301.
91 George Shuster, *Adenauer and Moral Re-Armament*, 10 April 1972, 2–3, SHU, 2/07, UNDA.
92 Eastman, *Report from Europe*, 19.
93 Buchman, *Remaking the World*, 216–17.
94 Ibid., 218.
95 Irene Laure, 'A Socialist Welcomes the World,' in Marcel, *Fresh Hope for the World*, 25.
96 Philippe Mottu, 'The Story of Caux from La Belle Epoque to MRA,' ACV, PP 746/2.1/726, 113.
97 Eastman, *Report from Europe*, 19.
98 Spoerri stated that 'Most [Germans wanted to make amends], nearly all; I met only a very few with closed hearts.' Spoerri interview.
99 Spoerri Interview.
100 Lean, *On the Tail of a Comet*, 356.
101 Mottu, 'The Story of Caux,' 114–15. Pierre Spoerri was part of the tour groups, and can attest to the impact that the tour, and the plays, had in Germany. On the tour, the victims of Nazism – including Jewish, French, Swiss, and British MRA members – brought the message of forgiveness and hope to the vanquished German people. Spoerri himself was directly involved with Germans on the tours, meeting all of Adenauer's future cabinet members – and being billetted in their homes – and befriending Adenauer's son. He was also very involved with Germans who came to Caux. For instance, he roomed with Peter Peterson in 1947 and described his job as being to 'listen, translate, and encourage.' Spoerri interview.
102 Mottu, 'The Story of Caux,' 116.
103 Quoted in Lean, *On the Tail of a Comet*, 357.
104 Spoerri interview.
105 For Lukaschek's views on civil rights in Germany, see conversation recorded between Lukaschek and the mayor of Düsseldorf, Mr Gockeln,

found in Rupieper, 'Der Bund für Bürgerrechte,' 96. Lukaschek was instrumental in drafting the co-determination law, or equalization law, which introduced into Germany a scheme in which people with resources shared part of their income with those in dire need. Also see Buchman, *Remaking the World*, 304.

106 'Moralische Aufrüstung: Das deutsche Echo auf Caux' (1947), ACV, PP 746/2.1/1247.
107 Eastman, *Report from Europe*, 21.
108 Lean, *On the Tail of a Comet*, 351.
109 For example, eight German minister-presidents extolled MRA, in 1948, in a collective statement sent to Frank Buchman. They asssserted: 'Germany is ready for your message ... the spirit of genuine unselfish love of one's fellowman is what is needed to bring Germany through her present distress and lead her to a better future. Moreover, the ideology of MRA is an indispensable foundation for the reconstruction and peace of Europe and the world.' Letter from Karl Arnold, Hans Ehard, Heinrich Kopf, Dr Luedemann, Reinhold Maier, Werner Hilpert, W. Kaisen, and Max Brauer, in Buchman, *Remaking the World*, 322–3.
110 Mottu, 'The Story of Caux,' 114. For more information on Adenauer's endorsement of MRA, see ACV, PP 746/2.1/6; see letter from Adenauer to Buchman, 22 Sept. 1948. Also see Eastman, *Report from Europe*, 24.
111 Mottu, 'The Story of Caux,' 113–14.
112 Schuman cabled Buchman on his 70th birthday in 1948, with this message: 'Inside nations people are seeking the reconciliation of liberty with authority and an understanding between the classes. I salute in moral rearmament one of the animating forces at work for inspired democracy which must reestablish the supremacy of all the spiritual values at the heat of our tormented humanity.' Buchman, *Remaking the World*, 321.
113 'Schuman an Deutschland: Alle Nationen sind Schicksalsverbunden,' *Badische Zeitung*, 13 Jan. 1949. See also 'Schuman zur Deutschland-Politik der Alliierten: Er erklärt: Der genesende Schwerkranke ist reizbar und ungeduldig,' *Frankfurter Neue Presse*, 13 Jan. 1949, and 'Kein Gedanke an Rache und Vergeltung: Aussenminister Schuman über Frankreichs Deutschlandpolitik,' *Schwäbisches Tagblatt*, 15 Jan. 1949.
114 An American journalist in Paris observed that 'fears in [France] about the future of the productive giant across the Rhine have not been put to rest by the recent London statute for control of the Ruhr or by the restatement in the six-power communiqué that Germany's steel production would be limited.' *New York Herald Tribune*, 17 Jan. 1949.

115 'Die deutsche Frage in Washington: Entscheidende Diskussionen über das Besatzungsstatut und Bonn,' 4 April 1949. Stuttgart, Document reporting on North Atlantic Pact, BAK, B 120/332.
116 See 'Deutschland und England,' *Die Tat*, Zürich, no. 264, 26 Sept. 1949, BAK, B 120/331, 5.
117 'Die deutsche Frage,' 6.
118 Sack, *Moral Rearmament*, 158.
119 Spoerri interview.
120 See SED document drafted by Dr Gerhard Buchmann in Wolbeck, 13 May 1948, ACV, PP 746/2.1.9. Frank Buchman made some controversial remarks about Hitler and fascists in general during the 1930s, celebrating their anti-communism. For instance, in an interview in New York in 1936, Buchman said, 'I thank heaven for a man like Adolf Hitler, who built a front line of defense against the anti-Christ of Communism.' See Lean, *On the Tail of a Comet*, 239.
121 Tony Judt addresses this point – and the study of reconciliation in Eastern Europe after 1945 – when he states, 'If the satellite countries of the Soviet bloc engaged in international cooperation superficially comparable to developments further west, this was only because Moscow imposed 'fraternal' institutions and exchanges upon them by force.' *Postwar Postwar: A History of Europe since 1945* (New York: Penguin, 2005), 5.
122 Peter Monteath, 'Organizing Antifascism: The Obscure History of the VVN,' *European History Quarterly* 29 (1999): 289, 294.
123 'Programm der VVN,' SAPMO, DY55 278/1/1.
124 'Erste Interzonale Länderkonferenz der VVN, 15–17, März 1947 in Frankfurt am Main – Referat Karl Raddatz,' SAPMO, DY 55/V 278/2/3, 20.
125 Zweite Sitzung des Zentralvorstandes der VVN für die SBZ Deutschlands, 30 March 1947, Berlin, Statistisches Amt, Klosterstrasse, SAPMO, DY 55 278/1/1.
126 Document written by Pastor Gabriel, SAPMO, DY 55 278/1/1.
127 Pamphlet, 'Sonderrundschreiben an alle Ortsgruppen der VVN in der SBZ,' March 1947, written by Karl Raddatz, 1. Found in Bibliothek, Bundesarchiv Berlin.
128 Ausstellung, 'Das Andere Deutschland: Eine Schau der deutschen Widerstandsbewegung gegen das Naziregime.' Details of the exhibit's tour dates and attendance records are as follows: Berlin, 2 Sept. to 31 Oct. 1948 (33,934); Dresden, 1–10 June 1949 (25,828); Leipzig, 26 March to 9 April 1949 (34,567); Halle, 15 Jan. to 13 Feb. 1949 (28,090); Erfurt/Weimar, 5 Aug. to 25 Sept. 1949 (22,376); Schwerin/Rostock, 5–14 Nov. 1949 (5,298). See SAPMO, DY 55/V 278/2/9–10.

129 See the 1947 correspondence between international groups and Germans, in which non-German victims of Nazism initiated the plans for a Berlin meeting in 1948. SAPMO, DY 55/V 278/2/3.
130 Correspondence between Germans and Colonel Manhes, president of Federation Internationales des Anciens Prisonniers Politiques du Facisme, and General Secretary Maurice Lambe in France, 1948. SAPMO, DY 55/V 278/2/3.
131 Warsaw Meeting, 18 Jan. 1949, SAPMO, DY 55/V 278/2/3.
132 The Federation's Manifesto of 14 Jan. 1949 demanded that 2,000 FF be awarded to each person for each month that person was in prison; 10,000 FF for lost property, and considerable sums for widows and orphans. See SAPMO, DY 55/V 278/2/3.
133 Edward Kowalski reported on the Berlin meeting that included the VVN; the Federation; representatives of the Polish Association of Former Prisoners; the National Association of Italian Anti-Fascist Political Prisoners; and the National Association of Austrian Prisoners and Political Persecutees. The organizations viewed the remilitarization of Western Germany as threatening to peace, and to people who continued to bear the wounds of Nazi persecution. See Berlin Meeting, 11 May 1949, 'VVN Funktionärkonferenz,' SAPMO, DY 55/V 278/2/3.
134 'Delegationsaustausch der DDR mit anderen Ländern' and 'Beratungen, Konferenzen und Tagungen in der DDR mit internationaler Beteiligung nach 1948,' SAPMO, DY 30/IV 2/20/60.
135 'Zum 10. Jahrestag des Überfalls auf Polen,' 1, SAPMO, DY 30/IV 2/20/155.
136 Ibid., 1–2.
137 Ibid., 2.
138 Ibid., 4.
139 Ibid., 6.
140 Ibid.
141 Naimark, *The Russians in Germany*, 416. For further reading on the enforcement of this German-Soviet 'friendship' via the society, see Jan Behrends, *Die erfundene Freundschaft: Propaganda für die Sowjetunion in Polen und in der DDR* (Cologne: Bohlau, 2006).
142 Naimark, *The Russians in Germany*, 416.
143 One German author longed to have the work of the society establish itself in Halle in order to garner more library resources from the Soviet Union, and in order for German and Soviet academics to become more actively involved in academic exchange programs. 'Gesellschaft für

deutsch-sowjetische Freundschaft,' 1948 letter, Martin-Luther Universität, Halle, BAK, B 137/1353.

144 'Das ist Wahre Freundschaft – Durch die Senkung der Reparationen schenkt die sowjetunion jedem Bürger DDR – 450 DM,' 3. Found in Bibliothek, Bundesarchiv Berlin.

145 Mary Fulbrook asserts, 'The USSR was extracting huge reparations from its zone (Saxony). At first, machinery and stock was simply removed to the USSR; when this proved inefficient, certain enterprises within the USSR were taken into Soviet ownership as Soviet Joint Stock Companies (SAGs) and their profits appropriated. See *A Concise History of Germany* (Cambridge: Cambridge University Press, 1990), 207.

146 'Das ist Wahre Freundschaft,' 5, 6.

147 Ibid., Appendix: 'An den Vorsitzenden des Ministerrates der UdSSR, Generalissimus J.W. Stalin,' from O. Grotewohl.

5. The Politics of Reconciliation in the Two Germanies, 1949–1954

1 German banker Hermann Abs and West German Finance Minister Fritz Schäffer prioritized German debts accrued during the Third Reich over reparations payments to the Jews. Geller, *Jews in Post-Holocaust Germany*, 233–4.

2 Ibid., 235.

3 Kuster's radio speech, titled 'Von Tag zu Tag,' aired on Süddeutsche Rundfunk; excerpts from it are included in the article, 'Schwere Beschuldigungen gegen Bonn,' *Allgemeine Wochenzeitung der Juden in Deutschland*, 11 April 1952, 1.

4 Ibid.

5 Geller, *Jews in Post-Holocaust Germany*, 236.

6 'Deutsche Angebot,' *Allgemeine Wochenzeitung der Juden in Deutschland*, 20 June 1952, 1.

7 'Die Unterzeichnung in Luxembourg,' *Allgemeine Wochenzeitung der Juden in Deutschland*, 12 Sept. 1952, 1.

8 See 'Re-Awakening in Germany?' *Economist*, 30 July 1949.

9 Brian Colonnell, 'The Ingratitude of Germany,' *Continental Daily Mail*, 20 July 1949.

10 'Germany Today like Yesterday,' *Témoignage Chrétien*, 12 Aug. 1949.

11 'The Failure of Allied Policy in Germany,' *New Statesman and Nation*, 27 Aug. 1949.

12 Herf, *Divided Memory*, 3.

13 'So That We Do Not Forget,' *Continental Daily Mail*, 2 Aug. 1949.

14 'Germany Today like Yesterday.' See also Maurice Duverger, 'Die Notwendigkeit deutsch-französischer Zusammenarbeit,' *Le Monde*, 17 Nov. 1948.
15 Naimark, *The Russians in Germany*, 10–11.
16 See letter from Otto Dibelius to Wilhelm Pieck, in which Dibelius chastises Pieck for claiming his legitimacy as GDR president. Similar attitudes appear in other correspondence. See letter from Dibelius to Pieck, 13 Oct. 1949, BAK, N 1439/7, 1, and conversation between Otto Grotewohl, Otto Dibelius, and Heinrich Grüber, 24 March 1950, BAK, N 1439/8.
17 The first postwar Kirchentag was held in Hanover, in 1949, with the theme, 'Kirche in Bewegung.' For details on this meeting, and the difficulties for churchmen to travel over the East-West boundary, see EZA, Bestand 104. See also, 'Kirchenfeindliche Aktion der "DDR": Interzonenpässe für Kirchentagungen verweigert,' *Tagesspiegel*, 19 July 1952.
18 For instance, when Thadden-Trieglaff addressed the all-German meeting at the Olympic Stadium in Berlin in 1951, he claimed that 'we have not gathered here to proclaim a political pilgrimage because it is not the duty of the church to align itself with a worldly political system,' but then went on to clarify that 'it is the cross of Christ, in this divided city, that binds our brothers in east and west ... [and] we remain brothers in spite of the borders.' Reinhold von Thadden-Trieglaff, 'Im Olympia-Stadion,' *Wir Sind doch Brüder, Berlin, 1951: Der Deutsche Evangelische Kirchentag in Wort und Bild*, Conway Collection, BX 4844 G489 1997 File 2, 90–1.
19 'Weil sie Faschisten waren? Hunderttausende Getötete quälen das Gewissen der Belgrader Machthaber,' *Christ Unterwegs* 3/3 (1949): 6–11.
20 See, e.g., 'Wir dürfen heim! Südtirol ruft seine geliebten Söhne zurück,' *Christ Unterwegs* 3/4 (1949), and 'Vom kirchlichen Leben in der alten Heimat: Die Lage des polnischen Katholizismus' and 'Wie sieht es "drüben" aus?' *Christ Unterwegs* 3/5 (1949): 20, 23.
21 See, e.g., 'Von Potsdam und Nürnberg zum Vereinten Europa: Gedanken über die Austreibung der ostdeutschen Bevölkerung,' *Christ Unterwegs* 3/8 (1949): 12–15. See also, 'Zwischen den Parteien: Um die politische Eingliederung der Ostvertriebenen,' which guided expellees politically regarding the next election. *Christ Unterwegs* 3/11 (1949): 9.
22 Eugen Gerstenmaier, 'Unsere Christliche Verantwortung für Europa,' Rede auf dem Deutschen Evangelischen Kirchentag in Essen, 25 August 1950, in *Eugen Gerstenmaier: Reden und Aufsätze*, 171, 166–7.

23 Eugen Gerstenmaier, 'Rede zur Beendigung der Entnazifizierung,' Rede auf dem 40. Sitzung des I. Deutsches Bundestages, Bonn, 23 Feb. 1950, in *Eugen Gerstenmaier: Reden und Aufsätze*, 154–5, 160.
24 Gerstenmaier, 'Unsere Christliche Verantwortung,' 175. The Protestant Relief Work's periodical, *Das Hilfswerk*, printed numerous articles after 1949 extolling German unification. See 'Vor polnischen und tschechischen Gerichten: Aus der Arbeit der Rechtsschutzstelle des Hilfswerk,' *Das Hilfswerk* 57 (Dec. 1951): 8; 'Dank aus dem Osten,' *Das Hilfswerk* 58 (Jan. 1952): 4; 'Unser Hilfswerk in der Ostzone: Wachsendes diakonisches Bewußtsein,' ibid.; and, Christian Berg, '"Oekumenische Hilfe" – das Rückgrat unserer Arbeit,' ibid., 5.
25 See 'London Documents,' 1 July 1948, and 'Charter of the Allied High Commission for Germany,' 20 June 1949, in von Oppen, *Documents on Germany under Occupation, 1945–1954*, 315–18 and 398–406, respectively.
26 Jeffrey Herf claims that 'Adenauer quoted an unnamed "very influential American" official who had told him that a West German agreement with Israel and with Jewish organizations would be a "political event that can be placed in the same league with" the treaties establishing West Germany's sovereignty.' *Divided Memory*, 286. Here, Herf cites Adenauer, '6. September 1952: Anspruch vor dem Bundesparteiausschuss der CDU in Bonn (Bundeshaus),' in Hans-Peter Schwarz, *Konrad Adenauer: Reden 1917–1967* (Stuttgart: Deutsche Verlages-Anstalt, 1975), 267.
27 Thomas Dehler's speech to the Bundestag on 4 Nov. 1950, 'Rückerstattungsgesetz Nr. 59,' BAK, B 136/1124, 1.
28 Ibid.
29 Henry Friedlander, *The Origins of Nazi Genocide: From Euthanasia to the Final Solution* (Chapel Hill, NC: University of North Carolina Press, 1995), 18, 30, 253–4.
30 Dr Redecker's internal memo of 2 Jan. 1951, 'Bundesministerium des Justiz, im Hause: Wiedergutmachung von Sterilisierten,' BAK, B 106/62728. The Bundesentschädigungsgesetz also included compensation for illegal sterilizations, following the 1948 Hessian Law Nr. 2/208. See 'Das Hessische Staatsministerium des Innern, Abt. IX, Wiedergutmachung Durchführungsverordnung über die Bildung und das Verfahren der Betreuungsstellen für Verfolgte in Hessen,' Wiesbaden, 13 May 1948, BAK, B 106/62728.
31 See letter from Otto Krakau to Bundesministerium des Innern, Bonn, 14 Aug. 1951, regarding 'Entschädigung für Sterilisation aus

rassischen Gründen während des NS-Regimes.' Krakau claimed that his Jewish brother-in-law, Arthur Wolff, was ordered to divorce his Jewish wife in 1942. After he refused, Wolff was sterilized, BAK, B 106/62728.

32 Land laws governed compensation until the Federal Compensation Act of 1953. *Compensation for National Socialist Injustice: Indemnification Provisions* (Berlin: Federal Ministry of Finance, 2006), 5.

33 Letter from Karl Stürke to Dr Dehler, 21 Oct. 1951, BAK, B 106/62728, 1.

34 Letter from Dr Redecker to Karl Stürke, regarding 'Wiedergutmachung für Sterilisierung: Ihre Eingabe vom 21 Oktober 1950 an den Herrn Bundesminister der Justiz,' BAK, B 106/62728.

35 Schultheiss' statement declared an application was invalid if it 'did not prove that the sterilization took place in violation of the Law of Hereditarily Diseased Offspring.' Applicants needed to provide evidence of having been 'sterilized on grounds of race, political affiliation or religious beliefs.' Dr Schultheiss, 'Wiedergutmachungsansrprüche von Sterilisierten,' BAK, B 106/62728.

36 'Sterilisierte gelten als Verfolgte des nationalsozialismus,' *Die Neue Zeitung*, no.16, 19 Jan. 1951, BAK, B 106/62728.

37 John McCloy confirmed the renewal of the Restitution Law in *Die Neue Zeitung*, June 1951.

38 Thomas Dehler, 'Wiedergutmachung,' in *Der Spiegel*, 18 July 1951, BAK, B 136/1124.

39 An in-house speech by Ministerial Director Dr Redecker, 'Wiedergutmachung von Sterilisierten,' 2 Jan. 1951, BAK, B 106/62728.

40 Ibid.

41 Königer's letter printed in the association's newsletter, no. 4, 20 Aug. 1951, BAK, B 106/62728.

42 Letter from Bundeskanzleramt to Verband, 16 Sept. 1951, BAK, B 106/62728.

43 For examples of government ministries avoiding responsibility for sterilization claims, see internal letter written by Redecker, 2 Jan. 1951, 'Wiedergutmachung von Sterilisierten,' BAK, B 106/62728.

44 For example, the Yugoslav embassy expressed its disapproval of Germany's handling of cases of medical abuses during the Third Reich. See letter from Federal Finance Ministry to the Foreign Office, 6 Nov. 1952, in BAK, B 106/91890. Also see 'Sühne für medizinische Experimente,' *Allgemeine Wochenzeitung der Juden in Deutschland*, 21 May 1954, BAK, B 106/91890.

45 Quoted in Pross, *Paying for the Past*, 18, 36.

46 'German Opinions on Jewish Restitution and Some Associated Issues,' in Anna J. Merritt and Richard L. Merritt, eds., *Public Opinion in Semi-Sovereign Germany: The HICOG Surveys, 1949–1955* (Chicago, IL: University of Illinois Press, 1980), 146.
47 Numerous articles appeared regularly in the *Allgemeine Wochenzeitung der Juden in Deutschland* in 1950. See 'Antisemitismus existiert noch,' 6 Jan., 5; 'Wissenschaftlichen getarnter Antisemitismus,' 21 April, 12; 'Nationalismus = Antisemitismus,' 26 May, no page number; 'Gerechte Strafe für Antisemitin,' 24 March, 11; and, 'Das Hakenkreuz im "Stern,"' 30 June, 2.
48 Ritzel 'Jetzt ist's genug,' *Allgemeine Wochenzeitung der Juden in Deutschland*, 28 April 1950, 1–2.
49 Pross, *Paying for the Past*, 22.
50 Ibid., 23.
51 Carlo Schmid, *Errinerungen* (Bern: Scherz, 1979), 510, quoted in Geller, *Jews in Post-Holocaust Germany*, 225.
52 See Granieri, *The Ambivalent Alliance*, 48–9, and Pross, *Paying for the Past*, 173.
53 Jay Geller asserts, 'Israel had consented to negotiations only because Adenauer had accepted a billion dollars (approximately 4.35 billion DM) as a basis for talks.' *Jews in Post-Holocaust Germany*, 235.
54 Ibid.
55 'Starke Spannungen im Haag,' *Allgemeine Wochenzeitung der Juden in Deutschland*, 11 April 1952.
56 Pross, *Paying for the Past*, 5.
57 'Professor Böhm sprach über Antisemitismus,' *Allgemeine Wochenzeitung der Juden in Deutschland*, 16 June 1950, 13,15.
58 'Zur christlich-jüdischen Verständigung,' *Christ und Sozialist: Mitteilungsblatt der religiösen Sozialisten* 1/9&10 (1949): 1.
59 Ibid., 2.
60 'Eine Frauenstimme aus der jüdischen Gemeinde,' ibid., 2.
61 'Zwei protestantische Pfarrer,' ibid., 3.
62 Dibelius' address, Conference Report, 'Deutsche Evangelische Ausschuss für Dienst an Israel: Kirche und Judentum,' held 27 Feb. to 3 March 1950, in Kassel, EZA, Collection 4/445.
63 Conference Report, 'Kirche und Judentum.'
64 For Freudenberg's presentation at Kassel, see *http://www.ekd.de/bulletin/2000/2908.html*, and Hockenos, *A Church Divided*, 167–72.
65 Rendtorff and Henrix, *Die Kirchen und das Judentum*, 548–9. Also see Hockenos, *A Church Divided*, 167–72.

66 Rendtorff and Henrix, *Die Kirchen und das Judentum*, 549.
67 Ibid.
68 The committee's third meeting, held at Dusseldorf, 26 Feb. to 2 March 1951, was titled 'Der Neue Stadt Israel und Christenheit,' and its fourth, held at Ansbach, 3–7 March 1952, was titled 'Der Mensch in Christlich und Jüdische Sicht,' EZA, Collection 4/445.
69 The *Wochenzeitung* printed a response by Protestant pastor Dr Helmut Lamparter, which began with a recognition of the complicity that Protestants had in the 'crime that was committed against the Jews by our people.' See 'Schweigende Kirche?' *Allgemeine Wochenzeitung der Juden in Deutschland*, 23 March 1951, 2.
70 Examples of Jewish conferences in the FRG include: 'Kongress jüdischer Studenten in der US-Zone,' 23 June 1950, and the first meeting of the World Jewish Congress, held in Germany on 14 July 1950.
71 By 1951, four of the Societies – Berlin, Stuttgart, Munich, and Bremen – were nearly financially self-sufficient, Sterling Brown's Report, BAK, B 259/188, 7.
72 A cross-state, cross-zonal project, like the establishment of a society in the British zone, had yet to be accomplished in 1950 (Düsseldorf's society opened in 1951). See Foschepoth, *Im Schatten der Vergangenheit*, 246.
73 Letter from Frankfurt society to Cultural Minister Christine Teusch, 11 June 1950, which highlights A. Kopisch's poem "Histörchen," which is antisemitic, and Ludwig Auerbacher's work that referred to the 'eternal Jew.' The society maintained that the works taught children, 'not only animosity, but abhorrence' towards the Jews and demanded their removal from the curriculum, BAK, B 259/153.
74 Letter to Cultural Minister Teusch.
75 Reply from Teusch to the Society, 12 June 1950, and her letter banning the books, 13 June 1950, BAK, B 259/153.
76 The 'Decree' from Teusch to the school board, on 14 June 1950, reads as follows: 'All additions, omissions, changes made to this [book] edition must be cleared by my office ... if changes happen in any way without my knowledge and my approval, I will by order forcibly have the books returned and ensure your removal from the school,' BAK, B 259/153.
77 Ibid. In another example, the Bavarian society's April 1950 meeting was held to combat antisemitism in the school curriculum and to develop an interfaith curriculum. See 'Liegt es am Religionsunterricht? Christen und Juden beraten in München,' *Blick in die Welt* (April 1950): 62.
78 Letter from the Frankfurt society to Teusch, 15 June 1950, BAK, B 259/153.
79 Muckermann's speech, 'Grundätzliches zum Problem der Solidarität von Juden und Christen,' auf der Kundgebung der Gesellschaft für

Christlich-Jüdische Zusammenarbeit in Berlin, Rathaus Schöneberg, 4 March 1950, 2, 4, 9, BAK, B259/67. See also, Bentley Glass, 'Racism and Eugenics in International Context,' *Quarterly Review of Biology* 68/1 (1993): 61–7. Glass points out that Muckermann supported sterilization in some cases but opposed the Nazis' criteria and cruelty.

80 Muckermann's speech, BAK, B259/67, 7.
81 Ibid., 10.
82 Friedrich Deich, 'Es gibt keine reine Rasse,' *Umschau: Der Gesellschaft für christlich-jüdische Zusammenarbeit*, Stuttgart, 1952, 5. The *Umschau* reprinted Deich's article, which originally appeared in *Die Neue Zeitung* earlier in 1952. In it, Deich claimed that racial biologists the world over have been unable to 'define and distinguish ... scientifically ... the absolute differences between the races.'
83 See 'Erste "Woche der Bruderschaft" in Deutschland,' *Allgemeine Wochenzeitung der Juden in Deutschland*, 16 Feb. 1951, 12.
84 'Für Eintracht zwischen Christen und Juden,' *Allgemeine Wochenzeitung der Juden in Deutschland*, 10 Feb. 1950, 11, and 'Engere christlich-jüdische Zusammenarbeit,' *Allgemeine Wochenzeitung der Juden in Deutschland*, 27 Oct. 1950, 11.
85 'Christlich-Jüdische Zusammenarbeit,' *Allgemeine Wochenzeitung der Juden in Deutschland*, 10 Nov. 1950, 2.
86 'Opening Remarks, ' Joseph Brandlmeier, *Sonderheft zur Woche der Brüderlichkeit in Bayern, 1951*, BAK, B 259/53, 2–3.
87 See 'Tätigkeitsbericht für Monat Februar 1951, im besonderen über die "Woche der Brüderlichkeit" in Bayern,' BAK, B 259/5, 12.
88 Ibid., 14.
89 Ibid., 15.
90 'Der Bock als Gärtner: Antisemitismus in der Gesellschaft für christlich-jüdische Zusammenarbeit,' *Allgemeine Wochenzeitung der Juden in Deutschland*, 1 Sept. 1950, 5.
91 Brandlmeier's speech, quoted in Kauders, *Democratization and the Jews*, 144.
92 Ibid., 144–5.
93 Julius Spanier, 'Zusammenarbeit,' *Sonderheft*, 4, emphasis added.
94 Hans-Joachim Schoeps, 'Bin ich der Hüter meines Bruders?' *Sonderheft*, 5.
95 Ibid.
96 Ibid.
97 Ibid., 6.
98 'Der Dialog muß beginnen,' *Allgemeine Wochenzeitung der Juden in Deutschland*, 7 July 1950, 12.

99 Brenner, *After the Holocaust,* 109–10. Rabbi Levinson served as the Jewish chairman of the German Coordinating Council for Christian-Jewish Cooperation, and from 1976 on, as president of the International Council of Christians and Jews; for additional information, see 107–10.
100 Rabbi Freier of Berlin commented at the World Brotherhood meeting held 3–6 July 1951 that the Hebrew word 'brother' could be broadly interpreted, and that the word 'mercy' comes from the Hebrew word 'mother's lap,' and raised the question, then, whether there really was a difference between the old and new testaments. See BAK, B 259/238.
101 Geller, *Jews in Post-Holocaust Germany,* 208.
102 For information on the Auerbach Affair, see 'Der Tod Philipp Auerbachs,' *Allgemeine Wochenzeitung Juden in Deutschland,* 22 Aug. 1952, 1.
103 Letter from Mrs Grumbach to President Heuss, 7 Aug. 1952, BAK, B 106/91885.
104 Ernest Landau, 'Die JRSO und die heutigen Kultusgemeinden: Vollkommene Rückerstattung gibt es nicht,' *Allgemeine Wochenzeitung Juden in Deutschland,* 30 March 1951, 5.
105 Letter from Dr Hermann, of the Ministry of the Interior – on the President's behalf – to Mrs Grumbach, 6 Nov. 1952, BAK, B 106/91885.
106 Letter from Erwin Vossler to the Ministry of Interior, 14 Jan. 1953, BAK, B 106/91885.
107 Letter from Dr Fiegel to Erwin Vossler, 2 Feb. 1953, BAK, B 106/91885.
108 Letters from Erwin Vossler to the Ministry of Interior, 16 Feb. and 14 July1953, BAK, B 106/91885.
109 See 'Ich besuchte Frau Grumbach,' *Die Welt,* 20 June 1954, BAK, B 106/91885, 1.
110 Küster's June 1953 speech to the Frankfurt Society, Pross, *Paying for the Past,* 40.
111 G. Gedye, *Western Germany,* found at http://www.ajcarchives.org/AJC_DATA/Files/1955_10_CentralEurope.pdf, 380.
112 Minutes of the meeting at Bebenhausen, Baden-Württemberg, 30 July 1949, BAK, B 120/333, 1.
113 Ibid.
114 Ibid.
115 Ibid., 6.
116 Ibid., 7.
117 Ibid., 8.
118 Ernst Friedländer interview with Konrad Adenauer: 'Germany and France,' *Die Zeit,* 3 Nov. 1949, 1–2.

119 Untitled 'Denkschrift,' from the Saar Archdiocese to the German Office for Peace Questions in Nov. 1949, BAK, Z 35/275.
120 Geneviève Tabouis' article in *L'Information,* 19 (24 Jan. 1950), BAK, Z 35/275.
121 Ibid.
122 German Office for Peace Questions' response to Tabouis' article, BAK, Z 35/275.
123 'The German-French Reconciliation – A Pattern for Europe,' CSP 1993, ACV, PP 746/7.5.2, 6–7.
124 Spoerri notes: 'The friendship between the two men did not proceed without its ups and downs. A profound crisis broke out, both between France and Germany and between Adenauer and Schuman in the second half of 1949 [over] the Saar.' See 'The German-French Reconciliation, ibid., 6.
125 Ibid., 7.
126 Mottu, 'The Story of Caux,' 119.
127 Franz Johann Vock, 'Zur Bedeutung der Moral fur die Politik: Eine Untersuchung der Arbeit der Moralischen Aufrüstung an drei Fallbeispielen,' Book: geisteswissenschaftlichen Fakultät, Universität Salzburg, 1989, ACV, PP 746, 148.
128 Ibid., 149.
129 Mottu, 'The Story of Caux,' 119.
130 Ibid., 120.
131 Ibid., 121.
132 See Edward Luttwack, 'Franco-German Reconciliation: The Overlooked Role of the Moral Re-Armament Movement,' in Douglas Johnston and Cynthia Sampson, eds., *Religion: The Missing Dimension of Statecraft* (New York: Oxford University Press, 1994), 37–57, and 'Moral Re-Armament Is Credited for Role in Schuman Plan Talks,' *New York Herald Tribune,* 4 June 1951, cited in Lean, *On the Tail of a Comet,* 382.
133 Spoerri, 'The German-French Reconciliation,' 7.
134 Spoerri interview.
135 Vock, 'Zur Bedeutung der Moral für die Politik,' 236.
136 Ibid.
137 Vock asserts that the reconciliatory acts were tied to Germany's application for NATO membership, which Denmark could veto. Adenauer invited Danish Prime Minister H.C. Hansen to Bonn to seal the Bonn-Copenhagen Declarations of March 1955, which included identical

declarations that ensured cultural, educational, and political rights to minorities. Ibid., 236–8.
138 See Victims of Fascism, 'Tötung von angeblichten Geisteskranken und Durchführung von Zwangssterilisierungen,' Protokolle, 22 Feb. 1946, SAPMO, DY 54 V/277 1/19.
139 VVN Board Meeting, 9 Jan. 1949, in Sacrow. The board discussed race, seen in Stefan Heymann's address, 'Antisemitism and the Racial Question,' in which he affirmed that there are different races, but that 'there are none that are more important than the other,' and that 'Jews [were involved in] the amassing of capital [and were] the nomadic people who were naturally the brokers of commerce,' SAPMO, DY 55 278/1/1.
140 Letter from Dresden Jewish community to Julius Meyer at the Zentralvorstand Jüdischer Gemeinden in der Sowjetischen Zone, 24 Oct. 1949, CJA, 5B1:50, 1–2.
141 Letter from Julius Meyer to DDR Ministerium des Innern, 3 June 1950, CJA, 5B1:51, 1.
142 Letter from Adolf Kastendieck of New York (formerly of Magdeburg) to the Society for Christian-Jewish Cooperation in Berlin, 10 April 1950. Mr Kastendieck had been unable to secure the property he had been forced to leave behind when fleeing Nazi Germany and appealed, unsuccessfully, for the society's assistance, CJA, 5B1:66.
143 Wolfgang Vogel ignored specific mention of the Jews entirely in this book, focusing, instead, on general categories of 'religious, racial, and political' persecutees. *Die Wiedergutmachung faschistischen Unrechts in der DDR* (Berlin: Humboldt-Universität, 1952). His denial of collective restitution allowed for the refusal of compensation on an ad hoc basis (100–2, 163–4).
144 See 'Sitzung des Landesverbandes der Jüdischen Gemeinden in der DDR,' 15 March 1948,' SAPMO, DY 30/IV 2/4/399, and Meyer's report on the demise of the Jewish community at Kleinmenchow, SAPMO, DY 30/IV 2/4 /404.
145 See German American journalist Robert Ehrlich's letter, 26 Oct. 1951, and Leon Löwenkopf's document, 'Die Juden in der Deutschen Demokratichen Republik,' CJA, 5B1:50.
146 For examples of these cases, see Michael Meng, 'East Germany's Jewish Question: The Return and Preservation of Jewish Sites in East Berlin and Potsdam, 1945–1989,' *Central European History* 38/4 (2005): 606–36, and Jeffrey Herf, 'East German Communists and the Jewish Question: The Case of Paul Merker,' *Journal of Contemporary History* 29/4 (1994): 627–62.

147 Otto Nuschke moved to expunge Protestant and Catholic curricula from the schools in the GDR. See letter from Nuschke to Ministerium für Volksbildung, 9 June 1950, SAPMO, DY 30/IV 2/14/239. See also, 'Kirchenfeindliche Aktion der "DDR."' For the SED attack on Dibelius, referring to him as a Nazi, see SAPMO, DY 30/IV 2/14/1.
148 WCC Pastor Bengt Hoffmann's report, 'Journey in Germany's East Zone, June 1950,' ADW, ZB 338, 19.
149 Bishop Horning of Görlitz's report on events during April–June 1950, ADW, ZB 338.
150 Hoffmann, 'Journey,' ADW, ZB 338, 15. The *Täglische Rundschau* published an attack against 'the reactionary church leaders,' titled 'The Role of the Church in the German Democratic Republic,' 15 May 1950.
151 The SED claimed that 'hundreds of pastors have resolutely given evidence of their sympathy for the national struggle of their people and have joined National Committees of the National Front of the German Democratic Republic. These pastors must be supported and a broad movement of protest must be created within the church itself so that in future the church members and the pastors are given full freedom to fulfil their national duty.' Bishop Horning's report, 16.
152 Ibid.
153 Ibid., 20.
154 For example, Bishop von Scheven of Pomerania, Dr Schröter of Anhalt, and Bishop Mietzenheim of Thuringia did share the bishop's views, and 120–125 pastors of 700 in the GDR had joined the National Front. National Front membership was a dividing point among pastors, as 'this is one way and perhaps the most sufficient in which the state is trying to break the strength of the church.' Ibid., 22.
155 Ibid., 23.
156 Document from the WCC's Department of Inter-Church Aid and Service to Refugees, '1950 Programme for Europe: An Advance Plan,' ADW, ZB 338, 18.
157 Christian Berg's speech at People's Solidarity regional meeting in Weimar on 2 September 1949, 1–2. Berg's aim was to convince People's Solidarity that 75% of Protestant Relief Work endeavours were for the needy, elderly, refugees, and children, and that its work was, first and foremost, of a material nature. Still, he stressed that people could not live 'by bread alone,' justifying the distribution of Bibles and songbooks throughout the GDR, claiming that it was 'obvious that a church-based charitable organization would combine material assistance and the reinstatement of spiritual service.' ADW, ZBB 67A.

158 Ibid., 2.
159 Report on People's Solidarity activities, 'Bericht über die Sitzung des Zentralausschusses der Volkssolidarität am 28 Oktober 1949,' 1, ADW, ZBB 67A.
160 Ibid.
161 Manfred Hörhammer, 'Eine Neue Generation springt ein ... !,' PCA, Folder Ifd. Nr. 1/8, Nachlass Pater Hörhammer 1951, 4.
162 'Pax Chrsti in Lourdes,' *Pax Christi: Zeitschrift des Gebetskreuzzuges für die Nationen* 2/3 (1950): 10.
163 'Der Hl. Vater spricht über das Herzensanliegen von Pax Christi,' *Pax Christi: Zeitschrift des Gebetskreuzzuges für die Nationen* 2/5 (1950–51): 5.
164 A noticeable change is evident in Pax Christ's vision in 1954, which shifted towards international reconciliation and peacemaking, seen in efforts towards reconciliation by having Germans 'bring the message of peace' abroad. See Manfred Hörhammer, 'Von der Enns bis zur Ems,' PCA, Folder Ifd. Nr. 1/8, Nachlass Pater Hörhammer 1952, 1–4.
165 Manfred Hörhammer, 'Liebe Erinnerungen an Holland–uns zur Überlegung,' (Draft), *Pax Christi: Zeitschrift des Gebetskreuzzuges für die Nationen* 5/2 (1953): 1.
166 Manfred Hörhammer, 'Pax Christi – Fahrt nach England und Irland,' PCA, Folder Ifd. Nr. 1/9, Nachlass Pater Hörhammer 1953–1956, 4.
167 Letter from A. Micewski to Otto Nuschke, 22 Aug. 1955, SAPMO, DY 30/ IV 2/14/95.
168 'Da ist nicht Jude, nicht Grieche ... ,' *Pax Christi: Zeitschrift des Gebetskreuzzuges für die Nationen* 5/2 (1953): 11–12.
169 In a report to the Office for Peace Questions, Ulrich von Ketelhodt reiterated the horrific story of the massacred village and reported on how a group of Germans – the publishers of the newspaper *Benjamin* – called on German youths to rebuild the village of Oradour and petitioned the French government to allow them to rebuild the village because they 'wanted to make right a small part of what the Germans were responsible [for damaging]' in order to improve German-French relationships (5). There were a wide variety of responses to the petition in France. The relatives of the murdered wanted the French government to decline the offer. They wanted another form of reparation; they wanted the perpetrators of the crime to be found and brought to justice. See 'Können wir Oradour Wiedergutmachung?' 1 April 1948, BAK, Z 35/ 544, 5–8.
170 Hörhammer, 'Pionierarbeit in den ersten Jahren,' 10–11.
171 Friedrich Siegmund-Schultze, 'Kriegsdienstverweigerung einst und jetzt,' *Junge Kirche* (Sonderausdruck), 1957, Conway Collection, BX 8080 S.53 S53 (file 2) RRAR2, 2. Siegmund-Schultze continued his campaign

of pacifism in the postwar years. He disseminated his views in the periodical *Junge Kirche* throughout the 1950s in the FRG, accepting the presidency of the German Committee for Questions Concerning Conscientious Objection in 1950. See, also, *Friedensrundschau* of the *Internationale der Kriegsdienstgegner,* Feb., March, Nov. 1950 issues, and April, July, Sept. 1951 issues.

172 Mottu, 'The Story of Caux,' 122.
173 Konrad Adenauer, 'Address at Caux, 1959,' ACV, PP 746/5.2.3/2, 4.
174 Memorandum from Zietlow's assistant, Karl-Heinz Fehsenfeld, to Carl Zietlow regarding VVN activities in Freiburg im Breisgau and Dr Luckner, 5 Dec. 1950, 1, BAK, B 259/189.
175 See 'VVN – Nebenorganisation der KP,' *Freie Wort,* 5 Jan. 1950; see also, 'Bürger und Bürgerinnen von Gelsenkirchen!' *Freie Wort,* 14 April 1951.
176 The posters had captions that read: 'Willst du sowjetischer Arbeitssklave werden?' and 'Niemals werden unsere Kinder Kommunisten!' and 'Herunter ... mit der Maske! Entlarvt die kommunistischen "Friedens"-Agenten!' Gelsenkirchen Kongress Wiederkämpfer und VVN, April 1951, BAK, B 137/1352.
177 Ibid., 1–2.
178 Memorandum to Carl Zietlow, 3.
179 See Phayer, *The Catholic Church and the Holocaust,* 189, and Foschepoth, *Im Schatten der Vergangenheit,* 59–60, 169.
180 For numerous documents on this topic, see ACV, PP 746/5.2.2/23. See also, 'Moralische Aufrüstung: Die Bestimmung für Ost und West, ' Programm der Pfingstkundgebung der Moralischen Aufrüstung im Hans-Sachs-Haus in Gelsenkirchen, 28 May 1950, ACV, PP 746/5.2.2/29, 1, and 'Kundgebung der Moralischen Aufrüstung: Eine Ideologie, die die Welt gewinnen kann,' Saalbau Essen, 17 March 1951, 'Welt im Aufbau,' Presse Information – MRA Haus der Landesregierung, Düsseldorf, 20 March 1952, ACV, PP 746/5.2.2/29, 1.
181 Karl Arnold read Adenauer's Welcome, which stated, 'The purpose of the [MRA] events in the industrial heart of Europe is to provide this proof by demonstrating a basis of ideological unity for the nation which is a decisive battleground in the world war of ideas,' 'Dr Adenauer's Welcome,' 1950 Conference at Caux, ACV, PP 746/5.2.3/2, 2.
182 Monteath, 'Organizing Antifascism,' 290, 289, 297. See also Elke Reuter and Detlef Hansel, *Das Kurze Leben der VVN von 1947 bis 1953: Die Geschichte der Vereinigung der Verfolgten des Naziregimes in der sowjetischen Besatzungszone und in der DDR* (Berlin: Edition Ost, 1997), 451–519.

183 'Protocol on the Termination of the Occupation Regime in the Federal Republic,' 20–23 Oct., 1954 Paris, in von Oppen, *Documents on Germany*, 614–16.

Conclusion

1 See Jens Holger Schjorring, 'Moralische Aufrüstung und westeuropäische Politik bis 1954,' (Manuscript, 1976), Conway Collection, BR 10 S42 1976 File 1.
2 Friedrich Siegmund-Schultze, 'Versöhnung von Deutschtum und Judentum,' *Junge Kirche* 16 (1955): 292–4.
3 Pax Christi, *Pax Christi im Dienst der Versöhnung mit Polen: Dokumente und Analysen* (Frankfurt: Deutsches Pax-Christi-Sekretariat, 1984), 6–10.
4 Franz Böhm stated, 'the western Allies, especially the American occupation authorities, exerted an effective influence on the legislation of Wiedergutmachung.' 'Das deutsche-israelische Abkommen 1952,' in *Konrad Adenauer in seiner Zeit*, 440, cited in Arthur Smith, 'A View of U.S. Policy toward Jewish Restitution,' *Holocaust and Genocide Studies* 5/3 (1990): 256–7.

References

Primary Sources

Manuscript Collections

Archiv des Diakonischen Werkes der EKD (ADW), Berlin, Germany
   Grundung des Hilfswerkes [ZB 1–10]
   Polen [ZB 933]
   Politische Angelegenheiten [ZB 840]
   Sowjetisches Besatzungszone [ZB 74]
   Volkssolidarität [ZB 192a]
   World Council of Churches [ZB 331]
      Bengt Hoffmann [ZB 338]

Archives Cantonales Vaudoises (ACV), Lausanne, Switzerland
   Rearmament Moral [PP 746]
      Pierre Spoerri Peronal Papers [PP 746/7.5.2]
   Various Personal Papers [PP 174]

Archives of the University of Notre Dame (UNDA), George Shuster Collection (SHU) Notre Dame, IN, USA
   Adenauer and Moral Rearmament [SHU 2/07]
      Katholisches Pfarrblatt
      Nordbayerische Zeitung
   The German People (Untitled) [SHU Box 5]
      Advisory Committee on German Re-education

Department of State, German Re-education and Cultural Exchange
Munich's 'Good Neighbor Week'
Questions of European Unity, 1944, 'Vital Speeches'
Vassar College Conferences
Vassar Community Church
Graf Schwerin von Krosigk and Admiral Dönitz [SHU Box 17]
   Religious Opposition to Nazism
Post-defeat letter from the Bishop of Cologne [SHU Box 2]

Bundesarchiv Koblenz (BAK), Koblenz, Germany
  Allied Control Authority Coordinating Committee [Z 46]
  Allied Control Authority Religious Affairs Committee [Z 45 f]
  Bundeskanzleramt [B 136]
  Bundesministerium für Gesamtdeutsche Fragen [B 137]
  Bundesministerium für Heimatvertriebene [B 150]
  Bundesministerium des Innern [B 106]
  Bundespräsidentialamt, Amtszeit Prof. Dr Theodor Heuss [B 122]
  Caritas Verband [Z 18]
  Deutsches Büro für Friedensfragen [Z 35]
  Institut für Besatzungsfragen [B 120]
  Kirchliche Hilfsstelle [Z 18]
  Koordinierungsrat der Gesellschaft für christlich-jüdische Zusammenarbeit [B 259]
  Länderrat des amerikanisches Besatzungsgebieten [Z 1]
  Nachlass Otto Dibelius [N 1439]
  Zonenbeirat der britisch besetzten Zone [Z 2]

Centrum Judaicum (CJA), Berlin Germany
  Anschriftenverzeichnis internationale Hilfsorganisationen und Jüdischer Gemeinden [5A1:86]
  Gemeinde zu Berlin [5A1:1]
  Halle [5B1:54]
    Juden in der DDR [5B1:50]
  Julius Meyer, VVN [5A1:25]
    Magdeburg [5B1:66]
    Satzung der Juden in der DDR [5B1:5]
    Thüringen [5B1:51]
  Wiedergutmachung [5A1: 16]
    Wiedergutmachung in der DDR [5B1:107]
  World Jewish Congress [5A1:455]

References

Evangelisches Zentralarchiv (EZA), Berlin, Germany
  Bevollmächtiger des Rates der EKD bei der DDR [Collection 103]
  Deutscher Zweig [Collection 210]
  Internationaler Versöhnungsbund [Collections 31 and 69]
  Kirchenkanzlei der EKD [Collection 2]
  Kirchenkanzlei der EKD, Berliner Stelle [Collection 4]
    Israelitische Religion ab March 1947
  Kirchenkanzlei der EKD für Gliedkirchen der DDR [Collection 104]
    Israelitische Religionen, Judenfrage, Judenchristen, Nichtarier
  Kirchliches Aussenamt [Collection 6]

John Conway Collection, John Richard Allison Library, Regent College, Vancouver, B.C., Canada

Pax Christi Archives (PCA), Bad Vilbel, Germany
  Manuskripten für Pax Christi Zeitschriften [Collection 1/9]
  Nachlass Manfred Hörhammer [Collection 1/9 and 2/15]
  Pax Christi 1948 – diverse Manuskripte und Durchschläge [Collection 1/6]
  Wallfahrten Kevelaer und Lourdes [Collection 1/2]

Stiftung Archiv der Parteien und Massenorganizationen der DDR im Bundesarchiv (SAPMO), Berlin, Germany
  Arbeitsgruppe Kirchenfragen 1946–1962 [DY 30/IV 2/14]
  Deutsche Verwaltung des Innern [DO 1 7 / 69]
  Gesellschaft für Deutsch-Sowjetische Freundschaft
    Nachlass Paul Merker [NY 4102]
  Opfern des Faschismus (OdF) [DY 54/V 277]
  SED Zentrale Parteikontollkommission (ZPKK) [DY 30/IV 2/4/1]
  SED Zentralkomitee, Internationale Verbindungen 1946–1962 [DY 10/IV 2/20]
  Staatssekretäriat für Kirchenfragen [DO 4]
  Verband der Jüdischen Gemeinden in der DDR und BRD [DO 4 274]
  Vereinigung der Verfolgten des Naziregimes (VVN) [DY 55/V 278]

Newspapers

Allgemeine Wochenzeitung der Juden in Deutschland
Continental Daily Mail
Economist

Gegenwart
Le Monde
Die Neue Zeitung
Die Neues Abendland
New Statesman and Nation
Témoignage Chrétien

Periodicals

Amtsblatt des Alliierten Kontrollrats in Deutschland
Christ Unterwegs
Das Hilfswerk
Freiburger Rundbrief
Mitteilungen aus dem Hilfswerk
Stars and Stripes
Vierteljahrshefte für Zeitgeschichte

Other Published Primary Sources

Adenauer, Konrad. '6. September 1952: Ansprach vor dem Bundesparteiausschuss der CDU in Bonn (Bundeshaus),' in Hans-Peter Schwartz, *Konrad Adenauer: Reden 1917–1967*. Stuttgart: Deutsche Verlages-Anstalt, 1975, 263–80.

Besier, Gerhard. *Der SED-Staat und die Kirche: Der Weg in die Anpassung*. München: Bertelsmann, 1993.

Clay, Lucius. *Decision in Germany*. Garden City, NY: Doubleday, 1950.

Crocker, David. 'Reckoning with Past Wrongs: A Normative Framework.' In Carol A.L. Prager and Trudy Govier (eds.), *Dilemmas of Reconciliation: Cases and Concepts*. Waterloo: Wilfrid Laurier University Press, 2003, 39–63.

Diem, Hermann. *Kirche für die Welt: Kirche und Entnazifizierung – Denkschrift der Kirchliche-theologischen Sozietät in Württemberg*. Stuttgart: Kohlhammer Verlag, 1946.

Evangelisches Hilfswerk. *Eugen Gerstenmaier: Reden und Aufsätze, Zusammengestellt Anlässlich seines 50. Geburtstages am 25.8.56*. Stuttgart: Ev. Verlagswerk, 1956.

Frederiksen, Oliver. *The American Military Occupation of Germany, 1945–1953*. OMGUS, Darmstadt: Historical Division, 1953.

Gollancz, Victor. *In Darkest Germany*. London: Victor Gollancz, 1947.

Harmssen, Gustav. *Reparationen-Sozialprodukt-Lebensstandard: Versuch einer Wirtschaftsbilanz*. Bremen: Friedrich Truejen Verlag, 1947.

Herman, Stewart. *The Rebirth of the German Church*. New York: Harper, 1946.

HICOG. *Conference on the Future of the Jews in Germany*. Heidelberg: Office of Adviser on Jewish Affairs, 1949.

ICCJ. *Reports and Recommendations of the International Conference of Christians and Jews: Seelisberg, 1947*. Geneva: Author, 1947.
Luckner, Gertrud. 'Geleitwort.' *Freiburger Rundbrief* 1/1 (1948): 1–2.
Maritain, Jacques. 'Eine Botschaft Jacques Maritain,' *Freiburger Rundbrief* 1/1 (1948): 2–3.
McClaskey, Beryl. *The History of U.S. Policy and Program in the Field of Religious Affairs under the Office of the U.S. High Commissioner for Germany*. HICOG, 1951.
Merritt, Anna J., and Richard L. Merritt, eds. *Public Opinion in Semi-sovereign Germany: The HICOG Surveys, 1949–1955*. Chicago, IL: University of Illinois, 1980.
JCS 1779. *Denazification in the Four Zones*. OMGUS: 1947.
Schloss, Bert. *The American Occupation of Germany, 1945–1952: An Appraisal*. Chicago, IL: University of Chicago, 1955.
Schoeps, Hans-Joachim. *The Jewish-Christian Argument: A History of Theologies in Conflict*. Translated by David Green. London: Faber and Faber, 1963; German 1st ed., 1937.
Soehlmann, Fritz. *Treysa 1945: Die Konferenz der evangelischen Kirchenführer 27–31 August, 1945*. Lüneburg: Im Heliand Verlag, 1946.
Vogel, Wolfgang. *Die Wiedergutmachung faschistischen Unrechts in der DDR*. Berlin: Humboldt-Universität, 1952.
VVN. *Die Toten, Der Lebenden: Gedenkschrift zur Gedächtnis-Kundgebung OdF, Berlin-Neukölln, 9.9.45*. Berlin: Stadt Berlin Magistrat, 1945.
– *Zwei Jahre Hauptausschuss OdF*. Berlin: HA OdF, 1947.

Secondary Sources

Ambos, Kai, et al., eds. *Building a Future on Peace and Justice: The Nuremberg Declaration on Peace and Justice*. Berlin: Springer-Verlag, 2009.
Bell, George. *Christianity and World Order*. New York: Penguin, 1940.
Besier, Gerhard. *'Selbstreinigung' unter britischer Besatzungsherrschaft: Die Evangelisch-Lutherische Landeskirche Hannovers und ihr Landesbischof Marahrens, 1945–1947*. Göttingen: Vandenhoeck and Ruprecht, 1986.
Bethge, Eberhard. *Dietrich Bonhoeffer*. New York: Harper and Row, 1970.
Bishop, Daniel. "Der lange schwere Weg zurück in die Familie der Nationen." *Die Neue Zeitung*, 25 Oct. 1945, 1.
Brenner, Michael. *After the Holocaust: Rebuilding Jewish Lives in Postwar Germany*. Princeton, NJ: Princeton University Press, 1997.
– 'Epilogue or Preface? Five Decades of Jewish Life in Postwar Germany: A Balance Sheet.' In Otto R. Romberg and Suzanne Urban-Fahr, eds., *Jews in Germany after 1945: Citizens or Fellow-Citizens?* Frankfurt: Tribune, 2000.

Broszat, Martin, and Hermann Weber, eds. *SBZ-Handbuch: Staatliche Verwaltungen, Parteien, Gesellschaftliche Organisationen und Ihre Führungskräfte in der SBZ Deutschlands, 1945–1949*. Munich: Oldenbourg, 1990.

Brown, Amy Benson, and Karen M. Poremski, eds. *Roads to Reconciliation: Conflict and Dialogue in the Twenty-First Century*. Armonk, NY: M.E. Sharpe, 2005.

Brown-Fleming, Suzanne. *The Holocaust and Catholic Conscience: Cardinal Aloisius Muench and the Guilt Question in Germany*. Notre Dame, IN: University of Notre Dame Press, 2006.

Buchman, Frank. *Remaking the World*. London: Blandford, 1961.

Buscher, Frank. 'The Great Fear: The Catholic Church and the Anticipated Radicalization of Expellees and Refugees in Post-War Germany.' *German History* 2/12 (2003): 204–24.

Clark, Christopher. *The Politics of Conversion: Missionary Protestantism and the Jews in Prussia, 1728–1947*. Oxford: Clarendon, 1995.

Cohen-Pfister, Lorel, and Dagmar Wienröder-Skinner, eds. *Victims and Perpetrators: (Re)presenting the Past in Post-Unification Culture*. New York: De Gruyter, 2006.

Conway, John. 'Protestant Mission to the Jews, 1810–1980: Ecclesiastical Imperialism or Theologcial Aberration?' *Holocaust and Genocide Studies* 1/1 (1986): 127–46.

– 'How Shall the Nations Repent? The Stuttgart Declaration of Guilt.' *Journal of Ecclesiastical History* 38/4 (1987): 596–622.

– 'Resisting Militarism: The Peace Movement in the German Evangelical Church during the Weimar Republic.' *Kirchliche Zeitgeschichte* 4/1 (1991): 29–45.

Feldman, Lily Gardner. 'The Principle and Practice of "Reconciliation" in German Foreign Policy: Relations with France, Israel, Poland and the Czech Republic.' *International Affairs* 75/2 (1999): 333–56.

– 'Reconciliation and Legitimacy.' In Thomas Banchoff and Mitchell P. Smith (eds.), *Legitimacy and the European Union: A Contested Polity*. New York: Routledge, 1999, 1–9.

Foschepoth, Josef. *Im Schatten der Vergangenheit: Die Anfänge der Gesellschaften für Christlich-Jüdische Zusammenarbeit*. Göttingen: Vandenhoek and Ruprecht, 1993.

Frei, Norbert. *Adenauer's Germany and the Nazi Past: The Politics of Amnesty and Integration*. New York: Columbia University Press, 2002.

Friedlander, Henry. *The Origins of Nazi Genocide: From Euthanasia to the Final Solution*. Chapel Hill, NC: University of North Carolina Press, 1995.

Friedrich, Jörg. *Der Brand: Deutschland im Bombenkrieg, 1940–1945*. Munich: Propylaen, 2002.
Fulbrook, Mary. *A Concise History of Germany*. Cambridge: Cambridge University Press, 1990.
Geller, Jay. *Jews in Post-Holocaust Germany, 1945–1953*. Cambridge: Cambridge University Press, 2005.
Gerlach, Wolfgang. *And the Witnesses Were Silent: The Confessing Church and the Persecution of the Jews*. Translated by Victoria Barnett. Lincoln, NB: Nebraska University Press, 2000.
Gibney, Mark, and Rhoda E. Howard-Hassmann. 'Introduction: Apologies and the West.' In Mark Gibney et al., eds., *The Age of Apology: Facing Up to the Past*. Philadelphia, PA: University of Pennsylvania Press, 2008, 1–9.
Glassheim, Eagle. 'National Mythologies and Ethnic Cleansing: The Explusion of Czechoslovak Germans in 1945.' *Central European History* 33/4 (2000): 463–86.
Gordon, Philip H. *France, Germany, and the Western Alliance*. Boulder, CO: Westview, 1995.
Goschler, Constantin. *Wiedergutmachung: Westdeutschland und die Verfolgten des Nationalsozialismus 1945–1954*. Munchen: Oldenbourg, 1992.
Granieri, Ronald J. *The Ambivalent Alliance: Konrad Adenauer, the CDU/CSU, and the West, 1949–1966*. New York: Berghahn Books, 2003.
Grossmann, Atina. *Jews, Germans, and Allies: Close Encounters in Occupied Germany*. Princeton, NJ: Princeton University Press, 2007.
Grüner, Karl. 'Das Zugabteil war seine Klosterzelle,' *Münchner Kirchenzeitung* (27 Nov. 2005): 13.
He, Yinan. *The Search for Reconciliation: Sino-Japanese and German-Polish Relations since World War II*. Cambridge: Cambridge University Press, 2009.
Heenen-Wolff, Susann. *Im Land der Täter: Gespräche mit überlebenden Juden*. Frankfurt: Fischer Taschenbuch, 1994.
Herf, Jeffrey. 'East German Communists and the Jewish Question: The Case of Paul Merker.' *Journal of Contemporary History* 29/4 (1994): 627–62.
– *Divided Memory: The Nazi Past in the Two Germanys*. Cambridge, MA: Harvard University Press, 1997.
Hockenos, Matthew. *A Church Divided: German Protestants Confront the Nazi Past*. Bloomington, IN: Indiana University Press, 2004.
Hyman, Abraham. *The Undefeated*. New York: Gefen Books, 1993.
Jarausch, Konrad. *After Hitler: Recivilizing Germans, 1945–1995*. New York: Oxford University Press, 2006.
Johnston, Douglas, and Cynthia Sampson, eds. *Religion: The Missing Dimension of Statecraft*. New York: Oxford University Press, 1994.
Judt, Tony. *Postwar: A History of Europe since 1945*. New York: Penguin, 2005.

Kauders, Anthony. *Democratization and the Jews: Munich, 1945–1965.* Lincoln, NB: University of Nebraska Press, 2004.

Kessler, Ralf, and Hartmut Rüdiger. *Wiedergutmachung im Osten Deutschlands 1945–1953: Grundsätzliche Diskussionen und die Praxis in Sachsen-Anhalt.* Berlin: Peter Lang, 1996.

Klessmann, Christoph. *Die doppelte Staatsgründung: Deutsche Geschichte 1945–1955*, 5th ed. Bonn: Bundeszentrale für politische Bildung, 1991.

Komesaroff, Paul. 'Pathways to Reconciliation: Bringing Diverse Voices into Conversation.' In Fleming Rothfield and Paul Komesaroff, eds., *Pathways to Reconciliation: Between Theory and Practice.* Burlington, VT: Ashgate, 2008, 1–12.

Königseder, Angelika, and Juliane Wetzel. *Waiting for Hope: Jewish Displaced Persons in Post–World War Two Germany.* Evanston, IL: Northwestern University Press, 2001.

Krondörfer, Björn, Katherina von Kellenbach, and Norbert Peck. *Mit Blick auf die Täter: Fragen an die deutsche Theologie nach 1945.* Gütersloh: Gütersloh Verlaghaus, 2006.

Lacquer, Walter. *Generation Exodus: The Fate of Young Jewish Refugees from Nazi Germany.* London: London: I.B. Tauris, 2004.

Laity, Paul. *Britain's First Peace Movement, 1870–1914.* Oxford: Oxford University Press, 2002.

Lean, Garth. *On the Tail of a Comet: The Life of Frank Buchman.* Colorado Springs, CO: Helmers and Howard, 1988.

Lederach, John Paul. *Building Peace: Sustainable Reconciliation in Divided Societies.* Washington, DC: U.S. Institute of Peace Press, 1997.

Leonhard, Wolfgang. *Child of the Revolution.* London: Regnery Publishing, 1958.

Luttwack, Edward. 'Franco-German Reconciliation: The Overlooked Role of the Moral Re-Armament Movement.' In Douglas Johnston and Cynthia Sampson, eds., *Religion: The Missing Dimension of Statecraft.* Oxford: Oxford University Press, 1994, 37–57.

Marcel, Gabriel. *Fresh Hope for the World: Moral Re-Armament in Action.* Translated by Helen Hardinge. London: Longmans and Green, 1960.

Meng, Michael. 'East Germany's Jewish Question: The Return and Preservation of Jewish Sites in East Berlin and Potsdam, 1945–1989.' *Central European History* 38/4 (2005): 606–36.

Merritt, Richard. *Democracy Imposed: U.S. Occupation Policy and the German Public, 1945–1950.* New Haven, CT: Yale University Press, 1995.

Mertens, Lothar. *Davidstern unter Hammer und Zirkel: Die jüdischen Gemeinden in der SBZ/DDR und ihre Beziehung durch Partei und Staat 1945–1990.* Hildesheim: Olms, 1997.

Moeller, Robert G. *War Stories: The Search for a Usable Past in the Federal Republic of Germany.* Berkeley, CA: University of California Press, 2001.
Monteath, Peter. 'Organizing Antifascism: The Obscure History of the VVN.' *European History Quarterly* 29 (1999): 289–94.
Myers Feinstein, Margaret. *Holocaust Survivors in Postwar Germany, 1945–1957.* Cambridge: Cambridge University Press, 2010.
Naimark, Norman. *The Russians in Germany: A History of the Soviet Zone of Occupation, 1945–1949.* Cambridge, MA: Harvard University Press, 1995.
Nationalrat der Nationalen Front des DDR. *Vom SD-Agenten P38/546 zum Bundestags-Präsident.* Berlin: Staatsverlag, Drückerei Tribüne Berlin, 1969.
Ndulo, Muna, ed. *Security, Reconstruction, and Reconciliation: When the Wars End.* London: University College London Press, 2007.
Niven, Bill, ed. *Germans as Victims: Remembering the Past in Contemporary Germany.* New York: Palgrave, 2006.
Offenberg, Ulricke. *Seid Vorsichtig gegen die Machthaber: Die jüdischen Gemeinden in der SBZ und der DDR 1945 bis 1990.* Berlin: Aufbau Verlag, 1998.
Ostmeyer, Irena. *Zwischen Schuld und Sühne: Evangelische Kirche und Juden in der SBZ und DDR 1945–1990.* Berlin: Institut Kirche und Judentum, 2002.
Overy, Richard. *Interrogations: The Nazi Elite in Allied Hands.* New York: Penguin, 2001.
Pendas, Devin. *The Frankfurt Auschwitz Trial, 1963–1965: Genocide, History, and the Limits of the Law.* Cambridge: Cambridge University Press, 2006.
– 'Transitions to Authoritarian Rule: Nazi Trials in the Soviet Zone, 1945–1950.' Conference Paper, German Studies Association Meeting, Oct. 2007.
Phayer, Michael. *The Catholic Church and the Holocaust, 1930–1965.* Indianapolis, IN: Indiana University Press, 2000.
Philpott, Daniel. *Just and Unjust Peace: An Ethic of Political Reconciliation.* New York: Oxford University Press, 2012.
Poiger, Uta G. *Jazz, Rock, and Rebels: Cold War Politics and American Culture in Divided Germany.* Berkeley, CA: University of California Press, 2000.
Pross, Christian. *Paying for the Past: The Struggle over Reparations for Surviving Victims of the Nazi Terror.* Baltimore, MD: Johns Hopkins University Press, 1998.
Raina, Peter. *Bishop George Bell: The Greatest Churchman – A Portrait in Letters.* London: Churches Together in Britain and Ireland, 2006.
Rendtorff, Rolf, and Hans Hermann Henrix, eds. *Die Kirchen und das Judentum: Dokumente von 1945 bis 1983.* Munich: Kaiser Verlag, 1989.
Reuter, Elke, and Detlef Hansel. *Das Kurze Leben der VVN von 1947 bis 1953: Die Geschichte der Vereinigung der Verfolgten des Naziregimes in der sowjetischen Besatzungszone und in der DDR.* Berlin: Edition Ost, 1997.
Rock, Stephen. *Why Peace Breaks Out: Great Power Rapprochement in Historical Perspective.* Chapel Hill, NC: University of North Carolina Press, 1989.

Rogers, Daniel E. *Politics after Hitler: The Western Allies and the German Party System*. London: Macmillan, 1995.
Ruff, Michael Edward. *The Wayward Flock: Catholic Youth in Postwar West Germany, 1945–1965*. Chapel Hill, NC: University of North Carolina Press, 2005.
Rupieper, Hermann-Josef. 'Der Bund für Bürgerrechte: Transnational Relations and the Problem of Democratization in West Germany, 1949–1954.' In David Wetzel, ed., *International Politics and German History: The Past Informs the Present*. Westport, CT: Greenwood, 1997, 87–102.
Sack, Daniel. *Moral Re-Armament: The Reinventions of an American Religious Movement*. New York: Palgrave Macmillan, 2009.
Schaap, Andrew. *Political Reconciliation*. London: Routledge, 2005.
Schroeder, Steven. 'Mennonite-Nazi Collaboration and Coming to Terms with the Past: European Mennonites and the MCC, 1945–1950.' *Conrad Grebel Review* 21/2 (2003): 6–16.
Schwartz, Michael. 'Refugees and Expellees in the Soviet Zone of Germay: Political and Social Problems of their Integration, 1945–1950,' *Journal of Communist Studies and Transition Politics* 16/1&2 (2000): 148–74.
Smith, Athur. 'A View of U.S. Policy toward Jewish Restitution.' *Holocaust and Genocide Studies* 5/3 (1990): 247–59.
Spotts, Frederic. *The Churches and Politics in Germany*. Middletown, CT: Wesleyan University Press, 1973.
Stern, Frank. *The Whitewashing of the Yellow Badge: Antisemitism and Philosemitism in Postwar Germany*. New York: Pergamon, 1992.
Timm, Angelika. *Jewish Claims against East Germany: Moral Obligations and Pragmatic Policy*. Budapest: Central European University Press, 1997.
– *Hammer, Zirkel, Davidstern: Das gestörte Verhältnis der DDR zu Zionismus und Staat Israel*. Bonn: Bouvier, 1997.
Vock, Franz Johann. *Zur Bedeutung der Moral für die Politik: Eine Untersuchung der Arbeit der Moralischen Aufrüstung an drei Fallbeispielen*. Salzburg: geisteswissenschaftlichen Fakultät, Universität Salzburg, 1989.
Vogt, Timothy. *Denazification in Soviet-Occupied Germany: Brandenburg, 1945–1948*. Cambridge, MA: Harvard University Press, 2000.
Wildenthal, Lora. 'Human Rights Activism in Occupied Germany and Early West Germany: The Case of the German League for Human Rights.' *Journal of Modern History* 8 (Summer 2008): 515–16.
Willis, F. Roy. *The French in Germany, 1945–1949*. Stanford, CA: Stanford University Press, 1962.
Winkler, Heinrich August. *Germany: The Long Road West*, vol. 2, *1933–1990*. Translated by Alexander J. Sager. Oxford: Oxford University Press, 2007 (German original, 2000).

Index

Abendland, 106
Ackermann-Gemeinde, 62, 179n27, 183n90, 183n91
Additional Federal Compensation Act, 1953, 133, 151–2
Adenauer, Konrad: Caux meetings, 97, 114; on France and the Saar 147–9, 211n124; and the MRA 114, 116–17, 156, 199n102, 200n111, 215n182; and reparations 135–6, 205n26, 207n53, 211n137
Allgemeine Wochenzeitung der Juden in Deutschland, 128, 203n3, 203n6, 203n7, 206n44, 207n47, 207n48, 207n55, 207n57, 208n69, 209nn83–5, 209n90, 209n98, 210n102, 210n104
Allied Control Authority, viii, 15, 21, 169n17
Allied Control Council, 16, 19, 21, 23, 25, 31, 32, 35, 41–2, 46–8, 62, 162, 170n29; Coordinating Committee, 19, 169n17
Allied High Commission, 10, 131–2, 205n25
Allied High Commissioners, 76

Allied Military Police, 7
Allied occupation of Germany, 5–8, 10, 13–16, 17–18, 20, 23, 33, 35–40, 42, 65, 72–3, 79, 97, 126, 162, 165n4, 168n4, 168n10, 169n15, 192n127, 205n25, 216n183, 216n4
American Jewish Joint Distribution Committee, 31, 174n73
American Military Government, 13–16, 21–2, 25, 34–5, 39, 76–7, 79, 86–89, 118; Religious Affairs Branch, 85. *See also* Office of the Military Government, U.S (OMGUS)
American zone, 18, 22, 34, 64, 76, 89, 113, 133, 170n25, 177n101, 184n112
Amerika Haus, 16
Amsterdam, 38, 79, 103–4, 177n100, 195n31, 195n32, 196nn36–7
Ansbach, 139, 208n68
anti-Communist, 51, 54, 155, 157
anti-fascists, 24, 26–7, 28, 30–1, 66, 74, 78, 94, 119–22, 130, 172n51, 202n133
antisemitic, 67, 72–5, 84, 92, 135, 139–40, 151, 164, 190n79, 208n73

Index

antisemitism: and Christianity, 82–3, 87, 90, 92, 138–9, 190n78; in GDR 9, 11, 76, 78, 135, 151–2; opposition to, 75, 84, 128, 212n139; pleas for American intervention, 85; in postwar Germany, 69–73, 92, 94, 102, 142, 160, 188n60; and Protestant teachings, 81, 190n78
Arnold, Karl, 116, 149, 158, 200n109, 215n181
Asmussen, Pastor Hans, 6, 41–2, 44, 47, 63, 81, 161, 177n1, 178n2, 178n4, 188n56
Association for Expellees (Bundesministerium für Heimatvertriebene), 43, 65, 66
Association of Jews in Germany, 145
Association of Victims of Nazism (Vereinigung der Verfolgten Naziregimes, VVN): Allied criticism of, 157–8; attitudes towards, 152, 158; formation of, 64, 186n20; goals and ideology of, 120–2; and Jews, 173n63; placing Jews on victim scale, 74, 94; results of work, 125, 163, 172n48, 175n76; in Soviet zone, 98, 120 Auerbach, Philipp, 70–1, 121, 142, 144, 210n102
Auschwitz, 30, 144, 167n13, 186n15, 189n68
Australia, 87, 174n73

Baden-Württemberg, 76, 116, 137, 145–6, 147, 171n41, 176n91, 210n112
Baeck, Rabbi Leo, 82, 91, 189n65
Baptists, 39
Barmen Declaration (1934), 103
Bavaria, 55, 59, 69, 70, 114, 116, 121, 141, 144, 171n32, 176n91, 181n54

Bell, Bishop George, 34, 48, 100, 102–3, 175n81, 179n18, 195nn28–9
Beneš, Eduard, 19–20, 170n22
Berg, Christian, 51, 53, 154, 205n24, 213n157
Berlin Magistrate, 28
Berlin Restitution Law, 31
Berning, Bishop Hermann Wilhelm, 58, 169n11
Bersarin, Nikolai, 28
Bethge, Eberhard, 102, 193n9, 195nn29–30
Bishop, Daniel, vii, 6, 162, 165n1
Bittenfeld, Hans Herwarth von, 117, 149
Böhm, Franz, 127–8, 136–7, 146, 163–4, 207n57, 216n4
Bonhoeffer, Dietrich, 34, 102, 193n9, 195n29
Bonn-Copenhagen Declarations (1955), 150, 211n137
Bonn-Paris Agreements (1954), 159
Bornewasser, Bishop Franz, 108, 148
Boucquey, Louis, 117–18, 148–9
Brand, Heinz, 30, 174n64
Brandlmeier, Joseph, 141–2, 209n86, 209n91
Britain, 16, 174n73, 175n81, 194n10. *See also* England
British Council, 16
British zone, 36, 56, 64, 89, 107, 113, 170n24, 176n91, 184n112, 185n9, 191n96, 208n72
Brown, Sterling, 85, 86–8, 190n75, 190n78, 190nn84–5, 208n71
Buchberger, Bishop Michael, 56
Buchenwald, 70, 134, 170n26
Buchman, Frank, 96–7, 112–16, 118–19, 148–9, 162, 166n6, 193n5, 198n83, 198n85, 199n90, 199n93,

199n105, 200n109–10, 200n123, 201n120
Bundestag, 132, 135, 180n37, 205n23, 205n27

Cahn, Max, 71, 185n11
capitalist, 65, 75, 119
Caritas, 67, 182n69, 182n74, 184n113
Catholic Church, 38, 43, 50, 54, 56–7, 58, 166n7, 179n27, 189n71, 190n83, 215n179; Aid Society (Kirchliche Hilfsstelle), ix, 43, 50, 57, 58–62, 66, 130, 174n73, 179n27, 182n70; Catholic Congress, 149; German Catholic Youth, 62, 183nn88–9
Central Association of Sterilized and Physically Harmed People, 134
Central Committee of Jews in Germany, 144
Central Council for Jews in Germany, 71
Central Europe, 42, 165n5, 170n21, 212n146
Central Party Control Commission, 75
Christian Democratic Union, 116, 168n7
Christians of Jewish descent, 67, 79, 83, 87
Christ und Sozialist, 137, 207n58
Churchill, Winston, 99
Clay, Lucius, 34, 37, 39, 87–8, 113, 176nn86–7, 177n108, 190n84
Clinchy, Everett, 86, 88, 141
collective guilt, 44–5, 48–9, 51, 63, 108, 172n54
Communists, 15, 22, 25–6, 43, 51, 57, 61, 66, 73, 120, 129, 157, 186n20, 212n146

Conference on the Future of Jews in Germany (1949), 69
Confessing Church, 30, 45, 67, 103, 121, 188n51
Consortium of Christian Aid Societies for Racial Persecutees of Non-Jewish Faith in Germany (Arbeitsgemeinschaft christlicher Hilfsstellen für Rassenverfolgte nichtjüdischen Glaubens in Deutschland), 67, 80
Council of States (Länderrat), 21
CRALOG (Council of Relief Agencies Licensed for Operation in Germany), 37, 177n98
cultural exchange, 16, 218
culture, vii, 15, 16, 58, 101, 137, 140, 167n13, 169n11, 181n58, 194n10
Czechoslovakia, 19, 20, 59–60, 66, 152, 167n14, 170n21, 196n44

Dahlem, Franz, 27, 121, 172n55
Dahrendorf, Gustav, 27, 172n54
Dehler, Thomas, 132–3, 136, 205n27, 206n33, 206n38
denazification: calls to end, 131; demand for, 122; different Allied versions of, 74, 171n31; failures of, 20–3, 65–6, 170n30; and German accountability, 14; German attitude towards, 162; goals of Allies, 20–3; Protestant opposition towards, 48; and religion, 33–5; role in reconstruction, 75; successes of Allies, 20–3; in U.S. policy, 17, 35; and Volkshochsschule, 63
Denmark, 114, 146, 150, 211n137
Department of Reconstruction and Inter-Church Aid, 37, 105, 176n88, 177n99, 195n27, 196n41

Dibelius, Otto, 44–9, 50, 54, 130, 138, 153, 178n8, 178n10, 179n23, 179n29, 204n16, 207n62, 213n147
Diem, Hermann, 80
Displaced Persons, 28, 71, 131, 173n57, 185n2, 198n69
Dortel-Claudot, Marthe, 106, 111

Eastern Europeans, 18–20, 52, 60
Ecclesiastical-Theological Society, 80
economy, 6, 8, 15, 58, 65, 127
ecumenical, 37, 44, 46, 81, 102–3, 111–12
Ehard, Hans, 116, 141, 200n109
England, 47, 87, 155, 179n15, 179n19, 194n10, 201n117, 214n166; Oxford, 87, 112, 198n79. *See also* Britain
European Coal and Steel Community, 156
euthanasia, 32, 175n75, 205n29

Federal Act (1953), 145–6
Fehsenfeld, Karl-Heinz, 157, 215n174
Feltin, Archbishop Maurice, 112, 198n78
Flügge, Lydia, 102, 195nn24–5
Foreign Ministers Conference (1947), 43, 52, 64, 149
France: attitudes towards Germany, 146–8, 200n114, 211n124, 214n169; Franco-German reconciliation, 105–8, 110, 115, 117–18, 149; German pilgrimages to, 105, 111; German POWs in, 109; Maison de France, 16; Paris, 43, 148, 159, 199n87, 200n114, 211n132, 216n183
Frankfurter Hefte, 16, 70, 185n3
Free Association for Pastoral Care, 58
Freiburg Circle, 85–6
French Employers' Federation, 117
French Federation of Former Deported and Interned Prisoners, 122
French Military Government, 110, 148, 171n31
French zone, 22, 57, 85, 146, 184n112, 197n53
Frings, Cardinal Joseph, 56–7, 108, 110, 181n62, 197n53, 197n56, 197n64

Galen, Bishop Clemens August Graf von, 56, 107, 180n35
Galinski, Heinz, 74
Gegenwart, Die 16, 169n12, 184n102
Gemeinde, 28–9, 167n11, 173n59, 173n62, 174n72, 186n17, 204n16, 207n60, 212n140, 212n144, 212n146
German Administration for Work and Social Welfare, 33
German Institute of Psychology and Overcoming Antisemitism, 84
German Office for Peace Questions (Deutsches Büro für Friedensfragen), 43, 64–6, 76, 118, 148, 156, 193n7, 211n119
German Protestant Church: and the American Military Government, 86; Church Council, 45, 81; Committee for Service towards Israel (Deutsche evangelische Ausschuss für Dienst an Israel), ix, 80, 138; and the Confessing Church, 67, 121; Declaration of Guilt towards the Jewish People, 80; on denazification, 22; German Protestant Committee for Israel, 82; and German unification, 130; and German victimhood, 42–3; ideological divides within, 34–5, 44–5; interpretations of Nazi era,

45, 103; Jewish relations, 79, 94, 137–9, 144, 208n69; local expressions of guilt, 80, 137, 153–4; missions, 81–3, 187n48, 188nn49–50; in Poland, 38–9; and Nazism, 41, 46–9, 175n80, 178n6, 179n29, 180n37; and spiritual reconciliation, 49, 99, 104–5, 193n9; support for Victims of Fascism, 26

Gerstenmaier, Eugen, 50–2, 54, 67–8, 103–5, 130–1, 179n30, 179n31, 180n34, 180n36, 180n37, 180n38, 185n118, 195n32, 196n37, 196n41, 204n22, 205n23, 205n24

Geschke, Ottomar, 26–7, 30–1, 172n49, 172nn52–3, 174n67

Greenstein, Harry, 69, 78–9, 185n1, 187n45

Gröber, Archbishop Conrad, 57, 181n64, 181n66

Grolman, Traub von, 91–2

Grotewohl, Otto, 125, 174n70, 203n147, 204n16

Grüber, Pastor Heinrich 26, 32, 48, 67, 74, 83, 85, 138, 151, 172n49, 179n18, 179n29, 184nn111–12, 189n68, 204n16

Gypsies, 6, 31–2. *See also* Roma

Harder, Pastor Gunter, 82, 188n61
Harling, Otto von, 89
Harmssen, Gustav, 65, 183n99, 183n101
Hauff, Karl, 76, 187n36
Heidelberg Conference (1949), 69, 73, 76–7, 139, 144, 185n10
Heuss, Theodore, 92–3, 141, 144, 149, 192n121, 192n122, 210n103
Horning, Bishop, 104, 153–4, 196n36, 213n149, 213n151

Herman, Stewart, 38, 42, 49–50, 178n5, 195n27
HICOG, 88, 175n82, 185n3, 185n7, 187n35, 187n40, 187n45, 191n103, 192n115, 192n121, 192n125, 193n128, 207n46
Hitler, 25, 26, 27, 47, 50, 59, 92–3, 96, 117, 123, 127, 148, 153, 169n20, 201n120
Hoffmann, Pastor Bengt, 153, 180n36, 213n148
Holocaust: calls for Germans to address, 11; as cause for Jewish emigration, 69; gentile-Jewish relations after, 77–8, 87, 90, 94, 143–4, 207n53; struggles of Jews after, 142, 187n44, 203n1
homosexuals, 6, 32, 126, 132
Hörhammer, Father Manfred, xi, 106–7, 109, 111, 196n44, 196n45, 196n47, 197n58, 198nn72–3, 198n75, 214n161, 214nn164–6, 214n170

Institute for Occupation Issues (Institut für Besatzungsfragen), 43, 64–5, 146
International Council of Christians and Jews (ICCJ), 37, 86–7, 163, 190n85, 190n86, 191n88, 191n90, 210n99
International Federation of Former Political Prisoners of Fascism, 121–2
International Fellowship of Reconciliation (IFOR), ix, 37, 98, 99–105, 112, 156, 163
International Opposition to Military Service, 156
Israel: FRG-Israel agreement, 75–6; and the GDR, 94, 151, 159; German dialogue on reparations

to, 135–6, 205n26, 207n53; and the
Jewish Claims Conference, 127–8;
Protestant Church relations with,
81–3, 138–9, 188n63, 189n66
Iwand, Hans, 44, 101, 104, 178n7,
194n19

Jehovah's Witnesses, 30, 174n69
Jesus Christus Kirche, 13, 36
Jewish Claims Conference, 127–8,
135–6, 145, 160
Jewish Restitution Successor
Organization, 145, 210n104
Jews: American, 39; and Catholics,
84–6, 105–6; and Christians, 86–94,
136–46, 153–4, 188n62, 189n68,
192n112; and the Confessing
Church, 67; in the FRG, 69, 151–2;
in the GDR, 151–4, 158–60,
163–4, 173n58, 186n20, 212n146;
German Jewry, 90, 187n44; and the
Holocaust, 3, 11, 189n69; migration
of, 69–70, 173n56, 185n1, 185n9,
185n13, 187n35, 187n44; and Nazi
persecution, 6; and NGOs, 67–8,
159; and Protestants, 79–83, 188n52,
208n69; purged from SED, 129, 158;
reconciliation with Germans, 9, 27,
71–2, 77–9, 95, 126, 135, 163, 188n60,
208n73, 212n139; reparations for,
24, 27–31, 32, 72, 132, 158–60, 163–4,
203n1, 212n143; in the Soviet zone,
72–5; in the Western zones, 75–7

Katterer, Arthur, 157
Kauders, Anthony, 142, 166n10,
209n91
Keilson, Max, 122
Keller, Bishop, 108, 197n54
Kevelaer, 107, 109, 111, 196n44,
196n48, 196n50, 197n53, 197n60

Kiel Declaration (1949), 150
Klein, Rabbi Isaac, 79, 187n47
Kleinschmidt, Pastor Karl, 83
Knappen, Marshall, 13–14, 35, 168n1,
175n82, 176n90, 177n97, 177n111
Knudsen, Knud, 89, 191n104
Kogon, Eugen, 16, 70–2, 77, 78, 93,
121, 185n3, 185n5
Königer, Kurt, 134, 206n41
König, General Marie Pierre, 146, 147
Kowalski, Edward, 122, 202n133
Küster, Otto, 76, 127–8, 136–7, 145–6,
203n3, 210n110

Länder, 76–7, 133, 152–3
Landwehr, Eva, 100–1, 172n49
Laure, Irene, 96–7, 115, 193n2,
199n95
Law for the Prevention of
Hereditarily Diseased Offspring,
132, 206n35
Law Number 10, 21
Law on Purging Bavaria of National
Socialism and Militarism, 21
Lehmann, Helmut, 32–3, 74–5,
151–2, 154–5, 186n17, 186n20
Leipzig, 83, 174n64, 201n128
Levinson, Nathan, 93, 143–4,
210n99
Lichtenstein, Ernst, 88–90, 191n105
Lidice, 60, 66, 182n77, 184nn105–6
Lourdes, 107–8, 110–12, 155, 196n48,
197n53, 197n63, 197n66, 214n162
Löwenkopf, Leon, 32, 73, 152, 173n59,
186n17, 193n129, 212n145
Luckner, Gertrud, 85–6, 89, 137,
157–158, 184n112, 190n81,
215n174
Lukaschek, Hans, 116, 199n105
Lutherans, 38, 39, 176n88, 177n98,
177n105

Lutheranism, 38
Luxembourg, 108, 128, 164, 197n54, 203n7

Maas, Herman, 87
Maier, Reinhold, 116, 200n109
Maritain, Jacques, 87, 191n87
Marshall Aid, 43, 162
McCloy, John J., 69–71, 185nn3–4, 192n121, 206n37
Mecklenburg, 83, 170n25, 189n69
Mennonites, 39, 178n9
Merker, Paul, 73–5, 151–2, 173n63, 186nn16–17, 186n24, 186n27, 193n129, 212n146
Methodists, 39
Meyer, Julius, 32, 74, 151–2, 172n49, 173n59, 186n25, 1932930, 212nn140–1, 212n144
Michelis, Pastor Z., 38–9, 177n105
Milik, Father Karol, 59, 182n75
Moral Re-Armament (MRA), ix, x, xiii, 5, 37, 96–8, 112–20, 146, 148–50, 156, 158, 162, 166n6, 193n1, 193n5, 193n6, 198n86, 199n87, 199n91, 199n96, 199n101, 200n109, 200n110, 211n132, 215n180, 215n182
Mottu, Philippe, 116, 199n96
Muckermann, Hermann, 140–1, 208n79, 209n80
Muench, Bishop Aloisius, 108, 181n53, 197n54, 197n56
Müller, Joseph, 144
Müller-Claudius, Michael, 84–5, 190n76, 190n79, 190n87
Munich Society, 90, 141–2
Munich Volkshochschule, 63–4, 183n93

Najder, Pastor K., 38–9, 177n105
NATO North Atlantic Pact (1949), 118, 201n115

Nazi: anti, 24, 30, 31, 32, 34–5, 51, 103, 121, 172n54; crimes of, 31, 38–9, 47–8, 52, 54, 64, 66–8, 72, 107–8, 121–2, 125–6, 128, 132–3, 162; German responsibility for, 41–2, 46–7, 51, 57, 60, 65, 87, 100, 159, 161, 163–4, 172n55; and damages to Germany's reputation, 30; denazification, 14, 17, 18, 20–3, 33, 35, 48, 63, 65, 74, 75, 93, 122, 131, 148, 162–3, 170n30, 171n31, 171n36; elements in the Church, 39; era, vii, 4, 5, 8, 10–11, 13–14, 16, 19, 20, 22–4, 26, 32, 42–5, 47, 49, 53–4, 55, 60, 64, 67, 73, 76, 79–81, 84–5, 91, 93, 99–100, 105, 107, 114, 119, 121–2, 126, 137–8, 140, 151, 153, 162; German exiles from Nazi Germany, 24, 61, 212n142; pro-Nazi, 34, 44–5, 148, 153, 175n80, 178n6, 180n37; propaganda, 17; racial policies, 6–7; victims of Nazi persecution, 6, 15, 25, 26, 28–30, 31, 32, 64–5, 76–7, 90, 102, 105, 128, 140–1, 202n133; reparations for crimes of, 27, 32, 60, 70, 121, 125, 127–8, 134, 137–8, 151, 164, 174n69
Nazism: addressing, 8, 15, 40, 61, 63, 110–1, 142, 161–2, 164, 172n55; crimes of, 13–14, 16, 28, 46, 51–5, 76, 170n26; difficulties in addressing, vii, 34, 44–5, 49, 108, 119, 131, 151, 159, 162, 197n57; victims of, ix, 4–7, 9, 23, 31, 33, 45, 56, 66, 74, 95, 106, 124, 159, 172n51, 199n101, 202n129. *See also* Nazi
Neues Abendland, 16, 169n12
Neues Deutschland, 16, 174n70
Neue Zeitung, Die, vii, 15, 19, 165n1, 168n3, 170n22, 170n24, 187n33, 192n120, 206nn36–7, 209n82

Neuss, Wilhelm, 87
Niemczyk, Pastor, 38–9
Niemöller, Martin, 13, 35, 44, 103, 176n88, 194n19
North Atlantic Treaty, 149
Nuremberg, 18, 30–1, 60, 93, 142, 162, 167n15, 169n12, 173n63, 175n76, 189n66

Occupation Statute, 76, 131, 146
Oder-Neisse Line, 104, 154
Oepke, Albrecht, 80–1, 83
Office for International Cooperation (Büro für Internationale Zusammenarbeit), 98, 120, 122–5
Office of Labour and Social Welfare (SED), 73–5
Office of the Military Government, U.S (OMGUS), 21, 88, 169n15, 171n31, 171nn40–41, 175n82, 176nn88–89, 192n121
Order 82 (1948), 74
Ostertag, Benno, 71, 76, 89, 141, 185n10, 187n35

Parmoor, Marian, 99–100, 194nn10–11
Pax Christi, ix–x, 37, 98, 105–13, 155–6, 163, 166n6, 196n42, 196nn44–5, 196nn47–50, 197n53, 197nn57–8, 197nn62–3, 198n69, 198n72, 198nn73–4, 198n78, 214nn162–3, 214nn165–6, 214n168, 216n3
People's Solidarity (Volkssolidarität), 43, 64–7, 73, 154–5, 163–4, 184n107, 184n109, 213n157, 214n159
Peters, Hans, 117
Peterson, Peter, 96–7, 199n101
philosemitism, 77, 81–2, 188n60

Pieck, Wilhelm, 74, 186n24, 204n16
Pius XII (pope), 54–5, 84, 110, 155, 181n49, 181nn53–54, 182n68
Poland, 38–9, 52, 57, 59, 71, 104, 123, 155, 167n14, 174n73; Poles, 20, 39, 53, 59, 123, 159, 170n24, 196n44; Polish Foreign Ministry, 123; Polish Protestants, 38–9
Popp, General Vicar Richard, 59, 182n76
Potsdam Conference, 14–15, 17–19, 25, 168n3, 168n5, 169nn18–19, 170n27, 204n21, 212n146
Potsdam decree, 59
Preuss, Siegfried, 52–4, 180n38, 180n41, 180n44
Preysing, Catholic Bishop Konrad von, 26, 180n35
prisoner-of-war (POW), 36, 62, 106–7, 109, 183n89
Protestant Relief Work (Das Hilfswerk der EKD): aims of, 43, 49–51; distancing from Nazism, 50; nationalist agenda of, 130–1; and People's Solidarity, 154, 213n157; political goals of, 52–4, 64, 155; and reconstruction, 66–8; work in the Soviet zone, 51
Protestants: and the Allies, 35, 38, 48–9; fragmentation among, 44–7; in Poland, 38–9; Protestant-Jewish relations, 79–86, 94, 137–40, 144, 163, 188n63, 189n66, 208n69; in Silesia, 104; in the Soviet zone, 34; spiritual reconciliation, 49, 130–1, 178n9, 193n9; and the World Council of Churches, 103–5, 153

Raddatz, Karl, 32, 121, 201n124, 201n127
Radlauer, Curt, 67, 87, 184n111

Red Cross, 50, 66, 174n73
religious education, 36, 62, 64, 152
Rengstorf, Karl, 82, 85, 138, 188n63, 189n64
repentance, 17, 117
Restitution Law, 31, 75, 94, 151, 206n37
restitution laws, 25, 74, 137, 151
Ritzel, H., 135, 207n48
Roma, 31, 126, 132–3, 174n69. *See also* Gypsy
Roman Catholics: and the Allied Control Council, 35; and the American Military Government, 39; Catholic-Jewish relations, 84–6, 89, 94, 139–40, 144; dealing with the Nazi past, 54–7, 64, 198n70; and foreign culture, 169n11; German and Polish Catholics, 59; Pax Christi, 106–12, 155; in the Soviet zone, 61–2
Roosevelt, President F.D., 29, 99
Roots, John, 112
Rosser, Henry, 100–1, 194n18
Ruhr, 116, 118, 146, 148–9, 158, 200n114

Saar, 106–9, 147–9, 211n119, 211n124
Saliège, Cardinal Jules-Géraud, 110
Scharnagl, Karl, 63–4, 88, 141–2, 183n93
Schoeps, Hans-Joachim, 89–91, 93, 138, 143–4, 192n110, 192n113, 192n114, 209n94
Schuman, Robert, 97, 117, 148–9, 193n5, 200n112, 200n113, 211n124, 211n132
Schutz, Hans, 58–9, 62
She'erit Hapletah, 28, 46
Shuster, George, ix, 114, 141, 168n6, 199n91

Siegmund-Schultze, Friedrich, ix, 7–8, 99–100, 156, 163, 194n16, 214n171, 216n2
Sinti, 31, 126, 132–3, 174n69
Sladek, Paulus, 58, 61–2, 182n81
Social Democratic Party (SPD), 33, 146
Social Democrats, 15
Socialist, 6, 15, 34–5, 66, 96, 119, 120, 122–4, 126, 133, 199n95, 206n32
Socialist Unity Party (SED): aid for Nazi victims, 32–3, 64–5, 73–5, 158, 163–4, 173n63, 174n70; and Christianity, 34, 153–4, 213n151; creation of, 15; and Jews, 73–5, 129, 151, 163–4, 212n146, 213n147; and MRA, 119; and reconstruction, 66–7
Societies for Christian-Jewish Cooperation: activities of, 139–44; Böhm and Küster's participation in, 127–8, 136; Coordinating Committee, 93; formation of, 86–9, 95, 163, 190n84; gentile-Jewish reconciliation, 5, 72, 86, 137; antisemitism, 88–9, 137, 139–40, 142–4, 208n77; Coordinating Council of the Societies for Christian-Jewish Cooperation (Koordinierungsrat Gesellschaften für Christlich-Jüdische Zusammenarbeit), 89; Freiburg Society for Christian-Jewish Cooperation, 86
Society for German-Soviet Friendship (Gesellschaft für Deutsche-Sowjetische Freundschaft), ix, 98, 120, 123–5, 163
Society of Christ the King, 105
Soviet Administration, ix, 33, 53, 124, 125, 129, 163

Soviet Military Administration in Germany (SMAD), 18, 22, 25, 28–9, 31, 33, 74, 151, 173n63
Soviet Union, 25, 113, 123–4, 159, 168n4, 202n144; ideology of, 22, 121
Soviet zone, viii, ix, 5, 6, 15, 16, 18, 22, 25–6, 28, 30–6, 43, 45, 51, 53, 61–9, 72–8, 80, 83, 94–5, 98, 119–125, 128, 159, 163, 165n4, 170n25, 173n63, 180n36, 183n83, 183n84, 186n20, 196n36
Spanier, Julius, 88, 143, 209n93
Stalin, Josef, 10, 28, 53, 99, 124–5, 162, 173n58, 203n147; Stalinism, 72, 153, 154; Stalinist, 15–6, 74, 78, 128, 152, 159, 163–4, 173n63; ideology, 16, 78, 152, 159, 163–4; Stalinization, 8, 162
Stein, Erwin, 117
Stenzel, Hugo, 140
Stürke, Karl, 133, 206nn33–34
Stuttgart, 24, 46, 50, 53, 88, 171n33, 171nn40–41, 184n116–117, 185n118, 186n15, 196n42, 196n49, 208n71
Stuttgart Declaration, 46–7, 178n11, 188n58
Sudeten Germans, 60–3
Sudetenland, 59
Switzerland, viii–ix, 38, 51–2, 87, 96, 103, 198n83
Synod, 46, 80, 188nn53–4
Szerunda, Bishop, 104

Tabouis, Geneviève, 148, 211n120
Tagesspiegel, 15, 187n33, 204n17
Teusch, Christine, 140, 208n73–6, 208n78
Thadden-Trieglaff, Reinold von, 130, 204n18

Théas, Bishop Pierre-Marie, 106–11, 156, 196n50, 197n53, 197n57, 197n59, 197n61, 197n63
Thieme, Karl, 86, 89, 142
Tilge, Robert, 118
Tillmanns, Erich, 51
Tippelskirch, Werner von, 150
Tiulpanov, Major General Sergei, 124
Treysa, 45, 48, 50, 170n25, 178n7, 180n34
Trier, 108, 148, 197n54, 197n58
Trocmé, Pastor André, 100–1, 194n19
Truman, President Harry, 17, 39, 170n26

United Nations Relief and Rehabilitation Administration (UNRRA), 68, 185n2
United States, viii, 13, 16, 43–4, 76, 87, 93, 108, 168n4, 169n14, 171n31, 187n37, 187n44, 197n53

Vatican, 54–5, 84, 87, 144, 181n48
Velden, Bishop John Joseph van der, 109, 197n53
Victims of Fascism (Opfer des Faschismus): and the Allies, 32–3; Berlin chapter, 25–6; classification of victims, 30–1, 74, 151, 173n63, 175n76; dissolution of, 64, 186n20; formation of, 172n49; goals of, 26–7, 172n48; records of, ix; and reparations, 25, 73–4, 173n63; in the Soviet zone, 22, 43, 66, 73
Visseur, Pierre, 86, 89
Vossler, Erwin, 145, 210nn106–8

war crimes, 20, 59, 68, 170n29
Weeks of Brotherhood, 139–142
Weltbühne, Die, 74, 186n23
Werner, Arthur (mayor), 26, 150
Western zones: Allied non-fraternization law, 17–18; democratization in, 16, 65, 86, 97; Displaced Persons camps in, 28; Jews in, 75–6, 78; NGO work in, 119–22, 159; pacifist groups in, 125; progressive individuals in, 83; reconciliation in, 5; records from, viii; relief work in, 50; Soviet zone compared to, 33, 124–5
West Germans, 134–5, 151, 159
Wiesbaden Society, 92, 141
Wollheim, Norbert, 71, 89, 93, 185n10, 187n44, 191n104
Working Group of Christians and Jews, 86

World Council of Churches (WCC): Amsterdam conference (1948), 102–4; areas of work of, 105; collective statement of, 104; Department for Inter-Church Aid and Service to Refugees, 154; early work of, 37–8; financial aid of, 196n40; Provisional Council, 38; results of, 98
Wurm, Bishop Theophil, 22, 44, 47–8, 50, 171n34, 178n14, 179n15, 179n19, 179n29, 215n178

Zietlow, Reverend Carl, 86, 88–9, 102, 157–8, 190n83, 190n85, 195n25, 215n174
Zuckermann, Leo, 32, 74, 151, 186nn23–4
Zusammenarbeit (Working Together), 94, 191n96, 191n98, 191n101, 209n93

GERMAN AND EUROPEAN STUDIES

General Editor: Rebecca Whitmann

1. Emanuel Adler, Beverly Crawford, Federica Bicchi, and Rafaella Del Sarto, *The Convergence of Civilizations: Constructing a Mediterranean Region*
2. James Retallack, *The German Right, 1860–1920: Political Limits of the Authoritarian Imagination*
3. Silvija Jestrovic, *Theatre of Estrangement: Theory, Practice, Ideology*
4. Susan Gross Solomon, ed., *Doing Medicine Together: Germany and Russia between the Wars*
5. Laurence McFalls, ed., *Max Weber's 'Objectivity' Revisited*
6. Robin Ostow, ed., *(Re)Visualizing National History: Museums and National Identities in Europe in the New Millennium*
7. David Blackbourn and James Retallack, eds., *Localism, Landscape, and the Ambiguities of Place: German-Speaking Central Europe, 1860–1930*
8. John Zilcosky, ed., *Writing Travel: The Poetics and Politics of the Modern Journey*
9. Angelica Fenner, *Race under Reconstruction in German Cinema: Robert Stemmle's Toxi*
10. Martina Kessel and Patrick Merziger, eds., *The Politics of Humour in the Twentieth Century: Inclusion, Exclusion, and Communities of Laughter*
11. Jeffrey K. Wilson, *The German Forest: Nature, Identity, and the Contestation of a National Symbol, 1871–1914*
12. David G. John, *Bennewitz, Goethe,* Faust: *German and Intercultural Stagings*
13. Jennifer Ruth Hosek, *Sun, Sex, and Socialism: Cuba in the German Imaginary*
14. Steven M. Schroeder, *To Forget It All and Begin Anew: Reconciliation in Occupied Germany, 1944–1954*

www.ingramcontent.com/pod-product-compliance
Lightning Source LLC
Chambersburg PA
CBHW020403080526
44584CB00014B/1157